TANK WARFARE

STRATEGY AND TACTICS:

TANK
WARFARE

CHRISTER JORGENSEN AND CHRIS MANN

MBI Publishing Company

This edition first published in 2001 by
MBI Publishing Company,
729 Prospect Avenue, PO Box 1, Osceola, WI 54020-0001 USA

MBI Publishing Company books are also available at discounts in bulk quantity
for industrial or sales-promotional use. For details write to Special Sales Manager
at Motorbooks International Wholesalers & Distributors, 729 Prospect Avenue,
PO Box 1, Osceola, WI 54020-0001 USA.

Library of Congress Cataloging-in-Publication Data available.

ISBN 0-7603-1016-5

Editorial and design: Amber Books Ltd
Bradley's Close, 74-77 White Lion Street,
London N1 9PF

Project Editor: Charles Catton
Editor: Vanessa Unwin
Design: Floyd Sayers

Printed in Italy - Nuova GEP, Cremona

Picture credits

Chrysalis Picture Library: 23. **Robert Hunt Library**: 69, 129. **TRH Pictures**: 6-7, 8, 9, 11, 12 (IWM), 14 (Bundesarchiv), 15 (t) (Bundesarchiv), 15 (b), 16 (Tank Museum), 17 (t), 18-19, 20, 21, 24, 25 (Tank Museum), 26, 27, 28, 29, 31 (both), 32, 33, 34-35, 36, 37, 38, 39, 40, 41 (both), 42 (t), 42 (b) (US National Archives), 44 (IWM), 45 (IWM), 46 (t), 47, 49, 50 (US National Archives), 51 (t) (US National Archives), 51 (b), 52, 53, 54-55 (Bundesarchiv), 56, 57, 58 (IWM), 59 (both), 60 (both), 62, 63, 65, 66, 67 (US National Archives), 68 (US National Archives), 70-71 (IWM), 72, 73, 75, 76 (both), 77 (IWM), 78, 79, 80-81, 82, 83, 84, 85, 87 (both), 88, 89, 90, 91, 92 (both), 94, 95, 96, 97, 98-99, 100, 101, 102, 103, 104 (both), 106 (both), 108, 109 (IWM), 110, 111, 112 (Tank Museum), 113, 114 (US National Archives), 115, 116, 117, 118-119, 120, 121, 122, 123, 124, 125, 127 (both), 128, 130, 131 (US National Archives), 132-133, 134 (both), 136, 138, 139, 140, 142, 143, 144-145, 146 (t), 146 (b) (IWM), 147, 148, 149, 150, 151, 152, 153, 154, 155, 156, 157, 158-159, 160, 161, 162, 163 (US National Archives), 165, 167 (US MOD), 168 (USAF), 169 (US DOD), 171 (R. Stickland), 172, 173.

Artworks by Patrick Mulrey

CONTENTS

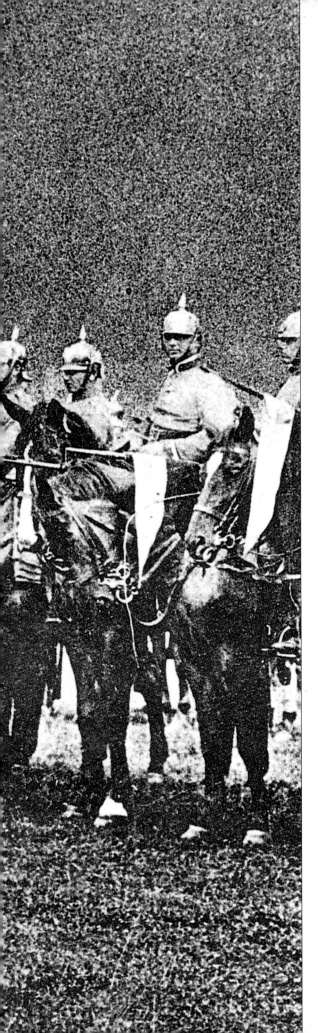

CHAPTER ONE

ENTER THE LANDSHIP

Like barbed wire, the submachine gun and the flamethrower, the tank first appeared in World War I.

Ever since he began fighting wars, Man has sought the perfect combination of speed, protection and firepower. The ancient Egyptians used war chariots to devastating effect upon their enemies, while the Indians used armour-plated war elephants with some success upon Alexander the Great's Macedonians. A millennium later, the medieval knights represented an almost perfect balance between the three elements above – they were the 'tanks of their age'. Armoured knights were, as tanks were later to be, masters of the battlefield, and almost always victorious against infantry armies. At Crécy, their defeat was as much due to being bogged down in mud (like tanks in difficult terrain) as to the killing efficiency of the English longbow in the hands of expert archers.

The development of the internal combustion engine in the latter part of the nineteenth century enabled a group of skilled engineers and officers to create the tank during World War I, as a means of restoring movement to the battlefield, something that had been lacking

LEFT: The elite Imperial German Cavalry regiment *Jaegers zu Pferde* ready for action at the beginning of the war. Unfortunately, this splendid display of horses and men was to prove to be an anachronism: with the development of the machine gun as a defensive weapon *par excellence*, the cavalry could no longer ride around the battlefield with impunity. As a result, the generals of both sides lacked an offensive shock weapon. Not until the emergence of the tank would large-scale movement return to the battlefield.

ABOVE: German infantry being conveyed to the front in lorries. A novelty at the beginning of the war, transport powered by internal combustion engines became a more common sight as the war progressed.

in the war until that point due to the awesome efficiency of the machine gun as a defensive weapon. The new mechanical oddity, called a 'tank' because of its resemblance to a water tank, would dominate battlefields for decades. In this and subsequent chapters, we look at the impact and changing role of the tank in warfare during the twentieth century, and ask whether the tank has now, like the armoured medieval knight, had its day?

WORLD WAR I, 1914–18

When Europe went to war in that fateful autumn of 1914, the massed multitude, politicians and military pundits alike placed their bets on a short, sharp war based on the experiences of the last great continental conflict: the Franco-Prussian war of 1870–71. While a more mobile war continued to be fought out in the east, the war on the Western Front came to a spluttering halt in the muddy fields of Flanders. The crushing impact of machine guns, trenches, mortar fire, shrapnel fire and barbed wire upon mass infantry attacks across open terrain was obvious for all to see. It was bleeding the the resources of the armies on both sides dry and something had to be done to break the murderous deadlock.

Designs for an armoured, mobile war engine had been presented well before World War I broke out. The invention of the internal combustion engine by the German Gottlieb Daimler in 1885 enabled engineers to develop an engine of over 100hp by 1914. Thus the 'military war engine' would eventually have an engine powerful enough to propel a large armoured body on tracks across the most difficult terrain. The British had the lead in the field of developing caterpillar tracks until, in 1912, a British firm sold its patents to the American firm of Holt. Holt had developed a tractor which moved on caterpillar tracks and this suc-cessful idea underlay most war engine designs. The only remaining ingredient was petrol fuel, which had been developed and refined so that it could be used in ever-more powerful engines. In 1907, a tracked car was tested at Aldershot

and, a year later, in May 1908, it took part in the Royal Review.

In 1911, an Austrian engineer, Gunther Burstyn, built a small, tracked vehicle with a cross-country speed of 8km/h (5mph), an ability to cross trenches, and a body that measured 3.65m long by 1.21m wide (12ft long by 4ft wide). He submitted plans of his device to the Austrian Ministry of War, which showed profound interest but equally exemplary financial prudence by suggesting that Burstyn find private finance to build it. Knowing that no one would put capital at his disposal in peacetime, Burstyn sent the plans to Berlin in the hope that Austria's ally, Germany, would show more support. In 1906, Germany had experimented with armoured cars, but now the German Ministry of War showed no interest, so Burstyn gave up. The Germans were later to regret their decision, but their negative attitude was typical of the period and British engineers also found the same lack of interest at the British War Office.

NECESSITY, MOTHER OF INVENTION
Only the horrors of an actual deadlocked war could make bureaucratic wheels

BELOW: The basic design for the tank: caterpillar tracks, armoured body on top and wheels at the rear to steer and help improve stability. This armoured prototype, nicknamed 'Little Willie', was to be the model for most tank designs during World War I. The resemblance to a water tank, the origin of the weapon's name, is marked.

move slightly faster. In October 1914, the unsung hero of British armoured warfare, Lieutenant Colonel Ernest Swinton, submitted a memorandum urging the War Office to provide finances and resources to mount an armoured car on top of a Holt tractor. His engineering colleagues knew that an 'Armoured Machine Gun Carrier' (AMGC) like the one that Swinton proposed was both a technical feasibility and a desirable weapon. Both GHQ and the War Office proved sceptical. They still held the view that tried and tested methods of warfare would, if correctly applied, prevail over the enemy. Although Swinton and other 'radicals' knew better, without the backing of a political heavyweight, their project would never get off the ground. In the end, backing came from a most unlikely quarter.

The First Lord of the Admiralty, Winston Churchill, threw his considerable political weight and determination behind the project. In February 1915, five months after Swinton had issued his memorandum, Churchill created the so-called 'Landship' Committee under the leadership of Eustace Tennyson d'Eyncourt, Churchill's Director of Naval Construction. At the same time, the army finally acted and General Sir John French set up the 'Invention' Committee. Swinton, who joined this committee, spelled out the minimum criteria for any AMGC: a crew of 10, a top cross-country speed of 6.5km/h (4mph), two machine guns, one

light gun and the ability to cross 2.43m (8ft) of trench.

In August 1915, construction of the Little Willie was begun and, a few months later, in February 1916, the first tank to be built for actual warfare faced a round of gruelling tests at Hatfield. Despite Kitchener dismissing them as 'pretty mechanical toys', the new Minister of Munitions, David Lloyd George, placed an order for 100 tanks with the armaments firms. With a turret on top, Little Willie was deemed to have too high a silhouette and was replaced with a new design. The new tank, the Mark I, was a rhomboid-shaped armoured box with caterpillar tracks that encircled its body. Its armaments were housed in a sponson on the tank's side.

FIRST USE

The new weapon was tested for the first time during the five-month–long Battle of the Somme in 1916. The British deployed the mysterious 'tanks' at Flers-Courcelette, between Albert and Bapaume, in support of the infantry. They were to operate in pairs. Of some 58 tanks, only 36 made it to the start line; of these, several were knocked out by artillery fire, some simply broke down and others were bogged down in ditches and mud holes. In other words, the tank was not initially a roaring success. Yet as these armoured monsters rolled out of the mist, the Germans were in for a nasty shock. Infantry, unused to armoured

BELOW: The first Mark I tanks used by the British came in two forms, the 'Male' and 'Female'. The only difference between the two was the armament, the 'Male' carrying six-pounder guns, while the 'Female' only had machine guns in its sponsons. This lozenge-shaped design was chosen as the best for crossing trenches. Note the anti-grenade netting on the roof.

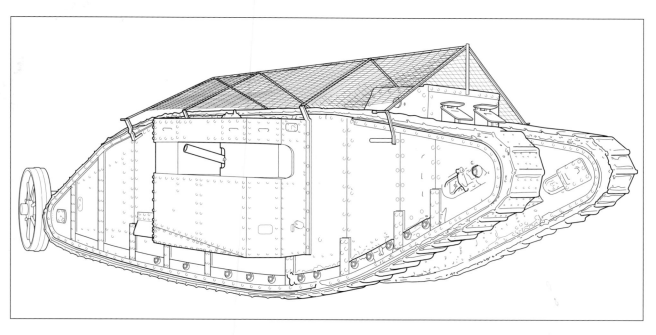

warfare, panicked and fled. Their officers showed great presence of mind and nerves of steel by ordering field guns to be manhandled into position to shoot at the grey 'monsters'. By noon, weakened by the insistence upon 'penny-packet' attacks and stiffening German resistance, the British attack had ground to a halt.

General Haig, the British Commander in Chief in France, was nevertheless impressed enough to claim that the tank was here to stay and had, by its very presence on the front, altered the war. Indeed, the tank had revolutionised land warfare forever. The question was not 'if' but 'how' the tank was to be deployed. Most officers in the British Army saw the tank as a passing fashion item that was specifically created for the conditions of the Western Front and which would be abandoned when 'normal' conditions returned. If, on sufferance, it was to be used at all, it was in the role of a mobile fort to support infantry attacks. Even Swinton, an officer noted for his quick, questioning mind, believed this was the limited role of the tank. Others, however, believed that the tank should be deployed as armoured cavalry, capable of cutting through the trenches and restoring much-needed mobility to an ossified front. This argument was to rage on for the next 20 years until the German tank

victories in World War II made the correct use of the tank in war obvious even to the most hidebound conservative.

NEW IDEAS

In October 1916, despite his experience, Swinton was replaced as commander of the British tank forces by Colonel Hugh Elles. His talented Chief of Brigade Staff was Major John F. C. Fuller, who set about writing manuals on tank tactics. Fuller believed that the tank would revolutionise warfare, and that the present war could be won by employing them in ever-larger formations. Tanks, he believed, should also be employed in mass attacks at a single point. If they were employed in pairs, like at Flers-Courcelette, the results would be disappointing. In November 1916, Fuller and officers of like mind urged the High Command and the British Government that thousands of tanks should be manufactured and formed into brigades, divisions, corps and even armies. The reality was quite different; by that same month, only enough tanks had been built to create the first Armoured Brigade.

In April 1917, the British deployed 26 tanks (out of 60 available) at Arras, where they wreaked havoc upon the German lines. At the same time, the British sent eight tanks to the Palestinian Front. There

ABOVE: An official photograph of a tank going into battle for the very first time. This type, a Mark I 'Female' with one of its machine guns visible, can be seen moving into battle at Flers-Courcelette on 15 September 1916. Its commander is wearing a metal skull cap as a crude form of head protection against protruding objects in the interior of the tank.

ABOVE: The 'Male' version of the Mark I going into battle on the Western Front. One of its six-pounder guns is clearly visible in the side sponson, as is a machine gun used to combat infantry. At this stage of World War I, the Mark I had no armoured opponents and its heavy armament was used purely for supporting infantry attacks or knocking out enemy artillery. However, the early tanks were unreliable and most broke down before they reached the enemy.

they took part in the First Battle of Gaza (April 1917) and had the same effect upon 'Johnny Turk' as they had had on German infantrymen. A few months later, however, opponents of the tank appeared to have their fears about the utility of the tank confirmed when a mass attack by 200 tanks at the battle of Passchendaele floundered and failed.

FURTHER SUCCESS

The critics were soon to be silenced. The attack failed at Passchendaele due to the nature of the ground. In the next battle the tanks took part in, the ground was dry, relatively flat and open. There were no major physical obstacles that could cripple a successful attack. Furthermore, Fuller had seen it to that the tanks were equipped with fascines (tree branches and long sticks) which could be dropped into the trenches and facilitate a crossing. Once across, the tanks would 'roll up' the trench line by firing from behind and

pick off machine-gun nests one by one. Other tanks would follow to support and protect the attacking infantry.

It was time to put theory into practice and see what a tank attack 'en masse' could achieve. The spot chosen by the British was Cambrai. On 20 November, Elles led 378 tanks in a massive assault on the fortified Hindenburg Line along a 9.6km (6-mile) front with the support of five infantry divisions behind him. This time the tanks led from the front, and in massed formation. The result was spectacular. By noon, the tanks had broken through four consecutive 'tank-proof' trench lines to a depth of over 6.5km (4 miles) and in the process had captured 100 guns and 4000 prisoners. What was even more spectacular was the fact that Elles had only lost 1500 men. With conventional methods, a similar advance would have taken three months and cost the lives of 400,000 troops. Unfortunately, the lack of reserves on the

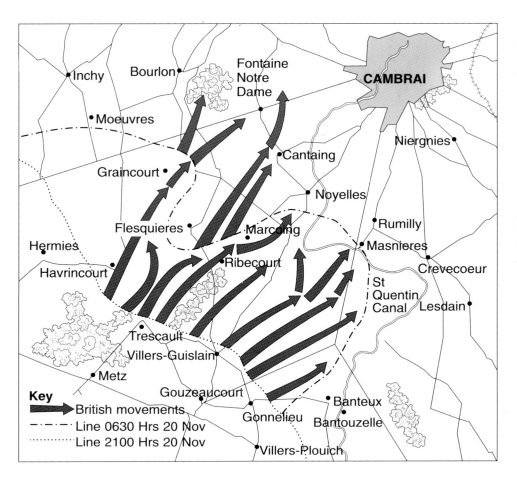

LEFT: The first mass tank attack took place near Cambrai and caught the Germans by surprise. Unfortunately, its success was as much of a surprise to the British and, in the delay in bringing up reserves to exploit the breach, the Germans recovered. Subsequent counterattacks recovered most of the ground won, but the battle showed how mass tank attacks could provide significant gains.

British side prevented them from properly exploiting the initial success and, by 30 November, the battle had bogged down in a stalemate. This time, however, there was no going back, since the tank had come to stay and its full potential had been demonstrated. Fuller and other tank enthusiasts had been vindicated.

FRENCH ARMOUR

Cambrai activated the atrophied French efforts to develop its own armour corps. In December 1915, Colonel Estienne, an inspired artillery colonel, had urged the French Army High Command to build mobile assault vehicles equipped with machine guns or artillery. He had got the idea from seeing the British using the Holt tractor to move heavy artillery. In early 1916, the newly formed French Ministry of Munitions acted upon Estienne's recommendations by placing an order for 400 *char d'assauts* (attack vehicles) with the French armaments firm Schneider. Estienne was promoted to general and commander of the *l'Artillerie d'Assaut* later in the year. The French were still unaware of British efforts, until

Flers-Courcelette showed British advances in the field. Estienne went to England to view the progress of the British tank and was impressed enough to recommend the building of a lighter tank model. Both the

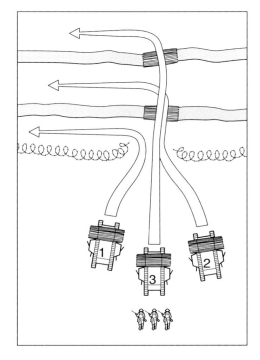

LEFT: Tank tactics in World War I. Tank 1 breaches the wire, and then follows the front line between the wire and the first enemy trench, clearing the latter with its guns. Tank 2 uses a fascine (sticks bound together with rope in a circular bundle) to cross the first enemy trench before turning in the same direction as Tank 1 and firing on both sides. Tank 3 crosses the first trench using Tank 2's fascine, then uses its own fascine to cross the second enemy trench, before moving in the same direction as the other tanks. Finally, the infantry moves up to consolidate the tanks' gains.

Schneider (at 15 tonnes) and the later St Chamond (24 tonnes) were heavy, cumbersome vehicles which proved disappointing when put to the test in real combat conditions. A production contract to build the new, lighter tank was given to the car firm of Renault.

Meanwhile, on 16 April 1917, the French used eight tank companies equipped with Schneiders to support 5th Army's assault at Chemin des Dames. Artillery and machine-gun fire led to heavy losses, but two French tank companies crossed three German defence lines. On 23 October, an attack at Malmaison in support of 6th Army saw the Schneiders perform reasonably well, but the St Chamonds failed to achieve their objectives. Both models were phased out the following year in favour of the more mobile, lighter Renault FT-17 tanks (7 tonnes). These proved their worth during the German offensive in the summer of 1918 when more than 100 were deployed to halt the German advance on Paris.

Cambrai not only woke up Britain's ally, but served as a warning call for her enemy, too. As we have seen, the German Ministry of War had shortsightedly rejected tank designs before the war. The tanks encountered at Flers-Courcelette and Arras therefore came as a nasty shock to them and left them with a major dilemma. How were they to counter this new weapon?

GERMAN COUNTERS

The Germans chose to improve their artillery and create new anti-tank weapons. The most effective was the 3.7mm light anti-tank gun, or 'PAK' (*Panzerabwehrkanone*). This effective gun was not produced in sufficient numbers but, when deployed, proved a dangerous tool in the hands of trained German artillerists. To counter it, the British deployed snipers to pick off PAK unit commanders. Special '*Tank und flieger*' (Tuf) ammunition was produced to penetrate armour at close range but a faltering German ammunitions industry, overburdened and with a malnourished workforce, did not produce sufficient amounts. Nor did the Germans produce

BELOW: The tank came as a complete surprise to the Germans and, as a consequence, Germany entered the 'tank race' at a later date (after September 1916) than the Allies. The Germans, after some initial trouble, developed the A7V (*Allgemeine Kriegsdepartment 7, Abteilung Verkehrswesen*), which saw service a year later.

ABOVE: An A7V in support of a storm troop detachment of German infantry in open country. The Germans were not as successful as their enemies in the use of tanks in World War I, and were much more interested in the development of infantry tactics for the new elite storm troops. When they did use tanks, the Germans preferred captured Allied Mark Is and Mark IVs to their own designs.

LEFT: In the absence of dedicated anti-tank weaponry at this early stage of armoured warfare, artillery was used instead with great effect against the relatively lightly armoured tanks. Here, British infantry passes what appears to be a knocked-out Mark I during the latter part of the war.

enough tanks of their own. The model they did produce, the A7V (*Allgemeine Kriegsdepartment 7, Abteilung Verkehrswesen*) was too heavy (32 tonnes) and, with a crew of 16 men, too cumbersome to be effective. The Germans, therefore, resorted to using captured British tanks instead. This proved an inadequate stopgap and the Germans lagged behind their enemies for the rest of the war. Fuller claimed that the German training was inadequate and their commanders continued to mistrust the tank as a weapon. The British, however, continued to make progress in the fields of both design and production.

TANK VERSUS TANK

The first tank-versus-tank battle in history took place at Villers Bretonneux in April 1918, and yet another chapter in the history of armoured warfare had begun. Some time afterwards, the Germans (having forced Russia out of the war) shifted their forces from the Eastern Front westwards.

With fresh troops and a numerical advantage, they staked everything from March 1918 upon one last, massive offensive to defeat France and Britain before the Americans could begin arriving in large numbers. During the retreat, the tank played only a very small part in the German plans and the British lost over 180 of 380 tanks during their retreat. The mere rumour, claimed Fuller, of German tanks approaching British lines would set off a panic among the infantry. Both French and British tanks played an important role in first halting and then rolling back the German offensive.

To exploit eventual breakthroughs, the British developed a much lighter and faster tank model, the 'Whippet', with a crew of three, four machine guns and a weight of only 14 tonnes. Once the German Spring Offensive had been halted, the Allies were able to break through their lines and exploit the new mobility of the tank. By November 1918, the British Army had 25 tank battalions;

BELOW: Although the Mark Is, IVs and Vs were a relative success, they were extremely slow. The British chose to develop a fast tank model, the Medium A ('Whippet') tank, seen here moving along a road in northern France during the offensive of 1918. Whippets were involved in the first tank-versus-tank battle at Villers Bretonneux on 24 April 1918.

Fuller concluded that the tank's potential was limitless and would totally change the face of warfare in the coming decades.

His prophecy was to be prove correct, but the road was both hard and long. One typical contemporary notion was that the tank was not a reliable new weapon, but an unwelcome apparition that would disappear during peacetime. It almost did, due to false economies and mistakes during the interwar period. Typical of this 'back to usual business' attitude was the officer who, when he heard that the war was over, told Fuller: 'Thank God that's over, [now] we can get back to real soldiering!'

ABOVE: Probably the best all-round tank of World War I: the French Renault FT-17.

BELOW: The FT-17 had a two-man crew. The driver sat in the front and the gunner inside the turret.

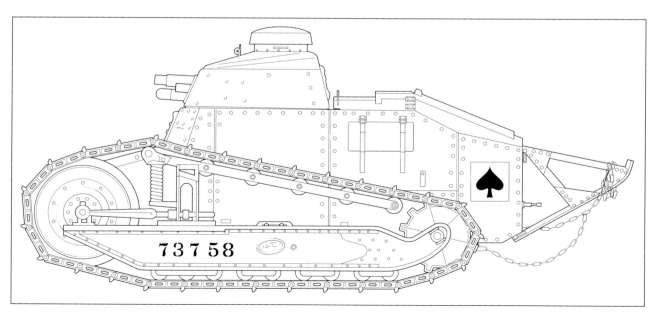

CHAPTER TWO

TOWARDS TOTAL WAR

The interwar period saw the development of the style of armoured warfare that would become known as *Blitzkrieg*.

After the bloodshed of World War I, the last thing Europeans wanted to do was to begin planning the next war. Those few that dared to think in terms of a new war where the tank was to play a key role were either silenced or ignored. Ironically, the victors of World War I were to be defeated by their opponents in World War II as a consequence of their neglect of the tank enthusiasts' warnings. Britain was the most glaring example of neglect and ignorance. Having invented the weapon, the British abandoned it in favour of a return to 'normal' soldiering. Even Douglas Haig stated in 1925: 'Some enthusiasts today talk about the probability of horses becoming extinct and prophesy that the aeroplane, the tank and the motor car will supersede the horse in future wars. I am all for tanks and aeroplanes, but they are only accessories to the man, and the horse.'

Haig summed up the feelings of military traditionalists of all the European armies who saw the tank as a cumbersome, slow and unreliable nuisance that – hopefully – would fade away. The tank, however, did not fade away, any more than the aeroplane or the car. Together, they were to bury the old style of warfare forever and, with it, the arguments men such as Haig propounded. Disturbingly, these

LEFT: Light tanks of the 2nd Battalion of the Royal Tank Corps advancing in formation during manoeuvres on England's Salisbury Plain in the early 1930s. The economising caused by the Depression had serious consequences for Britain's armoured forces. British tank design, which had been leading the world, became out-of-touch and would not catch up until the end of World War II. Tank numbers also fell, which meant that the British were forced into rushed rearmament programmes when the arms race developed in the late 1930s.

advocates of the increasingly old-fashioned 'horses and men' approach to war were not an isolated group of old 'Colonel Blimps', as one might think. They were the majority of the interwar officer corps and they were present in all of the European armies.

In Britain, the Tank Corps – renamed the 'Royal Tank Corps' (RTC) in 1923 – struggled to survive in the face of the overwhelming opposition from influential military figures. Those, such as Fuller, who believed in an independent tank arm with an armoured division as its core – with fully mechanised infantry and artillery as support – were in a small minority. Fuller, outspoken and controversial, was removed from his post as military adviser to the CIGS (Chief of the Imperial General Staff), while Elles lost faith in the tank and resigned from command of the RTC in 1934.

Some years earlier, in 1926, an 'Experimental' or Mechanised Force was set up for the Salisbury Plain exercises made up of the 3rd and 5th battalions of the RTC equipped with light Vickers tanks and armoured cars. For support, the tanks had a battalion of the Somerset Light Infantry in lorries and mechanised artillery. They showed the great worth of having tank units and mechanised infantry plus artillery operating as one unit. The logical answer would have been to set up an Armoured Division. But, in the 1920s, the emphasis was on economy and avoiding 'expensive experiments' such as tank units. At least two cavalry units, the 11th Hussars and 12th Lancers, were mechanised in 1928 and, three years later, the 1st Tank Brigade was formed at Salisbury with 95 light and 85 medium tanks. These tanks were operated and controlled through the use of radio telephones that simplified command and increased the tank unit's coordination in attack. Unfortunately, the unit was disbanded by the end of the year.

RIGHT: Tank training in Hampshire, England, between the wars. The Royal Tank Corps is seen here on a training exercise based on the initial stages of the Battle of the Marne in 1914. In this photograph, a tank commander of the 5th Battalion is making notes on his war map with a chinagraph pencil.

It was not until November 1933 that a permanent tank brigade was set up at Salisbury with 230 new Mark II light tanks. For some reason, the military establishment found the right man for the right job at the right time: Colonel Percy 'Hobo' Hobart. Hobart was an ideal choice. He was an inspired leader and educator of tank men. He had an outstanding knowledge and enthusiasm for the tank, both with regard to its application on the battlefield and its theoretical use and mechanical abilities. Although declared a god by his men, High Command and his superiors found him no less trying to deal with than they had found Fuller. Hobart, like Fuller, could not stomach opposition to tanks based on ignorance, malice or crass stupidity, and he made his opinions and ideas very clear. This earned him warm admirers as well as enemies.

Like all tank-producing nations in the interwar period, Britain had too many tank designs and this made production confused. There were always problems in relation to their practical use. In 1927, the British led the world in terms of tank design, production and application, but, during the following decade, they did not keep pace with other countries. The new models of the 1930s such as the MkI (A9) and MkII (A10) were fast, achieving 27km/h (17mph) on the road, but they were too thin-skinned. One design that was produced, the MkIII (A13), had thick front-turret armour combined with good speed, but its armaments (a two-pounder gun and single light Vickers machine gun) were inadequate. The MkIV, a reconnaissance tank, reached a speed of 48km/h (30mph), but had only two machine guns (one light and one heavy) and armour that was too thin.

REARMAMENT

If the RTC's equipment was not up to scratch, that was not true of the men that served in it. They were to serve as the core of the new tank force set up by the British during the early part of World War II. In the face of Nazi Germany's rapid rearmament, in particular from 1935, the British had to respond to this challenge, however reluctantly and slowly. Public opinion was against rearmament and the financial stringencies imposed by the Great Depression were a convenient excuse to

deprive the armed forces of much-needed financial support. But, in 1936, in response to the German occupation of the Rhineland, a further eight cavalry regiments were mechanised. At the same time, Germany was building up a series of Panzer units. Three years later, all British cavalry units had been mechanised and were using either light tanks or armoured cars instead of horses.

However, no one in the military establishment had addressed the problem of air power. Tanks could not function on the ground in the face of enemy air activity or without support from their own air force. In Britain, the attitude of the armed services was that of competing departments rather than as components of a single armed force. The Royal Air Force, having been under Army and Navy control before, was desperate not to lose its status as an independent arm. The RAF concentrated upon air combat and strategic bombing. Few, if any, pilots or

BELOW: Across the Channel the French, too, were training with tanks for war that few realised was not too far off into the future. Here, a French Hotchkiss H-35 is traversing a natural obstacle at some speed during training exercises in early 1939. On a one-to-one basis, French tanks were as good or better than their German rivals, but they were utilised in a way which put them at a disadvantage in combat.

RAF officers were interested in practising ground strafing and dive-bombing, elements which the RTC needed if it was to win tank battles on the ground.

Thus the British had neglected the one essential pillar of total, mechanised war in the twentieth century: the intimate cooperation between dive-bombers and tanks in destroying the enemy's tanks. The RAF, however, did not have a monopoly on chaos and confusion. When the dynamic and energetic General Edmund Ironside, who had been appointed to do something about tanks, asked for a heavier tank in March 1938, he was told that two separate committees were looking into the matter; these committees, however, had nothing whatsoever to do with each other. The British produced the Infantry Tank Mk I that same year. It had a crew of two, weighed only 11 tonnes due to its light armour and had a single Vickers machine gun: little use against the German panzers now being produced. A year later, the picture was quite different. The British finally had a tank that was impressive: the Matilda, a tank that was to prove a challenge to the Germans.

Across the seas, the Americans were in even worse shape in terms of tanks and tank tactics. During World War I, the American experience of tank warfare was quite limited compared to her allies. Lieutenant Colonel George S. Patton had led the first US tank unit, the 304th Tank Brigade, in support of the US 4th Army's attack upon St Michel on 12 September 1918. Patton's brigade destroyed a German artillery battalion and took 30 prisoners. The action went on for four days. It showed the value of the tank to the commander of the AEF (American Expeditionary Force), General John L. Pershing. He asked for five heavy battalions of tanks (375 machines) and 20 light battalions (1500 tanks) to be built.

Of this huge number, fewer than 100 had been produced by the end of the war.

The first US-built and designed tank – the MkVIII (International) tank of 25 tonnes, with 75mm howitzer and four machine guns in sponsons – saw the light of day in 1917. By the end of the war, the US Tank Corps consisted of 20,000 men and over 1000 tanks had been produced. During the interwar period, this number was cut back to 154 officers and 2508 men stationed at Camp Meade in Maryland, under Brigadier General S. D. Rochenbach's command. By 1920, the Corps had been disbanded and the two talented tank officers, Patton and Dwight D. Eisenhower, left a crumbling service for more promising careers elsewhere. The US War Department, like the British War Office, did not believe the tank had an independent role to play. Older cavalry officers and infantry commanders believed, like their British counterparts, in the future of their respective arms, while younger World War I veterans believed that mechanisation, both on land and in the air, was the wave of the future. The conservatives won out and, between 1920 and 1935, only 35 new tanks were produced in the USA.

FRENCH DEVELOPMENTS

In France, the situation was not much better, with some glaring exceptions. The German 'menace' was not a distant threat across the seas (as it was with the Americans and British); it was something

RIGHT: Tactics developed throughout the interwar period, led by the ideas of leading figures such as J. F. C. Fuller and Heinz Guderian. Forward-thinking armies looked to integrate motorised infantry with their tank forces to provide an armoured spearhead capable of breaking through the enemy's forces. This formation, developed by the Germans, was capable of immediate response to any threat over a 180-degree arc and gave protection to the infantry following closely in its wake.

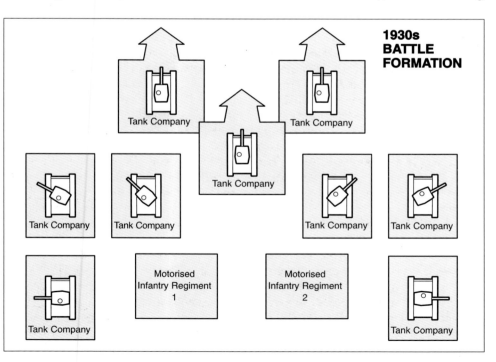

1930s BATTLE FORMATION

Tank Company
Tank Company
Tank Company
Tank Company
Tank Company
Tank Company
Tank Company
Tank Company
Tank Company
Motorised Infantry Regiment 1
Motorised Infantry Regiment 2

unpleasantly close and menacing across the Rhine. The French therefore kept up a large number of tanks of good quality in their army. Nevertheless, as with their wartime allies, the French still failed to comprehend the correct use and full potential of the tank. This, rather than a lack of quality tanks, was to prove their main failing in World War II.

When Churchill thought of the accession to power of Hitler he exclaimed: 'Thank God for the French Army!' His sentiments were fully shared by many other Britons and Europeans. The bulwark of Europe against the double menace of a new war and a new 'Kaiser' would be the French Army. But by the early 1930s, that army was a shadow of its former self. In 1931 Estienne, now General of Armoured Troops, called for the establishment of independent, armoured units, with the support of General Maxime Weygand. They were opposed by those, such as Generals Brécart and Dufieux, who believed that infantry-based tactics were superior. They put blind faith in the defence of France based on the old infantry divisions with artillery support,

coupled with the Maginot Line ('completed', if that is the right word, in 1932), with the result that production of tanks was given a low priority. In 1931, Estienne had worked out the design for the heavy and powerful Char B, which was superior to anything their potential German opponents had in their arsenal in both armour and armament. Yet it was not until 1935 that the first tank was produced, at a snail's pace of 10 tanks a year.

DE GAULLE

One man dared to challenge military 'orthodoxy' in France in his now famous book *L'Armée de Métier* (*Towards a Professional Army*) by arguing that France had to create a tank army to defend itself against a future German invasion. The title alone served to infuriate the senior officer corps. Neither British (such as Liddell-Hart) nor German (von Thoma and Guderian) tank experts were particularly impressed with the book. In the same year as the book was published, the author, Colonel Charles de Gaulle, received the support of the up-and-coming politician Paul Reynaud to increase tank production. However, France was fettered

ABOVE: The beginning of the world's largest and most diversified tank army. A tank officer in the Soviet Union in 1928 inspects a KS light tank model armed with a long 37mm (1.47in) gun. Without any baggage from World War I, the officers in the Red Army responsible for developing armoured tactics could integrate new ideas without having to overcome the opinions of conservative cavalry officers.

ABOVE: By the time of Hitler's accession to power in 1933, the Red Army already had a powerful tank army and was developing new tactics to take advantage of the capabilities of its tank designs. These advancing tanks (model BT-5s) are on exercise somewhere in the Moscow region.

by political divisions and refused to earmark enough money for the project. Even if money had been available, the military establishment would have been unwilling to spend it. They chose to believe in Marshal Pétain's reassuring claims that the Ardennes were impassable to tanks, the Maginot impregnable and the combination of anti-tank mines and artillery would stop any mechanised army in its tracks. None of these statements was in any way substantiated and they all proved utterly untrue when put to the test. It was only by the summer of 1943 that the Red Army was to demonstrate that a full-scale tank attack with aerial support could be stopped (with some difficulty) by the combination of anti-tank ditches, mines and artillery, but only then with massive aerial support and the use of massed tank formations as well.

In fact it was not in the west, but in the east, in the new state of the USSR – created out of the 1917 revolution – that the theories of total and mechanised warfare were to be applied and tested on a scale unheard of in the west. The Workers and Peasants' Red Army (RKKA) had no major tactical and strategic hangovers from World War I. It thrived, as an entirely new military force, upon being modern and daring, unfettered by past traditions and bourgeois conventional warfare. It was also operating in a controlled socialist economy that did not accept, as in the 'decadent' western democracies, financial constraints. Resources would be made available on a huge scale should the

political and military aims be important enough. The problem here, as in the west, was to find a political sponsor loyal and powerful enough to enhance the interest in the tank force. The Red Army had such a sponsor in the wily Georgian, Joseph Stalin.

STALIN'S ROLE

Having won the internal party feuds to succeed Lenin, by 1928 Stalin had the ambition to create the world's most modern and powerful army, as an instrument of conquest both against Asia and Europe, should the opportunity arise. The key would be mechanisation of the RKKA and the creation of a powerful tank army around which this ambitious programme could be based. Only the USSR's industrialisation, through the Five Year Plans (1928–37) enabled Stalin to realise his dreams. In 1930, the RKKA had hardly any modern tanks; by 1932, it had more tanks than the world's most powerful army, the French Army. Three years earlier, the RKKA's special Far Eastern Army, under the command of the brilliant General Vasily Bluykher, had demonstrated the skills of the pre-mechanised Red Army. In response to Chinese provocations, Bluykher conquered most of Manchuria in a fortnight through the inspired use of combined cavalry and tank units.

Over the next decade, the Soviet Union was to produce an unprecedented number and diversity of tanks, the likes of which the world had never seen. Like other nations during the interwar period, the Soviets divided tanks into several categories with very specific tasks. There were light tanks (*tanketka* or *legkiy*), amphibious tanks (*Plavainschchiva*) and medium (*sredni*) tanks – but the most numerous were the so-called *Bystrochodya Tank* (fast tank) and the heavy tank series.

In 1927, the T-27 tank was built in A and B series, based upon a Carden-Lloyd carrier with a single 7.62mm machine gun. Remarkably, this tank remained in production until 1941. The most numerous and successful of the Soviet light tanks was the famous T-26 series, produced as an infantry tank from 1931 onwards. The T-26 (A4 and A5) was produced with two turrets. In 1937, following service in the Spanish Civil War on the Republican side, the T-26 B2 was produced with twin spotlights and a welded turret, and some with a ball-mounted 7.62mm machine gun. The T-26 C and E models were later, improved models based on the original B2 series.

Given the numerous rivers in Eastern Europe and Russia (and the lack of bridges capable of bearing a tank's weight), the Soviets set great store upon the ability of tanks to cross rivers and therefore produced a series of amphibious tanks. The T-37 had thin armour and a single rudder. Improved versions (T-38) were introduced in 1936 and 1938.

SOVIET MEDIUM TANKS

The first of the medium or breakthrough tanks, the T-28, was produced with a 76.2mm gun and side turrets with machine guns. It was a fast tank despite its bulky body and was used to support infantry attacks. Both designers and the military theorists saw the potential of this tank, and from it developed the best of the medium tanks: the fast tank, or BT series. In 1932, two types came on line: the BT-2 (37mm gun), and the more powerful BT-5, which not only had a 45mm gun, but also a machine gun in an improved turret, and a radio for communication. This last development was crucial for effective control of larger tank units. In 1935, the famous BT-7 went into production with a conical turret and thicker 22mm (0.9in) front armour (compared to the BT-5's 13mm (0.5in)). A year later came the most impressive of the fast tanks: the BT-7M

(BT-8). With a diesel engine (to reduce the risk of fires), sloped glacis plate and, in theory, ability to travel at some 100km/h (62mph) on roads, this was the ultimate fast tank in the Soviet arsenal. Its sole purpose was offensive, as it was designed for operations in central Europe on Germany's good roads, should the RKKA ever be able to penetrate that far into the continent. If one could build a fast tank like that, argued Soviet designers, then perhaps these design improvements could be retained and developed further. During the late 1930s, the A-20/A-30 led the way to the development of the T-32, which was the prototype (based upon BT-7M model) that eventually was to become the famous T-34 series. The T-34 model was to play a great part in saving the USSR from military disaster and would spearhead the assault on the Third Reich during World War II.

HEAVY TANKS

A tank force had to have heavy tanks to destroy heavy fortifications. The T-35 was built for this specific purpose: 50 tonnes, a crew of 10, one main turret and four auxiliary ones, with improved suspension and a radio installed in 1935. The SMK (Sergei Mironovitch Kirov) tank was built to replace the unwieldy T-35, as was the T-100, but, at 56 tonnes, these behemoths were even clumsier. Production never began. Instead, the designers turned to another prototype: the Kliment Voroshilov tanks. The first model, the KV-1, appeared in September 1939, and went into mass production three months later.

If the sheer number of good designs seemed impressive, then these almost

BELOW: The mainstay of the RKKA's armoured forces in the 1930s: the BT-5, which was not only fast, but also very agile in offensive warfare. Shown here is the TU version with a cylindrical aerial around the turret for its radio. Radio gave commanders the opportunity to control mass tank formations, vital for the new tactics being developed.

paled in comparison to the huge numbers of tanks that were produced in the USSR before the war. By 1938, the Red Army had some 9000 tanks, of which the majority were mainly T-26s, BT-5s and BT-7s: thin in armour and weak in armament. Yet overwhelming quantity made up for weaknesses in quality. By 1939, the RKKA also had 2000 amphibious tanks, and production continued apace. In 1941, the Soviet Union had over 21,000 tanks, of which 75 per cent was BT models and T-26s. Aircraft numbers were also on the increase during the 1930s.

A mere accumulation of mechanised power, whatever its high quality, is of little consequence without a theory of operation based upon combination of arms and large-scale military exercises. As early as 1924, when a military commander and theorist of the highest calibre, General Mikhail Frunze, became Defence Commissar, and General Mikhail N. Tukhachevsky his deputy, the RKKA high command began to create a new, modern army. The political cavalry generals Semyon Budenny and Kliment Voroshilov opposed this trend. Frunze

died under mysterious circumstances a year later, while Tukhachevsky was exiled as commander of the Leningrad Military District (MD). In 1931, having been convinced of the need for mechanisation in the Red Army, Stalin recalled Tukhachevsky, who was appointed to head the RKKA office of armament and technology. Production increased by leaps and bounds during the following five years. Tukhachevsky encouraged the modernisation of tank plants at Chelyabinsk and Charkov, from which started to pour a huge, steady stream of good-quality, fast tanks.

A group of talented officers formed around Tukhachevsky, including the brilliant military theorists V. K. Triandafillov, N. N. Morchin, B. Kalinovsky and Isserson. Tukhachevsky encouraged development of ideas for mechanised warfare. To assault enemy defensive lines, mechanised infantry divisions would be supported by armour, self-propelled artillery and dive-bombers. To affect a breakthrough once this stage had been completed, armoured (tank) brigades and divisions would launch a massed tank assault, supported again by dive-bombing

BELOW: Here, a captured British Mark I tank from World War I is being used by German *Freikorps* (a semi-official right-wing military formation) in Berlin during efforts to crush the violent left-wing opposition. Germany was not, however, allowed to build or use any tanks according to the Treaty of Versailles (1919).

units. The tanks were not to overwhelm enemy units through frontal assaults based upon sheer mechanical power, but were to encircle and outflank enemy units. This explains why so many Soviet light and medium tanks were produced with one specific aim: speed and mobility at the expense of gun calibre and armour (which made tanks too heavy and cumbersome). As the enemy, cut up and confused, reeled under these armoured punches, a third wave of attacks would hit them, this time from the air. A deep airborne attack ('desant') would strike far behind their lines to seize and hold strategic points. The enemy would be paralysed and lose his ability to fight, rather than being physically destroyed through a direct attack upon his formations. Triandafillov had already concluded in 1929 that future wars would be won by large, mechanised armies with powerful combined arms formations, intimately supported and protected by air power in large, mobile battles.

Air power was emphasised in the USSR as an integral partner in this new style of 'deep war', and developed with as much speed as the mechanised formations.

The Red Air Force (RKKF) grew from 1100 aircraft (1930), to 3000 (1933), to 5000 (1935), to 10,000 (1939), and finally to over 12,000 in 1941. They were organised in Air Fleets and never developed, as in France and Britain, into fully independent, strategic armed forces devoid of contact with their army colleagues, but remained an integral part of the land forces. They had a highly specific purpose: to operate as aerial artillery in support of the armoured forces. To this end, the airborne arm (paratroops and air assault units) expanded as fast as the RKKF. By 1938, the Soviet Union had 70,000 airborne soldiers equipped with all sorts of support weaponry, including specially built lightweight tanks and armoured carriers. In this era the Soviet armed forces were years, if not decades, ahead of the west.

This was all well and good, but would it work in practice? Tukhachevsky and his enthusiastic associates were never in doubt. The Stalinists in the RKKA were hoping for, and expecting, total failure. They were disappointed. The Leningrad (North-West) MD, the Kiev and the Byelo-Russian (Minsk) MD were the most

BELOW: Denied tanks for so long, the German Army jumped at the chance to acquire them en masse after Hitler began his policy of rearmament. This parade in 1936 gives a false impression of German armoured might. In fact, these are light PzKpfw Is, with only twin machine guns as armament.

powerful in the USSR, both for defensive purposes should Poland attack and for offensive purposes should the RKKA want to strike west. The RKKA had two basic units for armoured warfare, which were to be tested. They were the Tank Brigade with four battalions – each with a large complement of light tanks and a minimum of 30 heavy T-28s – and the more flexible Mechanised Brigade, which was composed of five battalions: three light tank, one reconnaissance tank and one motorised infantry.

SUCCESSFUL DEMONSTRATIONS

General Ion Yakir, head of the Kiev MD, proved during the May 1935 exercise that aircraft could operate successfully in close cooperation with tanks, and that they should not be allowed to stray from their main purpose: a contribution to the ground war. The airborne units were landed and drove back 'enemy' units from the battlefield. A year later, it was the Byelo-Russian MD's turn, under General Uborevich, to prove the theorists right again. Uborevich's MD employed 1300 tanks and 630 aircraft in close cooperation. This time, foreign military observers were present and were duly impressed by what they saw.

It was exactly this admiration for men who did not owe their position to Stalin, were professional and promised to create a professional and excellent Red Army that was viewed by the dictator as a threat. The threat was against the Marxist purity of the so-called 'workers' state' and Stalin's own position – which was far from secure due to the economic and political mistakes associated with his policy of collectivisation in the early 1930s. Tukhachevsky was also outspoken in his criticism of Nazi Germany, and he wanted to strengthen Soviet defences in the face of that obvious threat. Stalin was not convinced that Hitler posed such a threat. From 1936 onwards, therefore, the Tukhachevsky group was marginalised. In June 1937, Yakir, Triandafillov, Uborevich and Tukhachevsky were shot, while Isserson was spared the bullets, but ended up in Stalin's 'labour' camps in the east. In 1937, the RKKA was the most modern, mechanised, well-equipped and well-led army in the world. A year later, it was reduced to a shambles by the deaths or arrests of 125,000 officers and the 'leadership' of such military incompetents as Voroshilov and Budenny. They blindly believed in the offensive based upon cavalry and 'proletarian' enthusiasm.

LEFT: German troops massed outside the Berlin Reichstag in 1935 to commemorate the fallen soldiers of World War I. That same year Germany had her first armoured unit and could begin the long road to revenge for their 1918 defeat. As this photograph shows, although the Germany Army was keen to increase its panzer arm, it still relied heavily on both horses (for transport) and infantry. In fact, in 1939 the only wholly mechanised force in Europe was the British Expeditionary Force in France.

Stalin had destroyed the Red Army and left the military initiative to Germany. In the Third Reich the theoretical basis of the deep mechanised war had not been formulated, but it was to be put into practice over the next few years with spectacular success. The Versailles Treaty of 1919 had stipulated that Germany was prohibited from manufacturing or using tanks. It was a prohibition the new German Army commander, General Hans von Seeckt, did his utmost to circumvent. In 1926, the first specifications for a tank were made. A year later, six *Grosstraktoren* with 75mm guns in fully traversable turrets were produced and shipped to the secret German tank school at Kama (near Kazan in the USSR). In October 1928, two six-tonne tanks with 37mm guns in fully traversable turrets had been produced and tested at Kama.

HITLER'S NEW ARMY
The coming to power of Hitler was, from a narrow German army point of view, a 'godsend', since the new leader ignored the Treaty of Versailles. On 1 November 1933, less than 10 months after Hitler's accession to power, the first panzer (tank) unit was set up outside Berlin in Zossen. A year later, 1 September 1934, General

Otto Lutz was made commander of the panzers. Lutz led the first proper exercise in August 1935 at Munster, where he put both machines and men (led by the Kama veterans) to the test.

Lutz came to some crucial conclusions: first, that the optimum unit for the panzers was an entire division; and, secondly, that there had to close cooperation between the tanks and the air force. Also, an attack had to be made on a narrow front and radios had to be installed to promote swift and safe communications between the tanks. In February 1935, several cavalry units were transformed into motorised regiments and, by 1 April 1936, the 1st and 2nd Panzer Divisions were combat-ready.

Both Lutz and his more dynamic deputy, General Heinz Guderian, saw the failure between 1936 and 1937 to establish more panzer divisions as a major setback. But it cost over 100 million Reichsmarks to create a panzer division and other sections of the armed forces needed money for rearmament. The German General Staff concluded that tanks were too expensive, and should be relegated to their proper role of supporting infantry. Lutz opposed these moves, but had to be content, for the moment, with the establishment of three

ABOVE: The new panzers close up. The PzKpfw IV was the heaviest of the four tanks developed by Germany before the war, and it was becoming more common by late 1938 and early 1939. The PzKpfw IV gave the panzer arm real strength and firepower, and was such a good basic design that, with modifications, it served until the end of World War II.

so-called light divisions (between 1938 and 1939). These had fewer and lighter tanks than a real panzer division.

FEWER DESIGNS

The Germans, unlike the Soviets, had neither the time nor the money available to experiment with several designs. Therefore they settled for four different models. The light *Panzerkampfwagen* (PzKpfw) Mark I had only two machine guns in a hand-traversable turret and only enough armour to protect its crew against solid-core bullets. The PzKpfw II had a 20mm gun and a single machine gun, but no better armour than the Mark I. The next model, the PzKpfw III, had a 37mm gun (and should have been produced with a 55mm gun), two machine guns, and thicker armour to protect it against heavier gunfire. The last model, the PzKpfw IV, was a good tank with a powerful, stubby 75mm gun.

It now remained to be seen which tank army, the German or Soviet, was the better. Both powers were given the opportunity to test their machines and the men who drove and led them under actual combat conditions when, in April 1936, the Spanish Civil War broke out. The USSR supported the Republican side, while the Germans and Italians supported Franco's Nationalists. During the war, the Soviets supplied the Republic with 731 tanks and over 1000 aircraft, while the Germans sent 600 aircraft (with 16,000 men in the Condor Legion) and 200 tanks (*Gruppe Imker*) led by Lieutenant General von Thoma. Mussolini was more generous and less calculating than his ally: he sent 75,000 troops in total, 660 aircraft and 150 tanks.

The Nationalist advance on Madrid had to be stopped if the Republic was not to fall to Franco. Time was short and this prompted a direct Soviet military intervention. On 29 October, the first Soviet tank attack, led by Captain Paul 'Greisser' Arman, was a massed attack with T-26s against Italian Ansaldo tanks and Nationalist cavalry. The more heavily armoured and armed Soviet tanks knocked out 11 Ansaldos without major problems. A week later, the same tanks, with inexperienced Spanish crews, failed completely to intimidate or defeat the Nationalists. The head of the Soviet Tank Brigade in Spain, General Dimitri Pavlov,

decided to take charge in person and, on 10 January 1937, managed to attack with his tanks in massed formations. Franco's bid to take the capital had failed.

At the battle of Jarama, a month later, some 25 of Pavlov's T-26s made an unsuccessful attack upon the Nationalist lines. This massed attack was thwarted through a combination of Italian 27mm anti-tank guns and more powerful anti-tank mines. In March, the roles were reversed. Colonel Rodimtsev, who led the Soviet armour in the battle of Guadalajara, totally destroyed what passed for Italian armour. The Fiat-Ansaldo, or L3/1935 (light tank) was no tank at all. It was based on the British Vickers light tank model, with a single machine gun as armour, a two-man crew and weighing 3.8 tonnes. It could reach a 'top' speed of 42km/h (26mph). It was too slow and too lightly armoured and armed to be called a real tank and showed its incapacity to fight in a modern war. The Republic was elated with a victory over a weak enemy. But Guadalajara was an example, on both sides, of how a tank battle should not be conducted. There was hardly any or no coordination between the tanks, artillery and air support, while the support units (especially the infantry) could not keep up with the tanks, which undermined offensive power.

Republican overconfidence led to General Rojo's May offensive against the Nationalists with 80,000 troops and 130 T-26s. It proved a costly failure. As if to confirm Republican incompetence, another offensive was launched on 6 July at Brunete. The Republican attack failed because their tanks were used as artillery support and, as stationary targets, proved to be sitting ducks for Nationalist artillery. They should have been used in their proper role as spearheads for a rapid, massed tank attack that could break through the enemy's lines and affect a breakthrough which could be exploited. Five days later, the Soviet commander General Rudoft reported to Pavlov that he had only 38 tanks left.

NEW LESSONS

Brunete ended on 26 July and from now on the tank was only to play a subordinate role in the war. It was time to draw some conclusions from this war; it had been used an experimental workshop

by both the Germans and the Soviets to test their theories and equipment. The Soviet tanks were superior in both armaments and armour to their outclassed Italian and German rivals. But Pavlov drew all the wrong conclusions from his experiences. He believed the tank was a mere supportive weapon for infantry and that all the larger tank units (divisions and brigades) should be disbanded and dispersed among the infantry units. His German counterpart, Thoma, came to the opposite conclusion. Light tanks, such as the PzKpfw I and

Ansaldo, were useless on a modern battlefield and heavier, more modern tanks that could match the T-26 and T-28 had to be produced if Germany was to win a future war against the USSR. He also concluded that tanks were more effective in larger units and when they were used in large numbers with close-up artillery and aerial support.

The Soviets were not the only ones to draw the wrong conclusions from the Spanish Civil War with almost fatal consequences for their survival. The Poles, uncomfortably stuck between the

ABOVE: Wounded being taken off the battlefield at Brunete, on the central front, in July 1937. The most successful tank of the Spanish Civil War, the Soviet T-26, can be seen in the background. Both German and Soviet tank commanders gained vital experience before World War II on the battlefields of Spain.

LEFT: Polish ski troops being pulled along by a tankette, the TK-3, during winter exercises in 1936. With its single machine gun as its only armament, the TK-3 was no match for the panzers three years later. Poland realised its lack of preparedness for armoured conflict in the late 1930s, but war broke out before she could build up her tank forces.

Germans and Russians, had realised that they lagged behind their neighbours in the development of tanks. But the Polish High Command, in charge of the world's fifth largest army, refused to mechanise its cavalry (some 70,000 men and horses) and came to the same conclusion as Pavlov: tanks were no threat since anti-tank mines and artillery could stop them in their tracks.

The Poles were therefore woefully short of tanks. The infantry divisions had some 18 companies of tanks (two platoons with 13 tankettes each), while the mechanised brigades possessed two tank reconnaissance squadrons. By September 1939, the Polish Army had 887 tanks, of which 293 were inadequate TKS tankettes and 300 obsolete TK tanks. Neither model could stand up to German or Soviet armour. The Poles had one good tank model: the 7TPjw, with a 37mm gun in a single turret, a strong 110hp engine and a speed of 37km/h (22.7mph). Unfortunately, there were not enough of them.

ZHUKOV'S VICTORY

At about the time that Hitler turned his attentions towards Danzig (Gdansk) and the Polish Corridor, a significant battle took place across the world in the eastern part of Asia on the border between the Japanese puppet state of Manchuria and the Soviet satellite of Mongolia. In May 1939, Manchurian cavalry violated the border of Mongolia and the border incident soon escalated into a full-scale war. In early July, when the new Soviet commander General Grigori Zhukov arrived at the front, his forces (the 1st Army Group) mustered 13,000 troops,

BELOW: War in the Far East: Japanese troops advancing behind an armoured car during fierce fighting with retreating Chinese troops in the streets of Chapei in December 1937. The Japanese only had a few tank designs, all of which were of poor quality in comparison with those of the Soviet Union and Japan's future enemies in World War II.

185 tanks and generous air support. His opponents had 40,000 troops, 135 tanks and 225 aircraft at their disposal and felt strong enough to attack. But their attacks on 2 and 4 July proved dismal failures. Zhukov halted their advances through the use of combined air strikes, artillery bombardments and massed tank attacks.

One would have thought the Japanese would have realised the danger they were in. But reinforcements for a final show-down kept on arriving. A month later the Japanese 6th Army (under General Ogisu Rippo) had increased in size to 80,000 troops, 180 tanks and 450 aircraft. Zhukov's Army was even more impressive: 35 infantry divisions, 500 tanks and 600 airplanes. In other words, the Russians had a marginal superiority in men and machines against the Japanese, especially in the number and quality of their tanks. But Zhukov was far superior to Rippo as a commander and convinced his enemy that he would remain on the defensive by building fortifications to cover his preparations for an attack. Having lulled the Japanese into a false sense of security, over 150 Soviet bombers flew in at dawn on 20 August and pummelled the Japanese lines. Under cover of a massive artillery barrage, laid down to erupt just after the air strike, Zhukov sent his 6th and 11th Tank Brigades around the Japanese flanks. They converged and met up at the village of Nomonhan. The entire Japanese 6th Army

was surrounded and Zhukov tightened the noose around its neck until the enemy capitulated on 31 August.

The Russians lost 10,000 men but the Japanese had lost five times as many: 55,000 troops (dead, wounded and captured). The Japanese learnt two valuable lessons: not to tangle with the heavily mechanised and powerful Red Army, and to stay out of Siberia. The USSR had removed the threat of a two-front war, while Zhukov had proved Tukhachevsky right: the only way to win modern wars was with the aid of modern, mechanised tank armies fighting in close cooperation with air and artillery units. Much of the Soviet victory was due not only to Zhukov's leadership and the quality of the RKKA's tactics and strategy, but also to superior tanks. The BT-5 and even more so the BT-7M (BT-8) were good offensive tanks: light, mobile, nimble in attack and, with sloped armour, able to resist most Japanese artillery. By contrast, the Japanese were outclassed. Their Type 95 Light Tank (37mm gun and 12mm (0.4in) armour) was shot to pieces when it confronted the BT tanks. The better Type 97 Medium Tank (57mm gun and 25mm (1in) armour) was not present at Nomonhan in sufficient numbers to make any difference to the outcome of the battle. This classic tank battle, played out on classic open tank country, had proved that armies ignored the offensive powers of the tank at their peril.

ABOVE: The Soviet success in the eastern part of Mongolia during the fighting around Nomonhan (Khalkin-Gol) in August 1939 with tanks like the fast BT-7 (medium) tank shown above [in 1942] discouraged the Japanese from attacking Siberia in conjunction with their German allies in 1941. The war in the Far East made the reputation of Zhukov, who would later lead the Soviet offensive against Germany in World War II.

CHAPTER THREE

BLITZKRIEG

When they were finally unleashed in September 1939, the German panzers appeared to be unstoppable.

Although it was in the Soviet Union under Tukhachevsky that the style of armoured combat later known as 'lightning war' was developed, it was the Germans who perfected it and turned the *Blitzkrieg* theories into deadly practice on the battlefield. Hitler's first victim was to be Poland which, although in possession of a fine army, was utterly unprepared for this new type of mobile war. The Polish Army amounted to 30 infantry divisions, 11 cavalry brigades, but only one light tank brigade. They had mobilised seven armies to defend their extended borders with Germany and her Slovakian satellite. The Germans, with East Prussia and Pomerania jutting into Polish territory, had not only a strategically more favourable position than Poland, but were also both numerically and technologically superior. In total, the German invading army had 40 infantry divisions, four motorised divisions, four light divisions and, crucially, seven panzer divisions at its disposal. Army Group South (7th, 10th, 14th Armies) had the lion's share of the panzers, while Army Group North (3rd Army in East Prussia and 4th Army in Pomerania) had the remainder.

On 1 September 1939, the Germans struck with the terror-bombing of airfields, wiping out the Polish ground forces' air cover. Guderian (XIX Panzer Corps) led from the front and, by moving through the 'impassable' Tuchola Forest, managed to cut the Polish Corridor in two by 5 September. The 10th Army had meanwhile covered half the distance to Warsaw by the same date, advancing along lines of least resistance such as 'impassable' swamps and forests. Colonel von Thoma's 2nd Panzer Brigade, for example, gave the Poles a nasty surprise by ignoring the Jablunka Pass and driving through

LEFT: In 1939, Poland had the fifth-largest and most modern army in the world. She was, however, woefully short of tanks. Here, on a pre-war manoeuvre, there is a display of what armoured might she possessed in the shape of massed formations of 7TP medium tanks with 37mm (1.47in) Bofors guns mounted in the turrets. The 7TP was the only tank the Poles possessed capable of matching the German panzers, but the the German advance's speed caught the Polish armour out of position and the tanks were unable to deploy before they were destroyed or captured.

ABOVE: The PzKpfw I showed itself to be completely inadequate as a frontline combat vehicle during the Polish campaign and was quickly phased out. The Germans also found out to their cost that tanks, as seen here at Warsaw in mid-September 1939, were completely unsuitable for street fighting.

thickly wooded ridges on either side. It proved better to attack with a few tanks via an unexpected route than with a mass attack by more obvious routes.

STRONG RESISTANCE

But the Germans were not having it all their way. In the north, only Guderian's arrival and support of the hamstrung 3rd Army had enabled the latter to advance. Polish resistance was fierce and they put their meagre resources to good use. The initial shock of the German assault had worn off and the Polish High Command ordered the uncommitted Poznan Army, with surviving units of the Pomorze Army, to attack the flank of the German 8th Army at the Bzura River. On the morning of 9 September, the Poles counterattacked with customary bravery. The German infantry was scattered to the four winds and the Poles hoped they could turn the tide of war around. At Warsaw, the Germans had discovered one of the tank's limits: its inability to subdue cities. That same day, the Polish defenders, led by Major General Czum, destroyed 57 tanks in three hours of street fighting with anti-tank artillery and 'petrol cocktails'. Disgusted with his losses and infuriated with his failure to take the

Polish capital, Reichenau recalled the 1st and 4th Panzer Divisions from Warsaw. The tanks were shifted with customary German efficiency to the Bzura front, where the Poles were defeated.

The legend that Polish cavalry units should have charged in closed formation against German tanks is a total myth. Despite their lack of tanks, however, the Poles did in fact delay or divert the panzers. During the battle of the frontiers, Colonel Maczeck's motorised brigade completely halted the advance of a German light division. No doubt this convinced the OKH (*Ober Kommando Heeres*, or German High Command) that these hybrid formations were useless and should be disbanded in favour of full panzer divisions. Another example which clearly showed that the Poles were not passive in the face of the panzers is the Wolynska Cavalry Brigade's three-day battle (1–3 September) to halt the advance of the 1st and 4th Panzer Divisions. The Poles put their faith in two 'miracles': that they could organise a deep line, river-based defence of the southeast and eastern part of their country, and that the French (with 99 infantry divisions and 2500 armoured vehicles) would take the offensive in the west.

French intervention was a forlorn hope and the defence line strategy received a deathblow from Guderian's advance at lighting speed north and east of the Vistula. On 14 September, the inhabitants of the strategically vital town of Brest-Litovsk were astonished to find Guderian's tanks in the streets. He had covered 182km (114 miles) in a fortnight and had destroyed one of the few tank units of the Polish Army as it was being loaded onto a train. Just south of Brest-Litovsk, Guderian linked up with tank units of the Southern Army Group and heard the worrying news that the USSR had invaded Poland from the east.

SOVIET INVASION

In the Kremlin, having banked on a slow-paced war to give him time to prepare his invasion, Stalin was displeased to find himself faced with the need to act fast or else see his German 'ally' steal the lion's share of Poland. On 10 September, the NKO (People's Commissariat of Defence) had ordered the mobilisation of one and a half million troops and, four days later, the Kiev Special Military District (under General Semion Timoshenko), and General M. P. Kovalev's Byelo-Russian Military Districts were 'activated'.

Timoshenko set up a 'Front Mobile Group' (25th Tank Corps, containing two tank brigades) to spearhead his advance into Poland, while Kovalev created a 'Cavalry Mechanised Corps' (one mechanised corps, one motorised division and one heavy tank brigade) under General V. I. Boldin. In total, there were some 750,000 troops in seven field armies with a total of 12 tank brigades. Between 0200 and 0400 hours on the morning of 17 September, in a poorly coordinated advance, the Red Army crossed the Polish border. The Poles, under Brigadier General Orlik Ruckemann, had 18 battalions and one under-strength brigade (some 30,000 men) to defend over 1400km (1531 miles) of frontier.

It was no wonder that the Soviet advance into Poland was as rapid and spectacular as the German one in the west. By 20 September, Kovalev's armoured units had moved beyond Wilno (Vilna), while Colonel S. M. Krivoshein reached Brest-Litovsk, where Soviet and German diplomats hammered out a withdrawal as Krivoshein and Guderian viewed a tank parade. On 22 September, at Lwow (Lvov), the Polish General Lagner argued that it was better to capitulate to fellow Slavs than the

ABOVE: Poland's broad and numerous rivers proved no serious obstacle to the invading Germans. Here a panzer unit fords one of many river obstacles — following a path marked out with stakes by German engineers — without visible Polish resistance.

detestable Germans. After Timoshenko had interviewed him about the Germans' use of tanks, he was flown to Moscow where the Soviet Chief of Staff, Marshal Shaposhnikov, picked his brains further. Lagner had expected questions about his own army, but was instead bombarded with questions about the Soviets' own ally. No doubt the Soviets were anxious to know as much as possible about their new neighbour.

The Stavka noted the glaring difference in performance between the German tanks (in the face of stiff Polish resistance) and their own forces. The German panzers had now been withdrawn, since the remaining Polish resistance on the Hel peninsula on the Baltic and in Warsaw was the job of the air force, heavy artillery and infantry. Only 25 per cent of the panzers had broken down due to mechanical failure, but all machines needed repairs. The Germans were lucky that the Poles had only a few outdated tanks so their crews

could gain the necessary experience for a much tougher task ahead: the invasion of France. But coordination with the *Luftwaffe* and the infantry units had to be improved significantly before victory could be assured. Overall, the panzers had performed more than satisfactorily and won a swift victory for Germany.

STALIN'S SATISFACTION

Their ally in the Kremlin was also smugly satisfied. While the Germans had lost 217 panzers in a hard-fought battle, the USSR had lost no tanks and only suffered some 3000 casualties to gain over 123,500km^2 (77,200 sq. miles) of new land and 13 million new subjects for Stalin. Bolstered by 'his' victories against Japan and Poland, the Soviet tyrant believed he could mete out the same treatment to the Finns. Negotiations between the two over territory led nowhere, so Stalin arranged a military incident through the NKVD which was staged on the Finnish frontier and which the Soviet Union used as a pretext to invade Finland. The Red Army had planned a short campaign in the mistaken belief the Finns would only offer token resistance. Again, the Soviets placed much confidence in their tanks' ability to defeat a technically inferior enemy. The Finns had only a total strength of 300,000 men, a handful of antiquated Vickers tanks and a weak air force. Soviet General Meretskov controlled 600,000 troops and thousands of tanks and aircraft. Each Soviet division had three times the firepower of a Finnish division and included a tank battalion with 40–50 tanks. The 7th and 8th Soviet Armies had six tank brigades, while the Finns had none.

On the Karelian Isthmus, 20,000 Finnish troops in the Mannerheim Line kept at bay for weeks on end 180,000 Soviet troops – in two field armies – supported by 1000 tanks and 1000 aircraft. On the northern front, the Soviet breakthrough was due to a single tank brigade. What Soviet advances there were on the isthmus were due to the application of tanks. North of the Ladoga, the Finns cancelled a proposed counterattack at Suvilahti when the Soviets used tanks in mass formation. Some tanks managed to break through lines and even the Finns, normally tough as nails, panicked and fled to the rear.

BELOW: 'White Death'. Whatever her weaknesses in terms of armour and modern equipment, Finland made up in the sheer morale, discipline and enthusiasm of her mobile infantry units. The terrain in Finland was often unsuitable for armour. Snipers such as the one shown posing with his rifle wreaked havoc upon the advancing Soviet armoured columns strung out along wintry roads in eastern Finland.

Until the Soviet invasion, the Finns had little or no experience of tanks. Yet after the initial shock, like the Poles, they had lost some of their fear and inflicted a massive defeat upon the invader at Tolvajärvi between 10 December 1939 and 17 January 1940. Using the famous *motti*-style encircling tactic, the Finns knocked out innumerable tanks and captured 60 others. They also used the lighter Soviet anti-tank guns (captured earlier) with great effect upon the enemy's tanks. Their own guns were too heavy, while their Vickers tanks had the opposite problem: they were too light and manoeuvred badly in the snow. Finnish tank forces thus only played a marginal role in the war.

STALIN ENRAGED

Stalin was infuriated with the Red Army's deplorable performance and, during a dinner at the Kremlin, upbraided Voroshilov for the Finnish fiasco. Stung by the accusations, Voroshilov struck back. His protégé, General Kyril Meretskov, was relieved of command and Timoshenko, whose performance in Poland had been commendable, replaced him. During late February and early March Timoshenko delivered mass tank, air and artillery attacks upon the Mannerheim Line until he broke it. Once through, the Soviets made for Viborg, rolled up the Ladoga front and, by 20 March, forced the Finns to cede Karelia to the Soviet Union.

The Soviet Union had won a dangerous victory against Finland. That country was now deeply hostile towards the USSR and would take the first opportunity to have its revenge. Finland could be relied upon to support any future German offensive against the USSR. The war also gave Hitler the fatal impression that the Red Army was rotten to the core and led by military blockheads. Given the sterling qualities of the troops, Timoshenko's shake-up and the quality of the pre-war RKKA, this was an entirely misplaced notion. The Soviets also drew some faulty lessons from the war. They began to divert tank production towards heavier, slower models of tanks that could break through fortified lines and forgot the special circumstances of the Winter War. The NKO would only switch production back to more mobile tank models after the fall of France in mid-1940.

ABOVE: Experiences from the Finnish War taught the Soviets one valuable lesson: slow, multi-turreted tanks had no future and the production of these was phased out in favour of the lighter and faster models. Above is an example of the multi-turreted types in vogue before 1939 in the Soviet Union: a knocked-out T-35 heavy tank. The soldier examining the T-35 gives a sense of the vehicle's scale.

From October 1939, the OKH of the *Wehrmacht* (German Army) had begun to plan the invasion of France. The Maginot Line, which was completed from the Rhine to Sedan along France's eastern frontier with Germany by 1931 at the cost of billions of francs, complicated Germany's military planning, since an

ABOVE: France's nemesis and Germany's panzer genius, General Heinz Guderian, who led the armoured spearhead into Poland and northern France. Guderian achieved much success by leading his panzers from the front. He is seen here during the French campaign.

assault through this 'impenetrable' line was practically impossible. North of the Maginot forts lay the forested Ardennes range that not only protected Belgium, but also shielded northern France from a German attack. Given these two major obstacles, the German General Staff planners wanted simply to dust off the old Schlieffen Plan of 1914 – in other words, to sweep through northern Belgium and the Netherlands with a broad, mixed assault force of panzers and

motorised troops. Following this first wave would come the horsedrawn artillery and infantry masses of the *Wehrmacht* plodding at a leisurely pace.

HITLER UNCONVINCED

Hitler was not entirely convinced of the wisdom of this plan, given its failure in 1914 to knock out France. He was terrified of a new two-front war that could get bogged down like the last world war. He believed, quite rightly, that the combination of massed panzer attacks and air power would knock out France and prevent a military stalemate on the Western Front.

One man, General Erich von Manstein, dared to question the logic of his peers by calling for a radical and drastic approach to the invasion of France. Instead of swinging through the Low Countries with the bulk of the panzers and trying to encircle the French from the east, the panzers (augmented by the conversion of the light divisions into the 6th, 7th, 8th and 9th Panzer Divisions) should be concentrated at a single point to deliver an armoured hammer blow to the French defences. Unlike his colleagues, Manstein was neither in awe of the French Army nor convinced that the Ardennes was unsuitable for tank warfare. On the contrary, the forest canopy could afford much-needed camouflage as the panzers moved through the 'impenetrable' Ardennes. Two further factors commended this region to Manstein: first, it was held by one of the weakest of the French armies, General Corap's 9th Army, made up with disgruntled and demoralised reservists; and, secondly, the French would not expect an attack to be delivered here.

Manstein's outspokenness and bold plans got him sacked, but not before copies of his plan, codenamed 'Scythe Cut' (*Sichelschnitt*) had reached Guderian and Hitler. Both the Führer and the panzer general liked Manstein's plan. Manstein was recalled by the spring of 1940 and Plan Yellow, the invasion plan, was revised dramatically to incorporate his ideas. Although Marshal Bock's Army Group was still to invade both Belgium and Holland with a large share of the German forces on the Western Front, this was only a diversion. It was important, as it would convince the Allies to advance

ABOVE: To replace older, more cumbersome heavy tank models, the Russians developed the KV (Kliment Voroshilov) Model 1 tank in 1940. It was tested in Finland and used as an assault tank to break through enemy lines. It was armed with a 76mm (3in) gun.

LEFT: The British also built heavy or infantry support tanks. This model is the 'Queen of the Battlefield', the infantry Mk II 'Matilda', which was impervious to all Italian and German dedicated anti-tank guns up to 1942. It lacked speed, however, and its two-pounder gun was quickly made obsolescent by the Germans up-armouring their panzers.

ABOVE: A posed photograph supposed to show Allied fraternisation and close cooperation. The British tank crew of the light Vickers tank seem worried.

RIGHT: After the Dutch, the Belgians had the smallest tank force on the Allied side in 1940. This tank, a Belgian AMC 35 (with 47mm (1.85in) gun), has been knocked out by anti-tank shells (note the entry holes in the turret) and abandoned during the Allied retreat to the Channel ports.

into Belgium in the mistaken belief that the main German blow would still fall upon that country. In fact, the main blow would be struck further south with seven panzer divisions supported by 34 infantry divisions led by Rundstedt. The panzer forces were made up of four Panzer Corps: Hoeppner's XIVth, Hoth's XVth, Reinhardt's XLIth and finally the XIXth under Guderian. Each corps had at least one motorised infantry division attached to it, the result of a lesson that had been

learnt in Poland. Panzers could not hold ground once it had been captured without infantry support, and that infantry had to be motorised if it was to keep pace with the panzers. The OKH conservatives continued to worry about allowing the tanks to race ahead through the Ardennes when they would be vulnerable to a French counterstroke as they emerged at the Meuse, and they even worried about Belgian resistance in the region itself. Guderian brushed aside these not entirely unfounded fears by pointing out that the bulk of the Allied armies were deployed away from the area and his only preoccupation was whether his target, once his panzers were across the Meuse, was to be Paris or Amiens. Capture of the first promised to bring political and military paralysis to the French, while the second would cut the Allied armies in two.

On the other side of the military fence, so to speak, the Allies were blissfully unaware of German plans. They only knew and expected the Germans to be as unimaginative as themselves in the use and organisation of tanks. A copy of the original Plan Yellow (*Fall Gelb*) had fallen into Belgian hands when a German staff officer made an emergency landing just across the frontier with intact copies of the plan tucked away in a briefcase. It could have been a plant; it was not, but the Allies were reassured by what they read. The Allies had learnt nothing from the Polish campaign; they believed that the Polish debacle was due to material deficiencies, not faulty tactics and organisation. The Poles had no Maginot Line, nor did they have as many tanks of the calibre the French did. By early 1940, the French had concentrated some 63 infantry divisions, seven motorised, three light mechanised and three armoured divisions along the northeastern front. The 7th French Army (under General Giraud) had one armoured division and the remaining two were allotted to the strategic reserve of General Billotte's 1st Army Group.

ALLIED SENSE OF SECURITY

The Allies felt strong. They were and, in terms of the quality and quantity of their tanks, were quite superior to the Germans. The Germans had started late with production, and their tanks were lighter and weaker in armour and armaments than their Allied equivalents. Of a total of about 3000 panzers, only 627 were of the latest Mark III or IV standard and 381 were Czech 38ts; the rest, some 2060 machines, were the inadequate Mark I or II. These machines had proved vulnerable to mortar and artillery fire during the war against Poland. The French had over 3000 tanks, plus a large number of obsolete World War I tanks in reserve formations. The best 1292 tanks were concentrated in the DLMs and DCM (*Divisions Cuirasée*). The British had 210 light tanks and some 100 heavy tanks (including 23 brand-new Matildas) in France. The Matildas, the Char B and British Mark I tanks could all stand up to the best of the German panzers and anti-tank guns.

Unfortunately, Allied technical and numerical superiority was not matched by a clear understanding of how to handle tanks effectively. The Allied tanks were scattered around infantry divisions to be used as support for the infantry, and not used as a proper independent arm that could dominate the battlefield. The Germans had perfected the panzer formation, communications between tanks and coordination with the Stuka dive-bomber squadrons used by the Germans as airborne artillery. They had installed radios in all their tanks (based upon Guderian's sound advice) and tightened up cooperation between the panzers and *Luftwaffe*.

This tank and dive-bomber combination was the secret ingredient of the success of the German *Blitzkrieg*. Another was that the German panzer commanders, following Guderian's example in Poland, led their units from the front, while their Allied counterparts were miles away from their men at their headquarters. This is not to say that the French Army did not contain good commanders or units. It did, but the dead hand of peacetime routine had killed off freer spirits and new ideas. One exception to the rule, as shown in the previous chapter, was General de Gaulle.

On the German side, there was great nervousness about whether they could pull off their armoured coup against the most vaunted war machine in the world. In this coming battle, the contest was like that of a heavily armed and experienced knight with a powerful mount facing a young upstart with a fast horse and eager lance. One false move on the part of the challenger and he could be felled. Everything now hinged upon the 200,000 young men in the Panzer Corps and their 3000 *Luftwaffe* colleagues. Could they pull it off: defeat France and bring a swift victory to the 'Fatherland'? Only the invasion itself could answer this question.

Following the invasion of Scandinavia and some six months of feverish preparations, the *Wehrmacht*, like a coiled spring, was ready to strike. On 10 May, the Germans launched Plan Yellow against the Low Countries. The 1st Panzer Division helped reduce Holland in a mere four days (despite fierce Dutch resistance), while two panzer divisions invaded Belgium. The remaining three panzer corps headed through the Ardennes, where the main headache for the Germans were endless traffic jams and

Guderian asked for and got massive air support. The Stukas were almost an integral part of the panzer forces and pounded the French defences west of the river to pieces. By noon on 13 May, all the panzer units were across the river. At this crucial juncture the French should have, as they had in the past, held their ground, whatever the cost in terms of blood and suffering. But General Corap, who was not at the front but relied upon secondhand reports that were overly pessimistic, gave the disastrous order to retreat from the 'indefensible' river line. It could and should, however, have been held, since Reinhardt's Corps was hanging on by its fingernails to a precarious bridgehead at Monthèrme. As the French begun their retreat, the panzers flooded through the lines like a tidal wave: by 14 May, the 1st Panzer Division was 24km (15 miles) to the west. The commander of the 7th Panzer Division, General Erwin Rommel, believed the French had no

the logistics of keeping this enormous military show on the road.

On the Meuse, the French Tank Divisions (DLMs) of the French Cavalry Divisions, despite having superior Somua S-35 tanks, were only deployed in penny packets with the infantry. Meanwhile, the feared German Stukas pounded the French tanks incessantly from the air until they were forced to retreat. By 13 May, all three panzer corps had reached the Meuse. Further north, XVI Panzer Corps had helped to push back and defeat the Belgian Army. The Belgian defences were in total disarray after the fall of Eben Emael fort complex. These events, however important as diversions, were mere sideshows to the main event taking place further south.

stomach for a real fight and rushed ahead. He was 42km (26 miles) west of the Meuse that same day as the spearhead of Hoth's Panzer Corps.

By the evening of 15 May, the German High Command, including Hitler and Rundstedt, were suffering from a case of cold feet. What if the French tanks and infantry units staged a counteroffensive in the flank of the panzers? When Kleist, the panzer sceptic, ordered Guderian to halt, the mercurial general, chomping at the bit to get moving even faster, refused and offered his resignation. Rundstedt had to keep his quarrelling generals apart and allowed Guderian to advance as fast as he could. Waving aside all orders to halt, Rommel rushed ahead and had occupied Le Cateau by 17 May.

French counterattacks with tanks did take place. South of Sedan, the 3rd French Tank Division (DLM) attacked with great élan, but the 10th Panzer Division brushed it aside. Having reorganised and equipped his forces at record speed, de Gaulle rushed his newly formed 4th DLM to the front. He made a determined but unsuccessful counter-attack at Laon. The 1st Panzer Division fought de Gaulle to a standstill and rushed on. Hour by hour, France was being sliced in two, and the best part of the Allied armies (moving into Belgium) was being cut off from the rest of the country. The northern 'pocket' included the entire BEF (British Expeditionary Force), the Belgians and the best units of the French Army. South of that dividing line – the Scape River – the French were ever more desperately constructing a defence line to protect Paris.

THE CHANNEL SIGHTED

By the evening of 20 May, men of the 2nd Panzer Division saw in the distance a broad blue belt of water: the English Channel. The 1st Panzer Division occupied Amiens, while the 6th and 8th were recuperating between Le Boisle and Le Bassé. The 7th Panzer Division, led at the peril of his life by Rommel from the front, swept on towards Arras, where it was to encounter a nasty surprise. On 21 May Rommel bumped into the British 7th Royal Tank Regiment (RTR). The RTR had 58 tanks, of which 16 were brand-new Matilda IIs, each with a two-pounder gun, 78mm (3.1in) armour and a massive weight of 26 tons.

By the standards of 1940, Matilda, despite its charming female name, was a monster of a tank. With these lumbering giants coming at them, both the German panzers and the accompanying raw SS *Totenkopf* Division infantry panicked. Their armour was like paper in the face of the Matilda's guns and her armour so thick that existing anti-tank guns were no better than popguns. These heavy tanks killed 600 troops and knocked out over 40 German tanks until Rommel, ever the brilliant improviser, found some 88mm (3.45in) anti-aircraft guns that he used with good effect on the British 'heavies'. Having had a taste of the '88s', the British

ABOVE: The French had good-quality tanks. One of the best was the Char B series with 76mm (3in) armour. Although it carried a 75mm (2.95in) gun, this was mounted in the hull rather than the turret, which meant the whole tank had to be pointed at the target. This Char B-1 was knocked out at Le Croisettes near the Somme during a failed counterattack.

RIGHT: France's man of destiny. Colonel Charles de Gaulle had warned France of the consequences of not keeping pace with tank developments elsewhere, but failed to convince the political establishment to modernise and expand the French tank forces. De Gaulle is seen here at manoeuvres in March 1938, with General Delestraint at his side.

RIGHT: The Battle of Arras was a bloody nose for Rommel's 7th Panzer Division. Originally intended to coincide with a French attack from the south, the Matilda Is and IIs of the 4th and 7th Royal Tank Regiments (RTRs) gave 7th Panzer its highest losses of the campaign, and were only stopped by the use of 88mm (3.45in) anti-aircraft guns used in an anti-tank role.

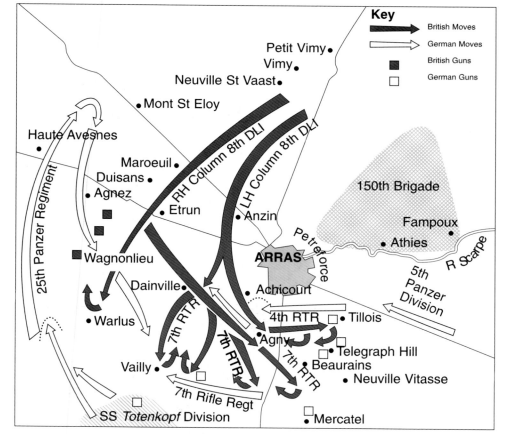

withdrew. It was clear to the Germans that their own machines were far inferior to some of the better Allied tanks. Rommel, too, had learnt a valuable lesson: tanks and anti-tank guns in combination made a formidable defence barrier against a mass tank attack. This lesson was rammed home again when his 25th Panzer Regiment was badly mauled by anti-tank guns. As we shall see, he was to apply these valuable lessons and experiences to the war in the desert.

Guderian and the other German panzer commanders wanted to pierce the Allied bubble around the Channel ports, but Hitler feared that, as demonstrated at Warsaw, they would lose scarce and valuable tanks and tank crews trying to take them. On 24 May, convinced the *Luftwaffe* could do the job of destroying the trapped BEF by itself, Hitler ordered a halt to the advance, allowing the British to escape across the Channel while the *Luftwaffe* relatively ineffectually strafed and bombed the beachhead. Guderian was infuriated that he had been prevented from achieving a total victory.

But the enemy had taken new heart. Given the paralysis at the head of the

French Army, it was high time that General Gamelin was replaced and the energetic Maxime Weygand was selected in his stead. Weygand was not marked by defeatism or the pessimism that had ensured the defeats of the preceding few weeks. His appointment seemed too little, too late; most of the army had been lost in the north. What men remained at Weygand's disposal, however, had been fired by a new patriotic glow and determination, which had, hitherto, been sadly lacking on the French side. The French had finally realised they faced defeat if they did not fight their ruthless foe with their traditional élan.

RADICAL THINKING

Weygand gave up the linear front line in favour of a radical solution. French units would be placed, with artillery and what remained of their armour, in strategic locations so as to dominate all approaches and roads nearby. A connected line of so-called 'hedgehogs' along the new front line north of Paris (and along the Somme and Aisne rivers) was named the 'Weygand Line'. Weygand told his troops they were fighting the 'Battle of France'

BELOW: The British had no proper armoured division (like the French) in 1940, but some of their equipment such as this Matilda tank was quite good. German air power forced the Allies to camouflage their tanks and ensured that they could not put their tanks to proper use against the panzers. The Matilda was later to serve in the Western Desert.

and had to stand and die where they stood; there was nowhere to run. The Germans on their part regrouped from the north to attack the centre of France in what was codenamed 'Operation Red'. As before, it was the panzers that would take the brunt of the fighting by spearheading the attack upon the Weygand Line and punching a hole through it. The XV Panzer Corps (5th and 7th Panzer Divisions) was stationed on the coast, the XIV Corps (9th and 10th Panzer Divisions) at Amiens, followed by the XVI Corps (3rd and 4th Panzer Divisions), and finally Guderian commanding a larger, new corps (1st, 2nd, 6th and 8th Panzer Divisions).

OPERATION RED

Hoth's XV Panzer Corps was first to strike and begin Operation Red on 5 June. But this time there was no Corap to order a headlong retreat. The French put up fierce resistance through a combination of artillery and what remained of their heavier tanks. Used to French 'flabbiness' in defence of the north, the Germans were astonished to find themselves faced with a foe that had

taken new heart and showed a will to fight. The French had learnt the lessons of tank warfare with surprising speed and had applied them. They had laid minefields, massed their tanks to give punch to their armoured units and concealed their artillery to lay a proper field of fire in the way of the panzers. It took even Guderian, with his powerful panzer group, over five days to get across the Aisne and through the French defence lines. Had the French had a determined war leader (such as Charles de Gaulle) at the helm in Paris, more territory to trade for land lost, or more aircraft and tanks, then in June 1940, they might have fought the Germans to a standstill. But the lack of all these factors, coupled with a shortage of ammunition and the German breakthroughs, made French defences break down. On 13 June, the French Government fled from Paris, which was declared an open city. Three days later still, Guderian had crossed central France in less than a week to reach the Swiss border. Thus General Prételat's 2nd Army Group of 43 divisions were cut off holding the Maginot sector.

BELOW: *Blitzkrieg* in action. The left-hand artwork shows German panzers pinning down the Allied defences, while a unit of panzergrenadiers in half-tracks bypass the defences and capture the vital bridge crossing. In this fashion, bridgeheads could be extended on the far side of the Meuse, Somme and Seine rivers. Should the bridges have been blown up by the retreating Allies, the right-hand artwork shows how the Germans would send panzergrenadiers across the river in rubber dinghies, while tanks would give fire support from the far bank.

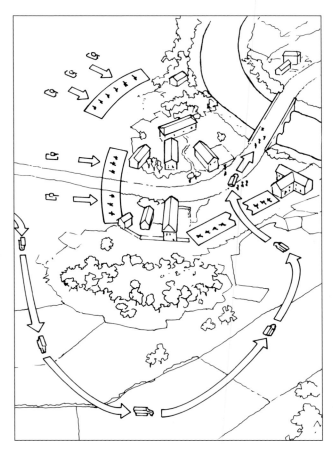
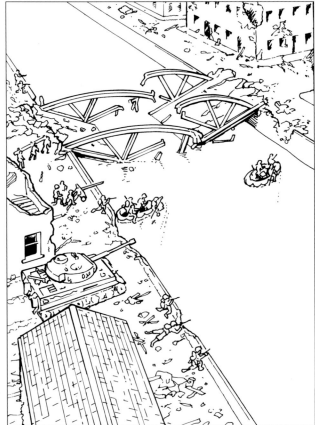

DEFEATISM

Until now, French defeatism had been under control, but at French HQ that 'spirit' began to creep in and the argument was heard more often; it could not go on like this. Churchill's badgering and support only made many of the French, even Weygand, resent their ally's interference. To boost French morale and show that Britain was giving its unstinting support, Churchill despatched a second BEF to France which included the British 1st Armoured Division with 174 light and 156 tanks. It was a commendable gesture, but it could not change the course of the Battle of France.

On 19 June, the irrepressible Rommel, having rampaged through Normandy and cut French units to shreds, reached Cherbourg, where the British 51st Division was forced to capitulate. It was only one of the worst pieces of news in an increasingly dismal situation and the French turned, as they had in 1917, to one man they trusted: Marshal Pétain. Unfortunately, the fighting general of World War I had gone to seed and was a convinced defeatist who blamed the British for France's woes. He called on Hitler to give him a soldier's peace and, on 25 June 1940, what Weygand had called the Battle of France was over.

Both sides were stunned by their fate: the French by their swift and humiliating defeat which left them in a daze, the Germans by their equally stunning success. What the Kaiser had been unable to do in four years of fighting, Hitler's panzers and Stuka squadrons, in deadly combination, had done in a little over four weeks. It was mainly the application of tanks to modern warfare, however, that had led to the amazing results of the campaign. The panzers had not only dominated the battlefield, but also achieved total victory over Germany's most traditional and dangerous foe.

Hitler was master of Europe by late 1940 and, but for the bungling incompetence of his ally, Mussolini, he could have turned his attentions towards the Soviet Union, his remaining and main continental enemy. As for the defeated British, the cancellation of Operation Sea Lion (the planned invasion of Britain) in late 1940 allowed them to absorb, at record speed, the lessons to be learnt from their debacle in France and to begin creating 10 new tank divisions.

The Germans, too, had lessons to learn from the campaign. Where their admiring allies and grudgingly respectful enemies alike saw a flawless military machine that seemed able to produce victories at the drop of a hat, the German

ABOVE: A German PzKpfw IV engages French defenders during the advance southwards into France after the evacuation at Dunkirk. The PzKpfw IV had proven itself to be an excellent tank, if a little lacking in firepower. Along with the PzKpfw III, it would form the bulk of the German panzer forces for the next three years.

ABOVE: In 1919, the French stopped production of this model of giant heavy tank, the Char 2C, and only 10 were in fact ever produced. In 1939, these were still in service with the 51st Tank Battalion. None of these behemoths saw actual combat, however, since the unit was knocked out while being transported on flat cars to the front by dive-bombing Stukas.

commanders saw the weakness behind the façade. German tanks were too thinly armoured and armed. So some Panzer IIIs and IVs were given new, long-barrelled 50mm guns for greater penetration of enemy tank armour. The lack of infantry to support the panzers' advance (the slower-moving infantry could not keep pace with the tanks) had been a constant problem during the invasion of France. The production of half-tracks was therefore stepped up and more infantry units were motorised.

NEED FOR ARTILLERY SUPPORT

There was also a great need for the tanks to have artillery support, so captured French tanks were converted into mobile 'assault guns' manned by artillery crews in special units that were attached to the panzer divisions. The lack of powerful anti-tank artillery was not properly solved, but the '88s' had proved even more effective against tanks than aircraft, so the production of these was stepped up, too. However, Hitler's refusal to burden the German people with the sacrifices of total war (in contrast to Churchill's 'blood, sweat and tears' approach in Britain) ensured that tank production remained at an unimpressive 1000 machines per year. Thus the panzer units did not have more or better tanks a

year later when they faced their most formidable foe so far in the war: the Red Army's tank forces.

Hitler remained obsessed with the USSR, but had to drop plans for an early invasion in October 1940 in favour of the spring of 1941. Before he could even contemplate such a move, which would extend the war eastwards, the Balkans – the Soviet Union's southwestern flank – had to be secured. Mussolini's declaration of war against Greece on 28 October and the subsequent invasion of that country had proved a dismal failure that reflected poorly on the Axis as a whole. That the Italians were equally unsuccessful in North Africa against the British did not improve the general situation.

Germany already dominated Hungary, Romania and Bulgaria when, on 25 March 1941, the alliance with Yugoslavia completed Hitler's dominance of the Balkans. But his initial euphoria at such a cheaply bought victory was soon to turn sour. Two days later, the Deputy Commander of the Yugoslav Air Force, General Bora Mirkovic, staged a military coup in Belgrade and repudiated the pact with Germany. That same evening, when the news arrived at Hitler's HQ, the Führer thought it was a bad joke. His initial 'humour' was rapidly transformed into furious outrage, the likes of which

LEFT: The Germans could use France's and the Low Countries' superb roads to advance at phenomenal speed. These crews are mounting their Czech-built 38ts before continuing their advance into the heart of France. The tank crews black uniforms and berets were discontinued during the latter stages of the war.

had never been seen. On 30 March, the orders for 'Operation Punishment', the invasion of Yugoslavia, were completed. The 9th Panzer Division, supported by the motorised infantry of the SS *Leibstandarte* Adolf Hitler Division, would spearhead Field Marshal von List's 12th Army (operating from Bulgaria) in an attack upon Skopje, the capital of Yugoslav Macedonia. Kleist's XIV Corps (from Romania), with three Panzer divisions, would strike against Nis and Belgrade. Finally, General Weich's II Army would invade Slovenia on its way to Zagreb, the capital of Croatia.

YUGOSLAVIA OVERCOME

Yugoslavia was the weakest of Hitler's foes so far. She was in no state, either militarily or politically, to face an armoured onslaught on the scale the Germans planned. Like the Poles, the Yugoslavians had a weak army, consisting of 28 infantry divisions and three cavalry divisions, to defend some 932km (1020 miles) of frontier. Like the Poles, the

LEFT: Another good French tank on the move: the Hotchkiss H-39. It first appeared in 1939 and gave a good account of itself during the campaign of 1940, although it was under-gunned – it only mounted a 37mm (1.47in) gun. Like all French tanks, it was hampered in combat by the flawed French tactics.

Yugoslavian High Command compounded their problems by spreading out their inferior and antiquated army along most of the frontier in a forlorn attempt to hold everything. France's political problems were nothing compared to Yugoslavia, where the Croats and Serbs fought for control of their multiracial state. The Yugoslav Army nowhere near the French or even Polish army's level of mechanisation and understanding of armoured warfare. One general told the country's ruler that tanks would only run out of petrol, and that horses and even bullocks were more reliable, if slower, means of transportation! They had no tank divisions or even brigades, only regiments and companies of tanks, 80 per cent of which were obsolete 1920s-era light Vickers tanks. Thus, Hitler had delayed the invasion of the USSR to divert an unnecessarily large number of units against a pitifully weak foe. He was using the equivalent of a huge sledgehammer to crack a peanut.

For the Germans, the Balkan campaign was a textbook example of

BELOW: In March 1941 Bulgaria was 'persuaded' to join the Axis and a month later the Germans crossed the Yugoslavian border to crush her remaining Balkan antagonists. This column of PzKpfw IIIs is crossing the Greco-Bulgarian border a week later.

panzer warfare in *Blitzkrieg* fashion against a much weaker foe crippled by political problems. On the entire Macedonian front, the Yugoslavs had not a single anti-tank gun and the Germans attacked from all sides. Skopje fell to List's panzer spearhead on 7 April; the day after Nis fell, Weich's army captured Zagreb, where 15,000 Croat troops capitulated without a shot being fired. The Hungarians, who had a friendship pact with Germany, only invaded Yugoslavia with great reluctance and even then with

the justification of 'protecting' their countrymen in the Banat (an area north of Belgrade). On 11 April, Hungarian tanks crossed the border and, showing a decided lack of 'German' efficiency, ran out of petrol, haggling with local chemists for more as there were no recognised petrol stations in Yugoslavia. The next day, Belgrade fell to the 8th Panzer Division. On 16 April, the last stronghold in Yugoslavia, Sarajevo, fell to advancing German tanks, and the day after what little remained of the Yugoslav Army capitulated.

Further south, the 2nd Panzer Division cut through Macedonia and outflanked Greece's Mataxas Line which protected the northeastern (and economically vital) part of Greece. The Greek faith in fortified lines without a properly organised and modern field army was as mistaken as that of the French. The panzers broke through the thin Greek defences along their border with Yugoslavia and managed to split two of the most powerful Greek armies (in Albania and the northeast) from each other. Like their northern ally, the Greeks lacked armoured units and experience of armoured warfare. General Papagos, the Greek Commander in Chief, ordered the 19th Motorised Division to block the 2nd Panzer Division's advance, but it proved unsuccessful. The Greek division achieved little in the face of the German tank units' obvious superiority and Thessaloniki fell to the panzers shortly afterwards. As in France, bad news followed bad news; on 10 April, the German XL Motorised Corps linked up with the Italian Army in Albania at the Monastir gap. Greece's best two armies — one along the Albanian border, and the 'Macedonian' one facing Bulgaria along the Mataxas Line — were forced to capitulate on 16 April.

FURTHER ALLIED DEFEATS

The burden of the fighting was now placed on the shoulders of the Expeditionary Force that Churchill had sent to Greece after German intentions became clear, the bulk of which was made up of Australian and New Zealanders (recognised as tough and durable troops). The British had hoped to hold the coastal plains while the Greek Army held the mountainous interior of

the country. However, they had to abandon that plan as well as their hopes to hold the Aliakmon River, as the advance of the German panzers made it impossible. A classical tank encounter took place on an ancient battleground when the British blocked the Pass of Thermopylae as the Spartans had done centuries before. The 2nd Panzer Division had in the meantime continued its swift advance from the north and was temporarily prevented from reaching Athens by the British tanks at the pass, which, along with British anti-tank guns, shot up 19 panzers in fierce and sharp skirmishes. The deadlock was only broken when the motorised infantry which accompanied the tanks dismounted and outflanked the Allied positions. The British were forced to

withdraw and finally, a few weeks later, evacuate the whole of Greece.

The Balkan campaign was hastily planned, but the professionalism and improvisation of the *Wehrmacht* had yielded great results. It seemed to Hitler and other German military planners that the panzers could conquer any enemy in any form of terrain and climate whenever the Führer pushed a button. This was a highly dangerous notion. In fact, the Balkan campaign was won with great force against a much weaker, poorly equipped and poorly organised set of enemies who could not hope to stand up to German military might. But this was only the beginning, and the Balkans was the last outright *Blitzkrieg* victory. In the east lurked a far more dangerous and determined foe for the panzers to defeat.

ABOVE: Once they reached the plains of Greece, the Germans cut up the Allied forces as they hoped they would be able to do in the Soviet Union. Yet again, Germany's panzers spearheaded a victorious campaign that left the Allies humiliated after another inglorious disaster. The Soviet Union would be a tougher prospect, however, and new, more powerful tanks such as this 75mm (2.95in) armed PzKpfw Ausf F2 would be needed to combat the Soviet tank forces.

CHAPTER FOUR

THE EASTERN FRONT

Hitler's invasion of the Soviet Union in 1941 was his greatest gamble of the war and, as usual, his panzer forces led the way.

It was obvious from the start that the Nazi–Soviet Pact was to be a marriage of convenience and it was only a question of time before one or the other partner broke the 'marriage vows'. It was Hitler who struck first, and almost destroyed the USSR in the process. In his mind, the threat of a two-front war had been removed with the defeat of France. Accordingly, in July 1940, the OKH staff began plans for the invasion of the USSR, codenamed 'Otto'. They were confident that the Red Army could be encircled and destroyed before the winter set in. They wanted, therefore, to give the lion's share of the *Wehrmacht*'s tank strength to the central army group which was to occupy Moscow. They hoped that the defence of their capital would make the Russians willing to stand and fight, giving the panzers a chance to encircle them and destroy their main formations. Capturing Moscow would also, argued the planners, demoralise the Russians

LEFT: Short-barrelled Panzer IVs (Model E) belonging to the armoured forces of the *Waffen-SS* advancing along a road during Operation Barbarossa, the invasion of the Soviet Union. By the time of Barbarossa, the *Waffen-SS* was a sizeable force in its own right and a competitor to the *Wehrmacht*. After initial problems, it became feared and respected for its fighting ability, and claimed the latest German equipment for its units. The wide, open spaces visible in the photograph are typical of the Soviet Union, scene of many epic tank battles in World War II.

ABOVE: Ideal tank country. Another view of the terrain in the east, which, especially in the Ukraine, was perfectly suited for tank warfare. Panzergrenadiers are advancing with their tanks towards the enemy on the horizon. Yet the huge distances travelled and the poor roads in the region were to hamper the advance of the Germans towards their objectives.

while disrupting their administration and rail communications.

Hitler disagreed. He wanted priority to be given to the capture of the rich Ukrainian grain region and Caucasus oil. He believed, furthermore, that the capture of Moscow was less important than the 'cradle of Bolshevism', Leningrad. What Hitler failed to understand was that these targets were less important than the capture of Moscow and that absolute priority had to be given to the destruction of the Red Army's field strength. Once the RKKA had been destroyed, all the German objectives could be taken at their leisure. Both he and his generals and planners had, however, committed two fatal blunders: they had underestimated their enemy and failed to focus the invasion upon one overriding objective.

The workhorse of the Barbarossa plan (as it was renamed in December 1940) was to be the panzer divisions of the German Army. Following the experiences of France and Poland, a panzer division was made up of two components: one panzer brigade (160 tanks) and one motorised infantry brigade. These in turn were to be backed up by an expanded number of motorised infantry divisions (MIDs) made up of two infantry brigades with soldiers carried in armoured personnel carriers.

Morale in the German panzer force was high: having defeated the whole of Europe, they were ready to take on the Russians, and they were as confident of a swift victory as their commanders. They also had good material at their disposal. The 23-tonne PzKpfw IIIs and IVs were good machines and the Germans were clearly superior to the Russians in radio and optical instruments. In addition to the tank 'killer' 88mm (3.45in) gun, the Germans had also built up a large number of self-propelled guns that would give the panzers valuable artillery support on the battlefield.

Yet in essence the German invasion army was too weak for its allotted task, especially in tanks and aircraft. In total, the Germans had only 15 more divisions to conquer the Soviet Union (which occupied over 1,000,000 square miles of territory or an area 20 times larger than the area operated in during the 1940 campaign). Crucially, the Germans had only 30 per cent more tanks than they had in 1940 (19 panzer divisions and 14 MIDs), totalling some 3300 tanks to face 21,000 Soviet tanks. The *Luftwaffe* had only 2800 aircraft (with 1500 planes in the west) to face the Soviet air armada of 12,000 planes. Clearly there were insufficient tanks or aircraft to perform the task.

The main problem was Hitler's failure to give priority to his aims and group his forces accordingly. Thus Hoeppner's 4th Panzer Group (three panzer divisions) in Army Group North (Field Marshal von Leeb) was to invade the Baltic States and take Leningrad. At least Army Group

LEFT: In 1941, the Germans had perfected the combination of air power (to pound the burning town) and fast moving panzers. The German strategy was to fight a so-called *Kesselschlacht* (cauldron battle), where entire Soviet armies could be encircled and destroyed while avoiding huge casualties for the Germans. The prime example of a *Kesselschlacht* was the Kiev pocket (September 1941).

Centre (Field Marshal von Bock) had two panzer groups: Guderian's 2nd (five panzer divisions) and Hoth's 3rd (four panzer divisions). Their task was to surround and destroy the 3rd, 4th and 10th Soviet Armies in the Bialystok bulge led by West Front commander General Pavlov. After this had been effected (through a convergence of Hoth's and Guderian's forces), they were not to strike at Moscow. Both panzer commanders wanted to do just that, but no plans had been made for this eventuality. South of the Pripet marshes (an area of swamp the size of Bavaria), over half the length of the front, stood Army Group South (Field Marshal von Rundstedt) with only six panzer divisions (Kleist's 1st Panzer Group) to conquer the whole of the Ukraine. Rundstedt also faced the strongest Soviet Front, General Kirponos's South West Front, formed from no fewer than four powerful armies containing 16 tank divisions.

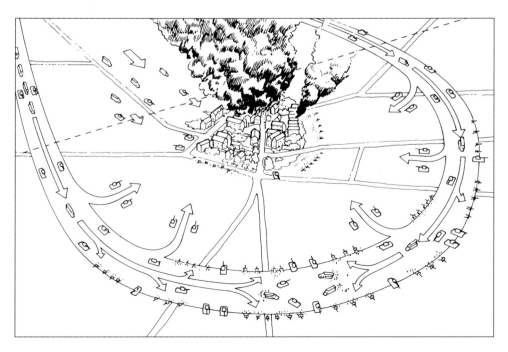

LEFT: An idealised version of the *Kesselschlacht*. The panzers, accompanied by panzergrenadiers, would bypass and surround a strongpoint, which would then be reduced by air power and artillery until its defenders were destroyed or forced to surrender. Huge numbers of prisoners were taken by the Germans during Operation Barbarossa, but the Soviets would learn from their mistakes in 1941.

On the Soviet side, confusion and uncertainty reigned over the proper use of its armoured forces. The last mechanised corps had been disbanded in late 1939 thanks to Pavlov's faulty conclusions from the Spanish Civil War. The swift fall of France had sent shock waves through the Red Army command and reached even Stalin. The Soviet dictator's ideas were finally abandoned and Timoshenko recalled 4000 purged officers to duty. Three new mechanised corps were set up with a paper strength of over 1000 tanks at Kiev (Lieutenant General Rokossovsky),

Moscow (Lieutenant General Romanenko) and Minsk (Lieutenant General Yeremenko). None of the remaining corps (13th, 17th, 20th, 24th) could be called mechanised due to their lack of tanks.

LOW TANK PRODUCTION

To compound Stalin's problems, the production of older tank models was discontinued before the models came on line. In 1940, only 115 T-34s and 243 KV-1/KV-2s were produced. Production between January and mid-June 1941 did climb to 1000 T-34s and 393 KVs (both

RIGHT: As in Poland two years earlier, natural obstacles did not prove a major headache for the invading Germans. Here a mixed column of PzKpfw IIs and IIIs cross a river during the advance into the Soviet Union.

models). These formidable machines were not concentrated in a single new mechanised corps, which would have been able to stem the flood of the panzers, but were dispersed among the existing 12 mechanised corps, lessening their impact on the German invading forces and thus the outcome of the campaign. Their effectiveness was further reduced by the Soviet practice of deploying them (like the French) in penny packets, which allowed them to be overwhelmed by the more concentrated panzers. Thus only nine per cent of the Soviet tanks were T-34s or KVs and, of the remaining tanks, over 29 per cent needed major overhauls and 44 per cent needed sizeable refits.

OPERATION BARBAROSSA

All hell broke lose on the western frontier of the USSR at dawn of 22 June 1941 as German artillery unleashed a storm of shell and grenades upon the unsuspecting Soviet border areas while the Soviet airfields were pounded from

ABOVE: The problems caused by dust and heat during the Russian summer were just as great for the panzers as those caused by the frozen winter.

BELOW: The early triumphs of Barbarossa disguised an important fact: most of the *Wehrmacht's* units were still infantry formations and the level of mechanisation was low overall.

ABOVE: Unlike their enemy, the Soviets mobilised their entire economy for total war from the very beginning of Operation Barbarossa and managed, through ruthless standardisation and exertions, to outstrip German tank production. Their best tanks, the T-34 (seen here on an assembly line behind the lines) and KV–1, proved far superior to their German rival's designs.

RIGHT: In Smolensk in 1941, a knocked-out T-26 tank is being used as a road sign, symbolically pointing to the east and the Soviet capital. Soviet tank losses in 1941 were enormous, but they would be replaced quickly and with better quality tanks.

the air. In the north, General Manstein's 56th Panzer Corps moved 88km (50 miles) in three days across Soviet-occupied Latvia and Lithuania, while Guderian's panzers penetrated 88km (50 miles) east of the Bug river and Hoth travelled the furthest at 88.5km (55 miles). Pavlov's 3rd, 4th, and 10th Armies were duly trapped around Bialystok in the first of many Soviet pockets. They were eliminated by 30 June with the loss of 40 divisions, 300,000 prisoners and 2500 tank. Pavlov had made one too many mistakes; he was recalled on 28 June and shot shortly afterwards.

Hitler was calling for, and getting, *Kesselschlachten* ('cauldron' battles) to liquidate the Red Army. But the Germans had already begun at this stage to realise the scale of their task. The destroyed Soviet 4th Armoured Division alone (Major General Potaturchev), for example, had 355 tanks to Guderian's entire corps strength of 855 panzers. However, in a week of war, the Red Army had lost 2500 tanks.

On 29 June, Guderian's and Hoth's corps converged at Minsk. This time the RKKA lost 250,000 troops and 3000 tanks in the pocket. Guderian's and Hoth's corps were combined into the 4th Panzer Army on 9 July and crossed the Dniepr to attack Smolensk as a first step to taking Moscow. But Hitler had other ideas. He wanted to swing the 4th Panzer Army to the south and surround the South-West Front, while Rundstedt took Kiev from the west.

Guderian and Hitler had a huge row at this point about where the panzers should be headed. Hitler unsurprisingly won. On 23 June, he ordered the 4th Army south against Kiev. Guderian ignored the order and had enough time to create another cauldron around Smolensk on 27 July. By 5 August, the pocket had capitulated and the German booty amounted to nine divisions, 300,000 prisoners and 3000 tanks.

The Germans were not, however, having it all their own way. General Yeremenko had made a powerful tank attack against Guderian and managed to halt a probe east of Smolensk (captured on 16 July by motorised German infantry). These attacks were frontal and had a weak punch, but the Red Army was learning fast. The Soviet 5th Army used the Pripet marshes to attack the panzers' open flanks. The Russians learnt to make attacks in the vulnerable joints of the German Army between the plodding infantry and the fast-moving panzers. A year earlier, the French had tried and failed at this, but the Russians had far greater reserves and resolve. Another problem for the panzers was the heat and dust in Russia (especially in the south), where the temperature could reach 35–40 degrees Celsius. The 3rd Panzer 'Bear' Division, made up of sarcastic and tough Berliners, joked that they had ended up on the wrong front, since Russia was as hot as the Western Desert. Indeed, the Russian and Ukrainian dust clogged engines and wore down machines, as in Libya.

PROBLEMS ON THE FLANKS

On the flanks, due to the lack of panzers, the Germans were not making as much of a success of Barbarossa as their countrymen back home may have believed. In the north, the Baltic States were far from ideal tank country and Soviet defences were stronger than expected. General F. I. Kuznetsov used his 8th Army's armoured strength to deliver some large but ineffective punches at the panzers. Leeb quarrelled with his panzer commander, Hoeppner, about the aim of their army group's thrust: was it to be Estonia (to mop up Soviet North Front Forces under General Popov) or Leningrad? An aristocratic Prussian general of the old stock, Leeb not only resented Hitler's constant interference, but also distrusted tanks. Already by late June his thrust had lost its momentum and the Germans found that, in this heavily wooded country, just a few Soviet tanks could hold them up on a single, narrow, winding road. Nevertheless, the 2nd Panzer Division captured Ostrov, thus breaching both the Velikaya River line and the Stalin Line. The road to Leningrad was open and, by late August, almost all lines of communication between the city and the rest of the Soviet Union were cut.

In the south, the Ukrainian plains were ideal tank country, but before these could be reached the heavily wooded regions along the border had to be crossed in the face of the strongest army group in the Soviet Army: the South West

ABOVE: Never squeamish about casualties, the Russian command had no problem in ordering infantry on top of tanks and using these vehicles as means of transport to the front line. The troops would jump off when they were needed to reduce an enemy-held position. Both the T-34 and troops are in winter camouflage somewhere in southern Russia (late 1941 or early 1942).

Front commanded by General Kirponos, after Zhukov, probably the best RKKA commander in 1941. Kirponos had not accepted Stalin's nonsense about avoiding 'provocations' and had, a few days before the Germans attacked, mobilised his front. Rundstedt's Army Group therefore had a tough job ahead of it. Kleist was hard pressed and only after some heavy losses did he defeat Kirponos's powerful tank attack at Korosten. On this front, the Soviet retreat was well ordered and Kirponos showed nerves of steel compared with Pavlov's panic-stricken mishandling of his front. There was only one 'minor' pocket, at Uman, where 100,000 Russians capitulated.

GUDERIAN HEADS SOUTH

It was only when the 4th Panzer Army (led by Guderian) finally swung southwards on 23 August with a powerful thrust towards Gomel that Rundstedt's Army Group could advance with greater speed and success against stiff Soviet resistance. Two days earlier, Kleist's 1st Panzer Group supported by Reichenau's

6th Army had begun the battle for Kiev. The Soviet commanders were too engaged to the west of them to notice how to the north, despite Yeremenko's frantic counterattacks, the Soviet front was caving in to Guderian's violent thrusts. Both Army Group Centre and South's entire armoured might (three panzer corps) was concentrated upon the Soviet South West Front. Kirponos was now alerted to the fact that his entire front and the third most important city in the country faced a German encirclement from the west, southwest and now the north.

Kirponos phoned in a frantic attempt to get Stalin's permission to pull out of Kiev with all haste across the Dniepr and Dnesna rivers to the safety of the east. He argued that the Red Army could not afford to lose an entire front. Stalin ignored the warnings and compounded his lack of competence to command by obstinacy in the face of adversity. He refused to allow a retreat from Kiev. Kirponos was to remain there. Kirponos's superior, Marshal Budenny, may not have

been the brightest (the Russians joke that his moustache was bigger than his brains), but even he could see the apparent peril. When he dared to question Stalin's dangerous order, he was recalled to Moscow and retired.

On 12 September 1941, Kleist and Guderian's panzers linked up 241km (150 miles) east of Kiev. It was the largest cauldron of the Barbarossa campaign. The 5th and 37th Armies were trapped inside. Kirponos refused to abandon his men and was killed along with many of them when he tried to break out to the east. Kiev and the pocket was reduced to shattered remains by 19 September: 600,000 prisoners and 1000 tanks had been lost due to Stalin's obstinacy.

COSTLY DETOUR

With the end of the Kiev operation, the 4th Panzer Army could be shifted back to its original task: the march on Moscow. But it was too late and the delay, due to Hitler's 'small' detour to Kiev, cost him the war. Guderian and Hoth's panzers (both men and machines) were worn out

and they would now face a gruelling task in the face of worsening weather.

The Germans concentrated 14 panzer divisions, eight motorised divisions and 49 infantry divisions to capture Moscow in Operation Typhoon, which began on 2 October with, by now, customary German successes and a speed of advance true to the operation's name. The plan was to do to Moscow what had been done to Kiev: namely, to encircle it from the north with Hoeppner's panzers and from the south with Guderian's by joining up well east of Moscow. Timoshenko's armies wilted under the onslaught and were trapped. The 2nd Panzer Army smashed through Russian defences towards Orel, while 4th Panzer Group, shifted from the push north, drove towards Vyazma. Timoshenko saw the 3rd, 13th, 43rd and 50th Armies trapped at Vyazma and Bryansk in new cauldrons. These pockets (crushed by 12 October) yielded 663,000 prisoners and 1200 tanks.

Despite these massive losses, the Red Army was still in existence and capable of delivering fierce resistance to the

ABOVE: Crew comfort was not at the top of a Soviet tank designer's priorities. The T-34's interior was designed for practical use and ease of mass production. Thus the turret and the gunner's position were extremely cramped, with as little room for the crew as practicable.

advancing Germans. The *Das Reich* SS Division, fighting its way towards Moscow, described the fighting of 19–20 November as the fiercest during the whole of Barbarossa. By this time the 'Typhoon' became an ever-weakening storm that was soon reduced to an asthmatic gasp.

The Germans finally realised, too late, that Russia was too vast, her resources too great and Stalin too impervious to losses to be defeated in one campaign; the *Blitzkrieg* had failed. Behind their lines arose hundreds of partisans (tying down five regular divisions in the centre alone) and, on the front line, they had encountered two Soviet tank models that were very potent threats.

The KV-1 and KV-2 were monstrous tanks that impressed with their sheer power and size. The KV-1 was a heavy tank of 43 tonnes, a crew of five, with three 7.62mm (0.3in) machine guns, a massive 76.2mm (3in) gun, and an impressive maximum speed of 42km/h (26mph). But it was its armour that proved too much for the Germans, their 37mm (1.45in) anti-tank gun being ineffective against the KV's 75mm (2.9in) armour

on its front and , with 60mm (2.3in) on its sides. Its heavier and massive 100mm (3.93in) howitzer-gunned cousin, the KV-2, was even more impressive in size at 52 tonnes. But it was too heavy, lacking in mobility and weakly equipped with machine guns, and so proved a disappointment. Production of the KV-2 was dropped by late 1941, although, to the Germans' horror, such a giant could be hit over 11 times with no apparent effect whatsoever.

THE WAR-WINNER

The tank which impressed the Germans the most was the medium T-34 tank, which was so good that Guderian wanted to start mass-producing it for the *Wehrmacht*. It was, indeed, the best all-round tank of the war and the pride of the Red Army's talented design department. It had a 76mm (3in) gun (upgraded to 85mm (3.34in) in 1943), two 7.62mm (0.3in) machine guns, 52mm (2in) armour on its turret, and 45mm (1.75in) armour on its sides, back and front. It had a top speed of 56km/h (35mph) on roads and 32km/h (19.9mph) cross-country, where its performance was excellent. Its armour

BELOW: The importance of supporting infantry for the momentum of *Blitzkrieg*. Panzergrenadiers in half-tracks could be dispatched to deal with any strongpoints or to take the surrender of demoralised Soviet troops, allowing the German panzers to push on unhindered to their objective.

was sloped to deflect shot and it had wide, strong caterpillar tracks, which enabled it to cross soft, marshy or snow-covered terrain with greater ease than the German panzers.

These tanks were eventually to tip the scales in favour of the Soviets, but for now the USSR was fighting for its short-term survival. During October, the advance of the Germans had reduced the Muscovites to the *Bolshoi Drap*, the 'Great Flight East'. But, by November, both military and civilian nerves had settled down. Hardened Siberian and Far Eastern troops were shipped in and all new tanks produced were concentrated in armoured brigades being set up in the rear. One such brigade, Colonel Mikhail Katukov's 4th, made up mainly of T-34s, gave the Germans a most unpleasant surprise at Mtsensk. The Russians had begun to rediscover the techniques of 'deep' mechanised warfare.

Stalin trusted no other general but Zhukov to attack the Germans with any hope of success. Timoshenko was replaced as commander of the Western Front. By 2 December, the Germans had reached the Moscow suburb of Chimki. They got no further. Four days later, Zhukov launched the Soviet counter-offensive with the 1st Shock Army and 10th and 20th Armies against the frozen, exhausted Germans. Zhukov's reconstituted Western Front had only 200 tanks (luckily all T-34s and KVs) and, when he asked for more, Stalin told him bluntly: 'There are no tanks. We can't give you any. But you're going to get aircraft.'

Zhukov improvised. It did not matter that the Russians were short of tanks. So were the Germans, since their's were immobilised or useless in the deep cold. He used fast-moving ski troops (copied from the Finns) and cavalry shock attacks to cut the retreating Germans to shreds. The proud panzer troops had to fight for their lives as infantry, shoulder-to-shoulder with generals, cooks and supply troops. In eight days, the Germans had retreated over 80km (50 miles) to the west. On 13 December, a proud 30th Army would recapture Klin, while Belov's cavalry rode down Guderian's panzers: the Germans lost 70 tanks in the process. All frozen or immobilised tanks were abandoned in the retreat.

Hitler was infuriated with these reverses. He feared (quite rightly) that what had happened to Napoleon in 1812 would now be the fate of his army: a panic-stricken retreat leading to total

ABOVE: As they had done from the beginning of the war, the Germans combined motorised infantry and tanks into a devastatingly effective armoured punch. On this road, the tanks rolled ahead to give cover and protection, while infantry (carried in half-tracks) would mop up Soviet infantry resistance on either side, or support an attack against any significant barrier. In general, however, the Germans preferred to bypass defences.

crippled and captured) and 1300 tanks. More importantly, the German myth of invincibility lay in tatters, and it proved to the USSR's allies (the Americans and British) that it could continue the war and was well worth supporting with a stream of supplies. It also gave heart not only to the Soviet peoples, but also to all the occupied countries of Europe that Hitler could be defeated.

On the more practical level, it meant that the initiative on the Eastern Front had passed over to the Red Army. Zhukov pointed out to Stalin that it was best to continue the counteroffensive on just one front since the Germans were still too strong and the Red Army too weak for a general front. As usual, Stalin would not listen and, despite Zhukov's strong protests, ordered a general offensive that led to the capture of the Kerch peninsula and Izyum bulge in the south, but which meant that the central offensive petered out. Demyansk, unlike Kalinin, was not captured and the general offensive soon ran out of steam.

STALEMATE

By February 1942, it was obvious that the Red Army's offensive had petered out, but it was equally obvious that the Germans had no intention of striking too early either. The fighting ended in a stalemate. Hitler now wanted to cut the Soviets' lines of communication along the Volga river and seize the Caucasus oil wells at the same time. Again he could not decide on a realistic objective. Army Group South was split in two: Field Marshal List's Army Group A with von Kleist's panzer army and Army Group B (Field Marshal von Bock). They were to spearhead a southern offensive called Operation Fredericus (changed to the less flamboyant 'Blue'). List was to march on the Caucasus, while Bock was to 'screen' List's offensive and seize Stalingrad.

Before Operation Blue got off the ground, the Soviets, who had no intention of giving up the initiative without a fight, launched a diversionary offensive at the Izyum bulge aimed at the capture of Kharkov. Timoshenko, South West Front commander, put two-thirds of his armour (600 KVs and T-34s) into the Barvenkovo salient. He quickly realised his mistake when he encountered no resistance, and he tried to pull back.

ABOVE: As more plentiful tanks of good and consistent quality started to pour out of the factories, the Soviet tank crews, gaining in experience, became ever more confident and difficult to beat. This young tankman is Lieutenant V. Golovin, who has been awarded a medal in recognition of his tank fighting skills.

defeat. He gave orders that not a single inch of land was to be abandoned without a fight. Guderian, aghast at this 'medieval anachronism', protested that his precious panzers had to be saved. Hitler, who had now appointed himself as Commander in Chief, fired Guderian and Rundstedt for making unauthorised troop withdrawals.

Zhukov's counterattack cost the Germans large chunks of conquered territory, 500,000 casualties (dead,

Again, Stalin forbade a withdrawal. A costly mistake became a total catastrophe due to his bungling interference. The 1st Panzer Army (two panzer divisions and one motorised division) struck eastwards, while the 14th Panzer Division advanced north against the side of the salient. On 22 May, they converged east of the Donets River and yet another cauldron had been created. Twenty-nine divisions, 1200 tanks and three armies (6th, 9th and 57th) were lost and another 250,000 troops were either captured or killed. Timoshenko lost three experienced commanders as well: Generals Kostenko, Bobkin and Khariatov. Both they and their troops would have been invaluable during the coming campaign.

The only merit of Timoshenko's failed offensive was that it delayed Blue by several weeks. This time, however, Timoshenko carried out a very successful retreat, while Hitler noted sarcastically how Bock's slow advance allowed the enemy to slip across the Don river and to safety. Rostov was finally taken on 23 July, but there were over 1125km (700 miles) to the Baku oilfields on the Caspian Sea and in between lay the Caucasus Mountains and well dug-in Soviet forces that offered fierce resistance to the German advance. By November, Kleist's depleted armour reached the most easterly point of their offensive: Ordzonikidze.

It was soon obvious that the two-pronged offensive was beyond the capacity of a weakened *Wehrmacht*. The panzers were worn from wear and tear inflicted since the opening of Barbarossa a year earlier. The Germans had not been able to get any rest for the men or proper repairs done to the machines since that time. Equally worrying was the lack of air cover and reconnaissance, which weakened the offensive. Hitler only compounded these problems by constantly switching his priorities.

In mid-July, Hitler needlessly diverted Hoth's panzers away from the Stalingrad offensive to support List's Army Group A. Thus Stalingrad was saved from an early attack when, had Hoth not been diverted, it would probably have fallen to the Germans. Moscow had avoided capture during Barbarossa due to Hitler diverting Guderian's panzer army southwards. Hitler was making the same mistake again and, by the time Hoth could return to the main attack, it was too late.

While Hoth was off on Hitler's wild goose chase to Rostov, the German 6th Army was making a slow and deliberate advance towards Stalingrad. This army had lost its dynamic and ruthless commander, General Reichenau, who had died of a heart attack and was replaced by his Chief of Staff, General Friedrich von Paulus. Paulus was a pedantic pen-pusher and quite unsuited to the role of a blood-and-guts commander in the field, unlike his predecessor. His appointment to command was most unfortunate.

BELOW: In Russia, the roads were commonly in such a poor state that it was often faster to move along riverbeds. The conditions caused far greater attrition of panzers such as this PzKpfw III than the Soviet defenders did. Furthermore, the success of the T-34 and KV-1 had shown the Germans that new tanks were needed. Hitler, however, still refused to turn the German economy into a war economy, meaning that replacements were not readily available.

On the Russian side, the opposite was true. Timoshenko and his corps clique of cavalry officers were removed from command, but not before more troops had been needlessly lost through a vain attempt to hold the Kalach bridgehead (west of Stalingrad). Zhukov replaced Timoshenko and created the Stalingrad Front on 12 July. To block any German move against Voronezh, Zhukov appointed his ally and protégé, General Vatutin, as commander of the Voronezh Front. To defend Stalingrad, Zhukov had 62nd and 64th Armies with the support of 1st and 4th Tank Armies (240 tanks). As before at Moscow half a year earlier, even the Red Army was running out of space to trade for time and reserves to throw into the battle. From the west General Wietersheim's 14th Panzer Corps was approaching Stalingrad, while from the south came Hoth's 4th Panzer Army. The 6th Army reached the Volga, at last, on 23 August. It was very late in the season for the city to be captured.

BATTLE FOR STALINGRAD

It was now that Hitler's command showed itself as one of the Red Army's greatest assets. Hitler used his ever more

slender resources of tanks and aircraft to take Stalingrad by frontal assault. The assault on Warsaw (and Madrid in the Spanish Civil War) had clearly proved that cities were not the right arena for the use of tanks. Stalingrad was no exception to this rule. While General Chuikov's small 62nd Army held Stalingrad's 3.2km by 29km (2 miles by 18 miles) city area street by street, Zhukov used the time provided by Hitler's simple-minded obsession with the city to prepare a counteroffensive, as at Moscow. His plan was so simple that it was difficult to understand how the Germans were defeated by it. He launched small diversionary attacks against Army Group Centre to prevent reinforcements reaching Paulus, while he built up the Soviet forces on the German flanks.

Meanwhile, Hitler played right into Zhukov's hands by concentrating all his attention on Stalingrad and forgetting his ever-weaker flanks (held by the German's disgruntled allies). The German assault on Stalingrad had begun on 15 September. A week later, the Germans had reached the city's centre and, by the end of the month, the northern factory district was in their hands. The 16th Panzer Division

BELOW: The deeper the tank columns plunged into the vast, open spaces of southern Russia's steppes, the clearer it became that Russia was no ordinary foe and that Germany was ever more distant from final victory. The panzers had not given Hitler his victory, and new designs were needed to counter the Soviet armour. In the meantime, stopgap measures were introduced with the up-gunning and up-armouring of the existing PzKpfw III and IVs.

supported by the 60th MID spearheaded this northern drive. The focus of the attack was shifted south, where the 14th and 24th Panzer Divisions attacked with the support of the 29th MID. Both tanks and machines were badly used. It would have been better left to assault infantry and artillery, but unfortunately the Allied victory at El Alamein diverted much-needed German reinforcements to the African desert. The war was turning full circle against the Germans.

The Soviets had been able to build bridgeheads along the Don River and, on 19 November, Rokossovksy struck southwards. Over 3000 guns roared, but, to begin with, the 3rd Romanian Army offered fierce resistance. After a while, the demoralised, outnumbered and under-equipped Romanians gave up and retreated southwards, attacked by 200 T-34s from Romanenko's 5th Tank Army. A single German panzer corps with some 20 unreliable old tanks could only offer feeble resistance. Yeremenko had 51st and 57th Armies to attack across the Yergeni hills in the south, but only 13th Mechanised Corps for armoured support. By 23 November, however, the two Soviet groups had joined together. The 6th Army and the 4th Panzer Army were trapped inside a huge pocket around Stalingrad with 20 German and two Romanian divisions.

DEFEAT ON THE VOLGA

Hitler appointed Manstein in charge of Army Group Don to recapture Stalingrad and restore a continuous front. He made good his promise to relieve Paulus and reached within 48km (30 miles) of the surrounded Germans. But Paulus could not escape and trusted that Göring's *Luftwaffe* would deliver as many supplies as were needed. They could not, however, and after Manstein's withdrawal the situation became intolerable. Incredibly, the Germans held out, despite privations and constant bombardments from the air and ground, until 31 January 1943. That day, Paulus, who had been made a Field Marshal by Hitler, capitulated to the triumphant Russians. The Germans lost 250,000 precious troops and a six-month equivalent of tank supplies. The war had turned for good against the Germans, who evacuated the Caucasus and Kuban as fast as they could. Only Manstein's brilliant counterattack at Kharkov saved the southern front from total disaster.

BELOW: At Stalingrad and after, the hammer blows that signalled the turning point of the war in the east were delivered. Although the Germans were still strong, the Red Army now had the equipment and skills to be able to fight on a more equal footing. Germany's battles became defensive and new tank design would reflect this change in attitude.

CHAPTER FIVE

THE WAR IN THE DESERT

With the arrival of Rommel in the North African desert, the world would witness one of the great panzer generals at work.

Mussolini's declaration of war in June 1940 left the British with an unpleasant situation. Their territories in Egypt could now be invaded from the Italian colony of Cyrenaica (part of what is now Libya). The Italians had a total of over 250,000 troops in that province and Tripolitania (which made up Italian Libya). Should they invade, an easy Italian victory seemed assured, since the British forces in Egypt – the Western Desert Force (WDF) – only amounted to 10,000 troops and lacked the latest equipment.

The problem for the Italians was not only that they were weak in armour (and all sorts of motorised materiel), but also that the modern tactics of armoured warfare had not penetrated the Libyan Army at all. In June, the British beat the Italians during a skirmish along the wire (the border between Egypt and Cyrenaica) and were amazed to

LEFT: The Desert Fox, General (later Field Marshal) Erwin Rommel, in a typically dynamic pose, pointing to an objective in the distance during his victory over the British at Derna in February 1942. The junior Italian officer on the right reflects his country's subordinate position in the Axis and his countrymen in general resented the inferior status many Germans gave them. However, Italian armour was extremely poor throughout the campaign, and it was increasingly left to the German panzers to provide a credible (and very successful) armoured force.

71

ABOVE: Having shown itself to be woefully inadequate in modern tank warfare, the thinly armoured Italian Ansaldo was put to other uses. Here it is being used as a flamethrower against the British lines. Its armour was so thin that ordinary rifle bullets could penetrate it.

discover that the Ansaldo tank – already outclassed in Spain – could be shot to pieces with machine-gun fire. Despite this conspicuous failing, the newly appointed commander of the Italian Army, Marshal Rudolfo Graziani, was pestered repeatedly by Mussolini to make an attack on Egypt and, as a result, in early September, General Berti's 10th Army made a slow and tentative advance towards Sidi Barrani.

The WDF was well equipped with tanks and motorised equipment. Their main tank was the A9 Cruiser tank, designed in 1934 and produced as a cheap battle tank with emphasis upon speed and armament, rather than armour. It had a two-pounder (40mm (1.57in)) gun and three machine guns, and weighed 12 tonnes, but had only 12mm (0.47in) armour. This enabled it stand up to any Italian tank, but it was vulnerable to Italian artillery fire. The British had 200 light tanks, 75 medium (A9, A10, A13) Cruiser tanks and some 45 Matildas, the 'Queens of the Desert Battlefield'. The Italians had only 60 medium M11/M13

tanks and 270 useless Ansaldos. The British also had the 7th Armoured Division, set up in 1936 at Mersa Metruh and superbly trained by the tank genius Major General Percy Hobart. It was now under the command of the energetic and resourceful General Richard O'Connor.

O'CONNOR TAKES THE INITIATIVE

Given the Italians' slow advance and their weakness in armour, as commander of the WDF, O'Connor was determined to seize the first opportunity to attack. He did so on 6 December, with the encouragement of his superior, General Archibald Wavell (Commander in Chief Middle East), when the 7th Royal Tank Regiment, equipped with Matildas, spearheaded the 4th Indian Division's attack. There was fine coordination between the Matildas and the artillery. The Italians found to their consternation that their puny anti-tank guns could not even begin to scratch the surface of the Matilda's 88mm (3.45in) thick armour. But the Italian artillery crews chose to fire and die with their guns rather than surrender, thus dispelling the myth of Italian 'cowardice'.

Sidi-Omar, Bardia and Tobruk (with 25,000 troops) fell to the advancing British, who took some 210,000 prisoners by mid-January 1941. Graziani was reduced to 40,000 troops (about equal in number to WDF's 36,000 troops) and the only unit that could block the advance of British armour was the Babini Armoured Brigade. It had some 120 M13 tanks (reinforcements had arrived from Italy) and this machine was almost adequate, if not as good as the Cruisers. Its 47mm (1.85in) gun could penetrate most British armour and its own 30mm (1.1in) armour could withstand 40mm (1.57in) shot at distances over 457m (500 yards). Its main weakness was its inadequate engine, which at 150hp only managed to give it a cross-country speed of 16km/h (10mph), or only half the British tank's speed. The fastest British tank, the A13, had a 340hp engine, weighed 15 tonnes, had 30mm (1.1in) all-round armour and was well armed (for the time) with a 40mm (1.57in) gun and a single machine gun. It outclassed the M13 during the battles for Mechili and Beda Fomm.

After six weeks of fighting, the British tank crews were exhausted and needed a rest, while their machines could have done with a much-needed refit and round of repairs. The fine desert dust played havoc with engines, fuel tanks and instruments. But the Italians, having learnt from previous mistakes, were not about to give their overconfident enemy a chance to rest and they fought at their best in the second phase of the campaign: the battle of Beda Fomm. On the morning of 24 January 1941, a massed attack by M13s chased off the 7th Hussars (with light tanks and Rolls Royce armoured cars) and knocked out the cruisers that came to the Hussars' assistance. The British were astonished to find their enemy, whom they had held in some contempt for their disorganised and lacklustre resistance, could mount a massive tank attack. They sent in the 2nd Royal Tank Regiment to support the Hussars and pulverise the M13s. But the Italians fought all the way and with some vigour, once their fear of tanks had worn off and their traditional bravado returned. They were forced to abandoned Derna

by 29 January, but kept up their resistance all the way back to the border of Tripolitania. Their performance in combat, especially their ever-disciplined and brave gunners and that of the Italian tanks at the battle of Beda Fomm, was more than respectable.

However, the Italians' lack of success in North Africa and in Greece was causing their ally major concern. In December, Hitler created the *Deutsche Afrika Korps* (DAK), composed of the 15th Panzer Division and the 5th Light Division (LD) equipped with PzKpfw IIIs and IVs with a supplement of 88mm (3.45in) guns. It was to be a small but well integrated and combined force. The 5th LD, despite its name, had 70 light tanks and some 80 PzKpfw IIIs and IVs. Hitler cast around for a suitable commander and found the right one in

the figure of his favourite panzer general: the 49-year-old Erwin Rommel, who had commanded the 7th Panzer Division in France with such success. His arrival in Tripoli in mid-February coincided with the Italian retreat out of Cyrenaica; it was to mark a new, exciting chapter in the desert war. A month later, on 11 March, the 5th LD landed with its men and machines in Tripoli's harbour.

O'Connor was resting in Cairo at this time, and the 7th Armoured Division was being refitted in the Nile Delta after an arduous campaign. This left only a scratch

BELOW: British tank crews cleaning and repairing their tank's tracks. An important and time-consuming job, it had to be done at regular intervals or the dust and grit of the desert would immobilise the tank. Other modifications had to be made for desert conditions: larger radiators, air filters and extra fuel and water containers.

BELOW: Events in the
Western Desert in 1941. At
first the *Afrika Korps* moved
forwards until they reached
the Halfaya Pass in mid
April. After Operation
Battleaxe in June, Operation
Crusader saw the British
push back the Axis forces in
November, until El Agheila
was reached in January 1942.
Tactics and movement in the
desert were limited by the
Sahara to the south, and only
the coastline possessed a
road, which meant that much
of the fighting took place
over the same strongpoints
or natural features.

force along the front, made up of the 2nd
Armoured Division, to hold Rommel at
bay. He was not a commander to miss an
opportunity to strike an enemy when he
least expected it. Both Wavell and
O'Connor thought that Rommel would
wait until he had collected his full force
before striking. Little did they know. On
31 March, Rommel attacked with 50
tanks, and the crack Italian *Ariete* and
Brescia divisions.

By 2 April, the 2nd Armoured
Division had retreated some 145km (90
miles) to the east. Rommel's style was to
keep his enemy off balance through
constant attacks. A day later, Benghazi fell
to his advancing forces and, on 6 April, a
German motorcycle patrol captured
General O'Connor and Lieutenant General
Neame. Thus both the WDF and 13th
Corps had been deprived of their
commanders and, in O'Connor's case, it

was a fatal blow to British morale.
O'Connor's drive and leadership were to
be sorely missed during the following
year and a half of campaigning. In two
weeks, having taken all the fuel and water
he needed from captured British supply
dumps, Rommel bounced the British
right out of Cyrenaica. The Australians,
dug in at Tobruk, distracted Rommel's
attentions while Wavell put his house in
order in preparation for a counterattack.

Operation Brevity (14–27 May 1941)
had two aims: to relieve Tobruk and to
push Rommel across the Libyan frontier.
The offensive was opened with a
combined attack by 4th Royal Tank
Regiment (RTR) and 22 Guards Brigade
against Halfaya Pass. They achieved total
surprise. The Italian gunners saved the day
by fighting to the death and knocking
out seven Matildas. When the 4th RTR
arrived at Fort Capuzzo, the Germans

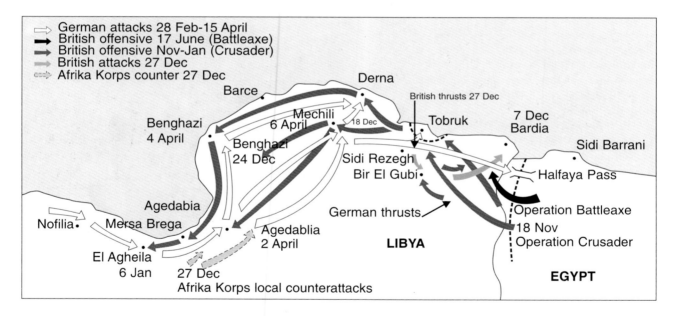

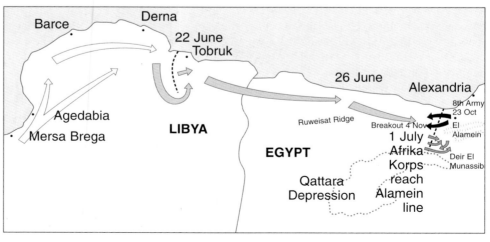

RIGHT: Rommel's offensive
of January 1942 took the
Afrika Korps to the Gazala
Line outside Tobruk. When
Rommel attacked again in
May, the British were
thrown back to the El
Alamein Line, where they
managed to hold Rommel
thanks to shortened lines
of supply.

were ready and greeted their unwelcome guests with a shower of hot metal. General Straffer Gott tried to push through the DAK guns, but the 4th RTR was pushed back by the Axis forces to Sollum, held by them until 27 May, when the failed offensive was called off.

'TIGER' TANKS

On 12 May, the 'Tiger' convoy arrived in Alexandria. Its cargo of tanks would give Wavell the forces to launch another offensive against Rommel. In addition to 21 light tanks and 135 Matildas, the convoy contained a consignment of 82 Mark VI Crusader tanks. The Crusader was a fast (42km/h (26mph)), 'stylish' tank with a two-pounder (40mm (1.57in)) gun, two 7.92mm (0.303in) machine guns, 40mm (1.57in) frontal armour, a crew of five and a weight of 19 tonnes. Yet it was under-gunned, an unreliable machine and had one fatal flaw: its water tanks, crucial in desert fighting, were troublesome. The 6th RTR received the Crusaders, while the 4th were given the Matildas.

Wavell had another plan, Operation Battleaxe, up his sleeve. Battleaxe was to destroy Rommel and end the desert war by relieving Tobruk. The garrison there was to join the 4th and 7th Armoured Divisions and drive Rommel out of Cyrenaica. Rommel may have had only

200 tanks (to 300 British ones), but he also had a large number of dug-in '88s' that shot to pieces the 4th RTR when it made a dawn attack against Halfaya on 15 June. By midday, the 4th was down to a single tank. When the Crusaders confronted the panzers, the result was not good: 17 were knocked out or broke down, and this model had an alarming tendency to catch fire. The next day Rommel struck the wrongfooted British again. He sent the 15th Panzer Division against Capuzzo and the 5th LD around the British flank. During the night of 16 June, Brigadier Alec Gatehouse (4th Armoured Brigade) put a temporary halt to the panzers with his sturdy Matildas. However, the 88s could penetrate the Matilda's armour at 1828m (2000yds) and the PAK 38 anti-tank guns had a 914m (1000yd) range.

Churchill relieved Wavell and replaced him as Commander in Chief Middle East with General Claude Auchinleck. To put Auchinleck in as good a position as possible, Churchill saw to it that he received three motorised divisions and 10 armoured regiments. Auchinleck had two new types of tanks: an improved version of the A10 Cruiser called the Valentine – but which nonetheless still had only an inadequate two-pounder gun – and the US-produced Stuart light tank, known to the British as the Honey, which had a high-velocity 37mm (1.45in) gun (with

ABOVE: Italian tanks were a sore disappointment: thinly armoured, poorly armed and slow. So many M 11/39 and M 13/40 tanks were captured by the Allies in 1940 and 1941 that they were pressed into service to make up a shortfall in Allied tanks, but they were so poor they were soon replaced.

greater hitting power than the British two-pounder) and a top speed of 58km/h (36mph). By contrast, Rommel was relatively starved of equipment: he had only thirty-five 88s. The tough 5th LD was renamed 21st Panzer Division.

Auchinleck was determined, given his superiority in tanks, to go on the offensive in Operation Crusader. It was similar to his predecessor's plans: destroy DAK and occupy Libya all the way to Tripolitania. The job was now given to the 8th Army, the renamed WDF, and its equally new commander, Lieutenant General Sir Alan Cunningham. While the 13th Corps pinned down the DAK along the wire, the 30th Corps would drive to Tobruk, where the garrison would come out and assist the offensive against Tripoli. Cunningham had three armoured brigades to do it: 7th (129 tanks), 4th (166 tanks) and 22nd (158 tanks) – in other words, a four-to-one superiority.

On 18 November, the offensive began with the 4th Indian Division attacking the wire, while the 7th Armoured Division swung around the southern flank of the German lines. The 22nd Armoured Brigade ran into the *Ariete* Brigade and lost 40 tanks to the accurate and devastating fire of the Italians' well dug-in anti-tank guns. On 20 November, the 7th Armoured Brigade (centre column) occupied the airfield at Sidi Rezegh. This was on the crucial plateau above Tobruk that commanded the approaches to the city. The Germans, however, blocked the road to Tobruk with their 88s and PAK guns, while Panzer Group *Stefan* (100 tanks) fought the 4th Armoured Brigade to a standstill along the Trigh Capuzzo.

It was only by 22 November that Rommel realised this was an all-out British attack; he abandoned his attack upon Tobruk and drove a panzer wedge between the 13th and 30th Corps at Sidi Rezegh. South of the airfield, the hapless 7th Armoured Brigade felt the full brunt of the DAK's combined armoured

strength, but were saved by the sheer bravery of their artillery gunners who (like their Italian colleagues) showed exemplary bravery by sticking to their guns. Three posthumous VCs were awarded to the artillerists. By the afternoon of 21 November, the 7th Armoured Brigade was down to only 40 tank. It was led, however, by an inspired commander, Brigadier Jock Campbell, who, like a cavalry officer, led his tank force driving in a flimsy staff car from the front. He, too, was rewarded for his foolhardy bravery and exemplary leadership (including that of 2nd RTR with only 12 tanks) with a much-deserved VC.

TOBRUK BREAKOUT

Meanwhile, the 70th Division had broken out of the Tobruk ring and headed towards El Duda, while the 13th Corps captured the DAK's forward HQ on 23 November. This was a sweet revenge for the British, in view of O'Connor's capture earlier in the year at the hands of Rommel. However, it could not change the fact that the British had

suffered yet another reversal from their arch foe Rommel, who was now being called the 'Desert Fox' and had assumed almost mythical powers of movement and leadership. As he told one glum British captive: 'What difference does it make to me if you have two tanks to my one, if you send them out and let me smash them in detail. You presented me with three brigades in succession.' This was very true. The British sent raw crews in untried and unseasoned tanks into the blue yonder of the desert in dribs and drabs. The inability to concentrate their armour was the main reason for their defeat at the hands of Rommel.

The British flight back to the 'safety' of the wire, known as the November Handicap, was covered by the South Africans, who lost 3000 troops and much equipment in the process. Rommel halted his 'raid' on the wire by 25 November and the British staged a remarkable recovery. Fifty tanks were recovered from the battlefield, while 4th Armoured Brigade received 36 new tanks. Despite his stopping Rommel, Auchinleck fired Cunnigham and

BELOW: The cost of muddle, confusion and flawed tank designs: a knocked-out British A-10 Cruiser, a victim of the last British attempt to break out from besieged Tobruk. A number of British designs saw service in the desert, but none was as good as the German panzers that they were forced to confront. The situation would not improve until 1942, when American tanks began to arrive.

ABOVE: One way of improving the protection of the British tanks was to bury them, but this had the disadvantage of rendering them immobile and vulnerable to artillery. Conditions inside the tank would not have been pleasant given the strong desert heat. This tank is an obsolescent Medium Mk II, a model which was pressed into first-line service due to a dire shortage of Allied armoured vehicles.

replaced him with General Neil Ritchie. Tailed by the 7th Armoured Brigade, Rommel was forced back across the wire.

Again Auchinleck received further reinforcements, by German standards on a lavish scale: an entire armoured division (the 1st) to replace the worn-out machines and men of the 7th. In January 1942, Rommel received 55 Panzers: 19 PzKw III Js with high-velocity long-barrelled 50mm (2.4in) guns, which gave the tanks 50 per cent better armour penetration. Auchinleck, like Wavell, expected Rommel to recover his strength before attacking. He had still not realised the calibre of the man he was fighting, nor the toughness of the men Rommel led. When Rommel did strike on 21 January, the attack came as a most unpleasant and unwelcome surprise to the British. The 2nd Brigade's three armoured regiments were defeated in turn by the panzers and the vast supply depot at Benghazi (stored for Auchinleck's planned Operation Acrobat) fell into Rommel's hands. By 4 February, the 8th Army had retreated 240km (150 miles) from Msus to Gazala.

In a line from Gazala into the desert proper, the British had constructed a series of fortified defensive boxes, held by a brigade and surrounded by a thick belt of mines and barbed wire, and known as the Gazala Line. Patrolling armoured

units covered the gaps between the boxes and the key box of the line was the last one, Bir Hacheim, held by General Koenig's 1st Free French Brigade, the tough Foreign Legion veterans. The elite 22nd Guards Brigade were detailed to hold the middle box, 'Knightsbridge'.

BRITISH OPTIMISM

The British had 700 tanks to Rommel's 560 panzers. The best tank on the British side was the US-built Grant, based upon the US M3 (Medium) Lee tank. It weighed 29 tonnes, had 57mm (2.2in) armour in front of the turret, carried a 37mm (1.45in) gun in the turret and a 75mm (2.95in) one in a sponson on the side of the hull, and was quite fast given its weight. The British at last felt that they had a tank that could stand up to the panzers. Rommel's tank park was less impressive. It was made up mainly of obsolete M13 tanks and he had only 240 PzKpfw IIs and 38 PzKpfw IIIs. Not much to take the offensive against the Gazala Line, although the PzKpfws IIIs were better tanks than the Grant.

General Gott's 13th Corps held the line, while 30th Corps (1st and 7th Armoured Divisions) held the south flank in support of Koenig's Free French. At dawn on 26 May, the South Africans spotted a huge tank force on the horizon in a southerly direction heading towards

Bir Hacheim. Even by Rommel's standards, this was a gamble. On the morning of 27 May, the panzers captured the 7th Armoured Brigade's HQ, but General Messervy managed to escape. Because of the speed and unexpectedness of the attack, 4th Armoured Brigade was committed piecemeal. For once, when up against a dug-in and prepared enemy, Rommel was hard-pressed to break through. The 'Cauldron' box held by 150th Brigade gave a good account of itself, but the Germans were more shocked and impressed by the fanatical resistance of the French at Bir Hacheim. Rommel, singularly impressed by Koenig's resolve and sheer endurance during four days of ferocious fighting, noted: 'Never in Africa was I given a stiffer fight than at Bir Hacheim.'

When Ritchie launched his counterattack on 2 June with his tanks, it was too slow, obvious and deliberate. It was easily repulsed by well-concealed 88s which wreaked havoc on the British tanks, which were reduced to 170 machines four days later. On 9 June, what remained of 4th Armoured Brigade tried to support the French, but were repulsed. The gallant Legionnaires were forced to withdraw on 11 June. 'Knightsbridge' was also evacuated as Rommel, seeing his enemy yet again in disarray, launched a full-scale attack. British humiliation was

complete when Tobruk fell to Rommel on 20 June. One observer noted sourly that British leadership was 'orders, counter orders and disorders'.

The 8th Army was now in full retreat, dubbed the 'Gazala Gallop' and, on 25 June, the Germans crossed the wire and captured Mersa Matruh that same evening. For the British, the only consolation was that British tanks mauled the Italian elite *Littorio* Division at Bir el-Temir. The British fell back to the Alamein Line outside Alexandria, which was their last line of defence and, due to the Quattara Depression, could not be outflanked from the south. With Rommel only 80km (50 miles) from Alexandria, Cairo in a panic about the German advance and Churchill breathing down his neck, Auchinleck fired Messervy and replaced him with Major General Renton. But Rommel's DAK was exhausted and had few tanks left. On 8 July, he made a feeble attack upon the line with 50 tanks and 2000 troops. Churchill now replaced Auchinleck with General Alexander and General Gott was given command of 8th Army. 'Gentleman' Gott was unfortunately killed in an aircraft accident and so, on 13 August, General Bernard Law Montgomery replaced him. A new and, for the British, victorious chapter was about to be written in the long tale of the desert war.

ABOVE: Both sides in the desert war learnt how to survive in this inhospitable and, to the inexperienced, potentially deadly environment from the Arab Bedouins. Here, a German tank regiment equipped with what appear to be PzKpfw Is has made camp for the night, when it was important to keep warm in the freezing desert air.

CHAPTER SIX

TANK WAR IN AFRICA AND ITALY

From the excellent 'tank country' of the African desert, the war moved to the very difficult terrain of the Italian mainland.

There was now a pause as both sides regrouped, re-equipped and reassessed the situation after the first battle of Alamein. For Rommel, although strategically defeated by Auchinleck's counterattacks, he had won a tactical victory, and the supply and re-equipment situation improved rapidly over July and August. The renewed German air offensive against the British-held Mediterranean island Malta, which sat astride the German–Italian supply route to North Africa, meant that Axis convoys were getting through more regularly. Thus, the *Afrika Korps* received a large number of new tanks, which shifted the qualitative balance some way back towards the Germans. The new up-armoured version of the PzKpfw III and several new long-barrelled 75mm (2.95mm) gun-armed versions of the PzKpfw IV were both able to deal with American-built Grant

LEFT: The wreckage of long-barrelled 75mm (2.95in) armed German PzKpfw IVs in Tunisia after the tide turns in the desert for the final time. Rommel could ill afford to lose such potent tanks, given Montgomery's vast superiority in all arms, particularly tanks, and the American and British landings in his rear in Operation Torch. The level of destruction in the photograph implies that the tanks have been caught in the open by artillery or aircraft. By 1942, the Allies increasingly had air superiority over the desert, making Rommel's task even harder.

81

ABOVE: Allied equipment capable of taking the fight to the Germans. A British tank crew brew up next to their American-built M3 Grant tanks. When these tanks were first deployed in May 1942 at Gazala, their combination of up to 50mm (1.96in) armour and armament of a 57mm (2.24in) weapon in the turret and, particularly, a 75mm (2.95in) gun in the hull, gave the *Afrika Korps* a considerable shock.

tanks employed by the British. Rommel also received the 164th Light Division, a fresh formation, which made up somewhat for the losses suffered in the early summer. However, when it came to his own health, Rommel's situation was not as positive, as he prepared to renew his advance. His stomach problems worsened, but he refused to relinquish his command until a replacement of which he approved was made available. Hitler refused to send him Guderian, who was still in disgrace, and thus Rommel remained in place, despite the fact that he could only leave his sick bed occasionally. It was a debilitated field marshal who would lead the last Axis push towards the Suez Canal.

In contrast to the physical state of the German commander were the energy and drive of his new adversary, Lieutenant General Bernard Law Montgomery, who immediately stamped his mark on his new command. Montgomery had led a division during the French campaign and spent the subsequent two years in Britain in positions of increasing responsibility. His commands were characterised by intensive training regimes coupled with an emphasis on physical fitness for all ranks. When one somewhat unfit colonel complained that having to run 11.2km (7 miles) would probably kill him, the

ascetic, teetotal, non-smoking (and totally unsympathetic) Montgomery responded that it would cause fewer administrative problems if he died in training, rather than on the battlefield. Montgomery brought this vigorous and uncompromising attitude to the admittedly dispirited 8th Army and set about instilling in his troops the will to win. He had a profound and energising effect on his battered army from the moment he arrived. This was important, as he had only two weeks to familiarise himself with his new desert command before Rommel attacked again.

ALAM HALFA
Rommel knew he had to attack quickly before the gathering British and Commonwealth strength became overwhelming. The fighting capacity and morale of troops remained high and he had received some more of the up-gunned PzKpfw IVs. Rommel was also under pressure from Hitler and Mussolini to continue the march on Cairo. Despite this, he remained worried about the German–Italian Army's chance of success, as he was at the end of massively overstretched supply lines and very short of fuel. He was also a very sick man. His doctor reported that he '[could] command the battle under constant medical

attention ... [but it is] essential to have a replacement on the spot' and concluded that that 'he was so ill with an infection of the nose and a swollen liver, that he could not get out of his truck'.

Montgomery had the advantage of Auchinleck's appreciation of Rommel's intentions, which accurately anticipated the German's move, as well as Auchinleck's very sound plan for defeating it. He also had the advantage of ULTRA intelligence from decoded German transmissions, which confirmed Rommel's plans. Despite similar advantages in the past, the British, to paraphrase Winston Churchill, had managed to snatch defeat from the jaws of victory many times before in the Western Desert. It is to Montgomery's credit, given his recent arrival and lack of experience in this theatre, that he won a comprehensive victory at Alam Halfa, although he did have a number of advantages, including more tanks and shorter supply lines than his opponent.

STATIC DEFENCE

Montgomery was not willing to fight a mobile battle, something at which Rommel excelled and in which, in contrast, Montgomery had little experience. He had enough troops to hold a line of defence as far south as Alam Halfa ridge. Along here, Montgomery had the 8th Army dig in its tanks behind an anti-tank screen. He did not intend to the repeat the mistakes of so many British commanders in the desert and take on Rommel at his own game. He outlined his plan to Brian Horrocks, the new commander of 13 Corps. As Horrocks recalled:

'The point was, he said to me, that our armoured formations are too brave. They always attack. And all the Germans do is withdraw their 88s behind the line and then knock out all our tanks. What's more their 88s have a far better range and the Germans have far better tanks than we've got.

'So the cavalry is really hunting the whole time. They're after the fox. They'll go, they'll always attack. That's their one element.

'Now, he said, I'm not going to have that. I want you to go up there, go up on to the Alam Halfa ridge, and I want you to arrange to lure the Germans on. And

when we've really got them into a trap, then we'll go for them. In other words all anti-tank guns must be dug in, and all our tanks dug in. Everything dug in. And let Rommel come on. Let him come down the side of the ridge ... And then when the moment comes, we come in at his soft stuff – because he's getting a bit short of fuel and one thing and another. In fact, he said, it's a case of dog eat rabbit. That was his phrase: "dog eat rabbit".'

As anticipated, Rommel attacked the southern British positions with his three veteran German divisions on the night of 30 August. The Italian XX Corps anchored his left flank. As the German armour pushed east, it was harried by the RAF, which had control of the skies. The density of British minefields and intensity of artillery fire meant that tanks of 15th Panzer Division and 21st Panzer Division made far slower progress than Rommel had anticipated. A number of high-

ranking casualties occurred in this early phase: 21st Panzer Division's commander General von Bismark was killed and Nehring, commanding the *Afrika Korps*, was wounded, thus unhinging the German leadership structure. Only the drive of Bayerlein, who took over at once, kept the attack going.

Rommel ordered the *Afrika Korps* to turn north, but here 15th Panzer Division's armoured assault on the British 22nd Armoured Brigade dug in on Alam Halfa ridge floundered in the face of the

ABOVE: The M4 Sherman – the best tank in the desert in late 1942. These American tanks were reliable and more than able to deal with any tank in the German–Italian army at that time. The Sherman proved its worth several times over in the second battle of El Alamein and subsequent pursuit of the *Afrika Korps*.

well-prepared Allied defences. Meanwhile, 21st Panzer Division made the tactical error of chasing a number of decoy British tanks, which led them into the fire of British heavy tanks in a hull-down position and forced the panzers to become involved in an almost static gunnery contest in extremely disadvantageous conditions. As Montgomery had noted, in the past, the British tanks had been inclined to charge the German armour, which usually ended in disaster. This time the British held their position and coolly reinforced the situation as necessary. It was the Germans who were forced to charge and they suffered accordingly.

By nightfall, the Germans began to fall back to regroup and refuel. Rommel faced a difficult decision: whether to renew his attack and fight a battle of attrition against a stronger enemy and take losses he could ill afford, or carry on to Alexandria, which was only 40km (25 miles) away. Rommel had neither the inclination nor the resources to contest an attritional battle and, on 2 September, he halted the offensive. There is some controversy as to whether Montgomery should have seized this opportunity and counterattacked, thus annihilating the

Afrika Korps, while the cream of Rommel's divisions lay scattered and short of fuel in the shallow depression between superior British forces at Alam Halfa and the Quattara Depression. Montgomery, however, was above all else a cautious and careful general. Perhaps, had he been Rommel, he might have launched a massive armoured counterstroke, but Montgomery had already planned for a future offensive and had no intention of pre-empting this. In his memoirs he gives two reasons for holding back: first, he did not feel the training of his army and levels of equipment were adequate and, secondly, he did not want Rommel to retreat too far from Alamein, as he wanted him to stand and fight when the British attacked.

SUCCESSFUL WITHDRAWAL

Thus Rommel conducted a consummate withdrawal and seriously mauled the 2nd New Zealand Division, which Montgomery did, in fact, order forwards against the German retreat on 3 September. In a matter of hours, these men suffered the bulk of the 1750 casualties the 8th Army suffered over the six-day battle. The Panzer Army lost 2910

RIGHT: Italian Semovente assault guns in the desert. According to Rommel, the standard of Italian tanks would 'make one's hair curl'. The Italian armoured formations were much hampered by the poor quality of their equipment.

men and 49 tanks. The loss itself was not too serious, but Rommel had failed to reach his objective and was now forced onto the defensive and, to a certain extent, had to abandon his concepts of mobile warfare in the desert.

EL ALAMEIN

'This battle for which we are preparing will be a real rough house and will involve a very great deal of hard fighting. If we are successful it will mean the end of the war in North Africa, apart from general "clearing-up" operations; it will be the turning point of the whole war. Therefore we can take no chances.'

Lt-Gen B.L. Montgomery
Orders about Morale
14 September 1942

Montgomery was a general who rarely took chances and he did not intend to do so at El Alamein. Alam Halfa had delayed his own offensive and he was determined not to be rushed. Churchill had been pushing Auchinleck to attack since March and his refusal, after the July battles, to undertake such an action until September had been part of the reason for his dismissal. Montgomery steadfastly resisted Churchill's exhortations until he was fully ready; that would not be until the end of October. Montgomery was determined that his troops would be trained to the peak of perfection and be completely within his grip, ready to do exactly what he wanted of them. As one of his generals, Oliver Leese, recalled: 'He was completely convinced he was going to win the battle. He made everything crystal clear.' Indeed, Montgomery was determined that the 8th Army was 'crystal clear' about its job in the forthcoming battle. In a series of lectures and inspections, he convinced his command that: 'All that is necessary is that each one of us, every officer and man, should enter this battle with the determination to see it through – to fight and to kill – and finally to win. If we do this there can be only one result – together we will hit the enemy for "six" right out of North Africa.'

To hit that enemy for 'six', Montgomery had built up a considerable weight in men and materiel. By mid-October, he had some 220,000 men whom he had rigorously prepared for the forthcoming battle. The 8th Army's tank force had increased from 896 to 1351. These included 285 of the newly arrived

BELOW: The PzKpfw III medium tank – mainstay of the *Afrika Korps*. In the early years of the desert war the PzKpfw III had proven superior to the lighter British tanks and far more reliable and manoeuvrable than the heavier infantry tanks. However, the qualitative balance was beginning to shift as the British received newer American models.

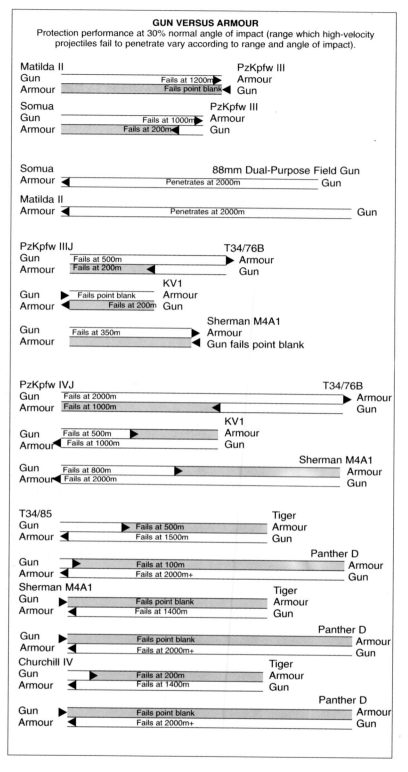

GUN VERSUS ARMOUR
Protection performance at 30% normal angle of impact (range which high-velocity projectiles fail to penetrate vary according to range and angle of impact).

Matilda II		PzKpfw III
Gun	Fails at 1200m	Armour
Armour	Fails point blank	Gun
Somua		PzKpfw III
Gun	Fails at 1000m	Armour
Armour	Fails at 200m	Gun

Somua Armour — Penetrates at 2000m — 88mm Dual-Purpose Field Gun Gun
Matilda II Armour — Penetrates at 2000m — Gun

PzKpfw IIIJ / T34/76B — Gun Fails at 500m Armour; Armour Fails at 200m Gun
KV1 — Gun Fails point blank Armour; Armour Fails at 200m Gun
Sherman M4A1 — Gun Fails at 350m Armour; Armour Gun fails point blank

PzKpfw IVJ / T34/76B — Gun Fails at 2000m Armour; Armour Fails at 1000m Gun
KV1 — Gun Fails at 500m Armour; Armour Fails at 1000m Gun
Sherman M4A1 — Gun Fails at 800m Armour; Armour Fails at 2000m Gun

T34/85 / Tiger — Gun Fails at 500m Armour; Armour Fails at 1500m Gun
Panther D — Gun Fails at 100m Armour; Armour Fails at 2000m+ Gun
Sherman M4A1 / Tiger — Gun Fails point blank Armour; Armour Fails at 1400m Gun
Panther D — Gun Fails point blank Armour; Armour Fails at 2000m+ Gun
Churchill IV / Tiger — Gun Fails at 200m Armour; Armour Fails at 1400m Gun
Panther D — Gun Fails point blank Armour; Armour Fails at 2000m+ Gun

ABOVE: A chart showing the penetration and protection of the major tank variants of World War II. As can be seen, some tanks stood little chance against opponents such as the German Tiger.

tank, if somewhat unreliable. These tanks were supported by 1000 field and medium artillery pieces supplied with plentiful ammunition. Montgomery's armoured and infantry division had 800 of the six-pounder anti-tank gun, which was capable of dealing with any tank in Rommel's inventory. He also had 100 105mm (4.1in) self-propelled guns. The RAF dominated the air above El Alamein, having roughly double the aircraft available to the Germans and Italians.

Against this Rommel could muster 108,000 men, of which only 53,000 were German. Nonetheless, the Italians had learnt from their early mistakes in the desert campaign and were now formidable opponents. The quality of their tanks, however, was another matter. Rommel had 489 tanks on the eve of the battle, of which 278 were the almost worthless Italian mechanised coffins, the M13 and M14. The bulk of Rommel's German tanks were PzKpfw IIIs. He had only 30 PzKpfw IVs with the long-barrelled 75mm (2.95in) gun, which was the only tank capable of dealing with the newly arrived Shermans. Rommel only had 24 of the much-feared 88mm (3.45in) anti-aircraft guns, which had proved so potent when used in the anti-tank role. Much has been written of the qualitative and quantitative superiority of Montgomery's army, but Rommel had had some time to prepare for the British assault and, while the 8th Army outnumbered its opponents roughly two to one in all weapons systems, a military rule of thumb is that a superiority of three to one is required for a successful assault.

ROMMEL ON THE DEFENSIVE
Rommel had resigned himself to going onto the defensive after Alam Halfa. His lack of troops, tanks, fuel and supplies made it the only sensible military choice. He was forced to return home due to ill health, but he had approved a large-scale series of fortifications, which he and his subsequent replacement Georg von Stumme put into place, establishing a defensive system of strongpoints set among deep minefields consisting of 445,000 mines. The mobile troops were to be held back in reserve to counter any penetration, but, due to the desperate fuel shortage faced by the Axis forces in North Africa, they were positioned much

American Sherman, the latest tank in the British arsenal and the best tank in the desert, and 210 Grants, whose 75mm (2.95in) gun the Germans had learnt to respect in recent months. Even the Crusader, latest of the long-suffering line of British cruiser tanks, with its six-pounder cannon, was a reasonable battle

ABOVE: An Italian M 13/40 is loaded onto a tank transporter before the battle of Alamein. The Germans, particularly, set great store on the recovery of their damaged tanks.

LEFT: A line of PzKpfw IIIs advances along a desert road in Tunisia. The increasing vunerability of the PzKpfw III is demonstrated by the tendency of the *Afrika Korps* crews to fix spare track to the front of their tanks in an effort to improve the PzKpfw III's protection.

ABOVE: The Desert Rats alongside their Valentine tanks in Tripoli in January 1943. The British tank men had largely had the worst of the desert war until the arrival of General Bernard Law Montgomery and their morale was suffering. This the new British commander set out to change with customary drive and energy. His success at Alamein gave his men a much-needed lift.

closer to the front than normal. Rather than having his armoured divisions concentrated ready to counterattack any Allied breakthrough, Rommel had to put them where he expected them to fight: in the north, he placed 15th Panzer Division, 90th Light and the Italian armoured division *Littorio*; and, to the south, 21st Panzer and *Ariete*.

MONTY'S PLANS

In the north, Montgomery intended to have his infantry of 30th Corps cross the minefields and clear two passages through the Axis defences for his 10th Corps' tanks to fight their way out and then post themselves defensively to the west. In the south, the 7th Armoured Division – the infamous Desert Rats – would make strong representations westwards to tie German forces down in the south.

Operation Lightfoot – a name somewhat in bad taste considering the 445,000 German mines – opened with a 908-gun artillery barrage on the evening of 23 October 1942. It took the Germans completely by surprise and seriously

disrupted Axis communications. Stumme, commanding in the absence of Rommel, went forwards to find out what was happening and suffered a heart attack while under shellfire. Ritter von Thoma temporarily took command, while Siegfried Westphal, the chief of staff, signalled to Germany, recommending that Rommel should return to the desert, despite his ill health.

Meanwhile, the British and Commonwealth troops battled across the minefields and into the Axis positions. By the evening of the 24th, some tanks of the British 2nd Armoured Brigade had cleared the western edge of the minefields, but they were not clear of the German defensive system. These tanks were part of the northern thrust towards Kidney Ridge, to the south over Miteiriya Ridge. The British advance stopped, enmeshed in the Axis minefields on the following morning. Therefore, neither of the two attacks had achieved its objectives of the first day's fighting. The bitter fighting continued over the next couple of days as the advance began

to falter. The coordination of the British armoured and infantry corps left much to be desired, but they managed to repulse a piecemeal attack by 15th Panzer against the northern attack, which cost the Germans many vital tanks. The fighting reduced the German panzer division's strength from 119 to 31 tanks. Despite the limited advance, the battle of attrition was clearly going Montgomery's way.

ROMMEL'S RETURN TO ACTION

Rommel arrived back at the front on 26 October, but the situation was quickly slipping away from him. He immediately concentrated what armour he had left north – including 21st Panzer Division – to launch a counterattack against a salient created by the British 1st Armoured Division on a slight rise on Kidney Ridge. Both 21st Panzer and 90th Light Divisions attacked the salient's tip, backed up by the adjacent elements of 15th Panzer and 164th Divisions. *Luftwaffe* support failed to materialise in the face of British air superiority. Well-served British anti-tank guns brought 21st Panzer

Division to a halt with serious losses, while 90th Light was prevented from effectively coming to grips with the British by artillery fire and air attacks. It was the largest German counterattack of the battle and it had failed. Nonetheless, the *Afrika Korps* attacked determinedly again the following day, although the attack produced similar results.

The British advance, however, had stalled and, when it finally restarted on 28 October, the thrust on the northern flank by the 9th Australian Division made little headway against 90th Light. Montgomery was forced to come up with another plan. Operation Supercharge shifted the weight of the British assault into the area of Kidney Ridge on the night of 1 November. British tank forces remained immensely strong, with 152 Shermans and 133 Grants, plus many of the less effective British models, available to Montgomery. Rommel had only 102 tanks ready, although 52 were under repair. Supercharge, however, was headed by two infantry divisions, which managed to infiltrate deep into the German and

ABOVE: The American-built M4 Sherman equipped both the British and American forces involved in the invasion of Sicily in 1943. This M4 is seen shortly after disembarking from its landing craft. The Browning machine gun on its turret is for anti-aircraft defence.

Italian defences. Once the British tanks surged forwards in the morning, however, the Germans and Italian anti-tank gunners made them pay. The leading British Armoured Brigade – the 9th – lost 70 out of 94 tanks. Yet still the British were grinding the Axis forces down. Losses amongst the vital anti-tank gun crews were particularly high. The 50mm (1.96in) and captured Soviet 76.2mm (3in) guns, which made up the bulk of Axis anti-tank forces, were only able to penetrate the Grants' and Shermans' front armour at close range.

AFRIKA KORPS UNDER PRESSURE

Von Thoma told Rommel that the line was holding but would not do so much longer. He launched the few uncommitted elements of 15th and 21st Panzer Divisions against the 4000m (4376yd) British penetration and again suffered extremely heavy losses. By the end of the day, von Thoma had only 30 battleworthy tanks left. Rommel had been preparing to withdraw since the failure of his first counterattack and, on 3 November, he began to pull back his armoured forces and issued orders for the rest of his hopelessly outnumbered men to disengage. It was a remarkable feat accomplished in the face of a vastly superior enemy, under constant air attack

and seriously constrained by the shortage of fuel. Rommel even hoped to get away most of his largely immobile infantry because, as he later remarked, 'the enemy was operating with such astonishing hesitancy and caution'.

Montgomery, however, found an unexpected ally in Adolf Hitler, who, upon hearing of Rommel's intentions, ordered him not to retreat with the instruction that 'there can be no other thought but to stand fast, yield not a yard of ground and throw every gun and man into the battle'. Hitler exhorted continued resistance: 'It would not be the first time in history that strong will has triumphed over the bigger battalions.' This, as with so many of Hitler's stand-fast orders, was clearly foolish, and would result in the destruction of the Afrika Korps, yet Rommel rescinded his own orders and attempted to continue to the hold the line. The following day, the New Zealand infantry and 7th Armoured Division finally broke through Rommel's defensive lines and threatened to encircle the bulk of his forces. He abandoned any pretence of holding on and gained the grudging consent of Hitler to withdraw his troops westwards. It was too late for many; 130 Italian tanks were caught and annihilated by the 7th Armoured Division, and much of the immobile

RIGHT: A rather forlorn Tiger with a rather forlorn soldier seeking shelter beneath it. The British and Americans first came across these monsters during the fighting in Tunisia. This one has probably been bulldozed off the road having lost its left track, most likely to a landmine. Italy was a difficult country in which to use tanks offensively, something which contributed to the slow pace of the Allied advance up its length.

infantry were left stranded in the desert, where 30,000 men were rounded up with little resistance over the following days. The battle of El Alamein was over. It had cost the British 13,560 casualties and about 600 tanks.

THE PURSUIT

According to Clausewitz, the fruits of victory are in the pursuit. Montgomery had won a key victory at El Alamein, but his army remained stationary in the aftermath. By the time Montgomery pushed forwards again on 5 November, Rommel's forces had gone. On the following day 22nd Armoured Brigade caught a remnant of 21st Panzer Division, immobilised through want of fuel, but was fought off until the Germans were re-supplied and slipped away. The chase then faltered in heavy rain, although admittedly the same weather seems to have barely affected the retreating Rommel. Both armies then settled down for the long march west of 2414km (1500 miles). Montgomery's experienced desert commanders pleaded to race after Rommel to bring him to battle, but Montgomery refused. He was determined not be caught by a surprise German counterstroke. In fact, Rommel was down to 10 functioning tanks. Despite this, there was real combat, as

Rommel occasionally turned and halted to hamper his pursuers. As General Oliver Leese wrote: 'In the retreat I never saw Rommel fight a real action; there was no battle crisis until Mareth. But there was a lot of fighting – a battle every day, because you couldn't take chances with German rearguards. Rommel fought every day with something.'

Meanwhile the strategic situation had changed drastically. On the night of 7 November, American and British forces landed in French Morocco and Algeria, seriously threatening Rommel's rear. After two days of fighting, the French commander Admiral Darlan accepted a ceasefire and subsequently began cooperating with the Allies. The Germans rapidly reinforced their forces in Tunisia with some 17,000 troops, including 10th Panzer Division, to prevent the Allies capturing Tunis and stranding Rommel in southern Tunisia.

The 10th Panzer Division successfully blunted the Allied advance 21km (13 miles) short of Tunis. Heavy rain and mud ensured that the Allies were forced to pause. The German reinforcements included five of the new monster 56-tonne Tiger tanks with the 88mm (3.45in) gun; two of these saw combat.

Back in Libya, Montgomery retook Tobruk on 13 November, tussled

ABOVE: Men from a panzer division's mobile workshop hurriedly replace a PzKpfw IV's tracks under fire during the battle for Monte Cassino, Italy, in April 1944. A tank without its tracks was extremely vulnerable and difficult to manoeuvre, and the Germans would go to great lengths to keep their precious few tanks in action.

ABOVE: A Sherman of the 1st Armoured Division, 5th Army, equipped with a bulldozer in Italy in September 1944. The difficulty of movement in such mountainous terrain prevented any serious hopes of a rapid advance. German roadblocks, landmines and booby traps made the employment of such specialised equipment vital.

RIGHT: British Churchill tanks of 51st Royal Tank Regiment move slowly across open terrain overlooking the River Foglia, suitably dispersed in case of enemy attack. Although slow and heavy – a classic British infantry tank design – the heavily armoured Churchill more than proved itself in Italy due to its toughness and ability to deal ably with the mountainous terrain.

ineffectively with the *Africa Korps* at Gazala, and captured Benghazi for the third and last time on 20 November. However, at his old defences at El Agheila, Rommel paused and appeared ready to make a stand.

Montgomery was not willing to risk a strong German riposte and halted to prepare for a set-piece assault. Rommel again slipped away. At times it seemed that the two commanders were working in collaboration, as Rommel was

determined not give battle and Montgomery appeared to have no wish to provoke the German into action. On 23 January 1943, Montgomery finally entered Tripoli and, on the same day, Rommel crossed into Tunisia.

KESSELRING'S DILEMMA

Although the German–Italian position in Tunisia had been heavily reinforced over the winter, Field Marshal Kesselring, in overall command of the Axis position in Africa and the Mediterranean, was in a fairly desperate situation. In western Tunisia, his forces under General von Arnim faced overwhelming Anglo-American might, while, to the south, Rommel had been steadily withdrawing in the face of Montgomery's 8th Army. Despite this, the Germans were to enjoy a brief period of tactical success at the tail end of the war in Africa.

Kesselring now had the advantage – despite the shortage of supplies due to the Allied control of the Mediterranean – of short interior lines of communication, and he could shift his troops from one front to the other with comparative ease. Detaching 21st Panzer Division from Rommel – somewhat to the latter's chagrin – Kesselring ordered von Arnim to attack the Americans in the vicinity of Sid bou Zid with the 201 tanks of 21st and 10th Panzer Divisions, backed up by the newly arrived Italian Superga Division and a company of 12 of the new Tiger tanks. The two panzer divisions encircled and crushed the advanced units of US 1st Armoured Division on 14 February, destroying 40 American tanks. The subsequent American counterattack, launched the next morning, suffered a similar fate; only four tanks out of two armoured battalions survived. The commander of the German attack, General Zeigler, did not push on as fast as Rommel urged and American resistance stiffened; nonetheless, his command had destroyed over 100 tanks and netted 3000 prisoners.

Meanwhile, after leaving a covering force to face Montgomery, Rommel pushed northwest with a combat group drawn from the *Afrika Korps*. His advance met little resistance and steadily gathered pace, capturing the American airfield at Thelepte. The British, American and French troops in his path fell back in confusion. He was desperate to continue the drive into the Allies' main communications and exploit the situation. However, von Arnim had already halted Zeigler and the 10th Panzer Division. Rommel was forced to plead with Mussolini for the advance to proceed and a vital day passed before his request to advance was approved. To his horror, however, its axis was changed from northwest, deep into the Allies' rear, to northwards behind the front line, which took the Axis forces perilously close to Allied reserves. Thus, Rommel's thrust came exactly where General Alexander, overall commander of the Allied land forces, expected it to come.

THE KASSERINE PASS

Failing to make much headway without some cost – the 21st Panzer Division was down to fewer than 40 tanks – Rommel decided that the key to his advance was the pass at Kasserine. Here he concentrated his limited forces on 20 February, hampered by the fact that von Arnim had held back half of 10th Panzer Division and perhaps the trump card of a company of Tigers. The Americans holding the pass broke and, in the telling and candid words of the American official history, 'The enemy was amazed at the quantity and quality of American equipment captured more or less intact.' Rommel pushed onwards, destroying 40 or so Allied tanks and capturing 700 prisoners on the road out of Kasserine and in positions around Thala, although he lost 12 tanks of his own in the process. However, he had advanced as far as possible given the presence of superior Allied forces; in a meeting with Kesselring on 22 February, they agreed to withdraw to the Kasserine Pass and concentrate their next attack on Montgomery's 8th Army. It was a considerable tactical victory and Rommel had come surprisingly close to achieving his strategic goal of driving the Allies out of Western Tunisia. It is interesting to speculate upon what he might have achieved had he received all of 10th Panzer Division from von Arnim.

Rommel and Kesselring now settled on attacking Montgomery, whose 8th Army sat at Medenine. It was a difficult operation, as Rommel readily admitted, given that he had almost no chance of surprise. Nonetheless, Montgomery's initial dispositions appeared vulnerable to an attack by the three German Panzer divisions. However, ULTRA intelligence provided Montgomery with the timing, strength and direction of the German attack. This enabled him to bring up reinforcements and prepare strong anti-tank defences, which were bolstered by the superb new British 17-pounder gun that was more than capable of dealing with any of the German tanks deployed. Montgomery held his tanks back as he had done at Alam Halfa and let the panzers come on to him. This they did on 6 March. The 21st Panzer Division was mauled carelessly crossing a ridge and never reached the British lines. The 15th Panzer Division managed to close, but was easily repulsed. The 10th did no better. This attack cost the Germans 700 men and 52 tanks, while the British lost no tanks whatsoever. This was the last offensive action by the Germans in Africa and a tired and sick Rommel was flown home. The Allies gradually closed the pocket, capturing 200,000 Germans and Italians when resistance finally ceased on 11 May 1943.

The loss of most of Rommel's veterans and the pick of the Italian Army in Tunisia left Sicily and Italy somewhat weakly defended. Mussolini was understandably hesitant to accept too many German reinforcements due to a mixture of pride and fear. Nonetheless, the Allies' next target – Sicily – was defended by four Italian divisions, the hastily formed 15th Panzergrenadier Division, and the rebuilt *Herman Göring* Panzer Division. The Western Allies argued about their next move over the winter of 1942–43. The British preference to continue the Allied campaign in the Mediterranean won out over the American wish to invade northwest Europe.

SICILY INVADED

Operation Husky, the invasion of Sicily, was launched on 10 July 1943. The Anglo-American invasion had absolute air superiority and the landings were carried out with minimal resistance. Most of the Italian units facing them had no wish to continue fighting, although one Italian unit in obsolete light tanks gallantly counterattacked on the first morning against one American landing beach. The main threat developed on 11 July from the *Herman Göring* Panzer Division, supported by a company of Tiger tanks. The Americans had few tanks

BELOW: An American M18 tank destroyer blasts enemy positions in Firenzuola in Italy on 17 October 1944. The Americans used tank destroyers to combat the thick armour of the panzers. Tank destroyers generally carried a large, high-velocity gun, but lacked the armour of conventional tanks.

and anti-tank guns ashore, but US naval gunfire broke up the attack. The British advance was initially faster, as Montgomery faced no immediate counterattack. Although Italian resistance collapsed rapidly, the same could not be said for the Germans'. The terrain was rough and favoured the defenders; this certainly was not tank country. Montgomery's troops slowly struggled northwards along the east coast, while General George Patton, commander of the US 7th Army, pushed north and then swung east and made better speed. The Germans decided to withdraw to the mainland after Mussolini's overthrow and managed to pull 40,000 German and 60,000 Italian troops, plus over 1000 vehicles and 47 tanks, from the port of Messina by 17 August.

Italy was not tank country either, as the British and Americans found to their cost over the long and bitter campaign to capture Italy. It might have been considerably easier had the haggling over Italian peace terms not delayed the invasion and allowed Hitler to move 16 divisions into Italy. Once the Italian surrender was agreed, the Allied invasion force set sail for Italy on 3 September. The new Italian Government wanted a landing near Rome, but the British and Americans were unwilling to operate beyond the range of Sicilian-based air cover. Montgomery's 8th Army landed without opposition at Calabria and sedately advanced inland, meeting no resistance. A landing at Taranto was carried out under similar conditions. The Germans seemed to be content to withdraw northwards.

MAIN LANDING

The main landing by a joint Anglo-American force of three divisions under US General Mark Clark took place at

ABOVE: British commandos file past a couple of Churchill AVREs (first used in any numbers at Normandy) on a lake shore in Italy in 1945, during the last months of the war. These versatile and specialised tanks operated by the Royal Engineers were capable of performing a variety of tasks, and were particularly useful when assaulting enemy strongpoints.

BELOW: The Panther – most potent of the new generation of German tanks that appeared in 1943. This one, coated in Zimmerit anti-magnetic mine paste, is a *Befehlswagen* command Panther, as indicated by the Fu8 radio antennae behind the commander's cupola.

Salerno on 8 September – the day the Italian surrender was announced – and met with a very different reception. Kesselring was now determined to fight for every foot of Italian soil, and the weak 16th Panzer Division – roughly 80 PzKpfw IVs and 40 assault guns, hardly the 600 tanks Clark talks of in his memoirs – launched a ferocious counter-attack against the Allied landings, which kept Clark's force of up to roughly the strength of five divisions confined in its narrow beachheads. The Germans were reinforced by the 29th Panzer-grenadier Division and elements of the refitted *Herman Göring* Division, and together they almost drove the Allies back into the sea. Bolstered by the massive application of air power and naval gunfire, including the 380mm (15in) guns of the battleships HMS *Warspite* and HMS *Valiant*, the British and American divisions held and began to push inland.

Despite this, Hitler was convinced by Kesselring's near success that Allied advance should be contested all the way. The construction of the Gustav Line of defences south of Rome began at once. Thus, as the Allied troops moved off the landing beaches into the valleys and mountains of Italy, they faced a long and relentless struggle northwards, interrupted by periods of sitting in the mud and rain when movement of men and vehicles became almost impossible.

'SLOGGING UP ITALY'

Tank warfare in Italy for the Germans consisted of the panzers and their supporting panzergrenadiers fighting rearguard actions – often from prepared and hull-down positions – as the Anglo-American tanks and infantry carefully edged their way forwards through the difficult terrain, a process described by Alexander, the Allied Commander in Chief, as 'slogging up Italy'. The Germans would subsequently slip away to prepared positions at their rear. Allied domination of the air took its toll on the German armoured formations, but it rarely proved decisive against the skilfully conducted withdrawals. Air superiority was no compensation for effective operations on the ground.

Clark's 5th Army in the west and Montgomery's 8th Army on the Adriatic side of Italy struggled forwards until they reached the Gustav Line, which was anchored on Monte Cassino, where their advance petered out in December 1943. Montgomery had never had much enthusiasm for the Italian campaign, the strategic rationale of which was that it was a battle of attrition to keep German divisions away from the proposed landing beaches in France. So it was with some relief that he handed over command of the 8th Army to Oliver Leese at the end of the year. He therefore missed the bloodiest fighting of the Italian campaign in the four great battles around Monte Cassino. These battles (12 January to 18 May) were not tank battles in the classic sense; rather, they resembled the vast attritional struggles of World War I, even if fought with more modern weapons. Comparatively few tanks were used by the Germans, who were inclined to hold their armour back to meet any break-through, as when 2nd New Zealand

Division managed to cross the River Rapido on 17/18 February. For the Allies, tanks were largely reduced to the infantry support role providing mobile and close firepower. As the history of one of the British armoured regiments, the 17/21st Lancers, notes: 'Italy was not to provide the opportunity to use [armoured division] at its best again. Fighting with an armoured division in Italy was like using a dagger to open a tin; the dagger is blunted and the tin is jagged and twisted.'

ANZIO LANDINGS

At the simultaneous landing at Anzio, north of the Gustav Line, however, armour played an important role. The Anzio landings on 22 January 1944 were an attempt to outflank the Gustav Line and force the Germans to thin out their defences to meet the threat and allow Clark to break through the weakened line. Kesselring was taken by surprise and the British and Americans landed unopposed. However, the commanding general, John Lucas, was extremely sanguine about the operation's chances of success and made little effort to push inland. This allowed Kesselring to reshuffle his forces with remarkable skill and speed, shifting 1st Parachute Corps

and 76th Panzer Corps to an area of the beachhead. The German counterattack began on 16 February, but air and naval support ensured the beleaguered beachhead held on, despite the German pressure and the use of new Goliath remote-controlled explosive tanks. The final successful battle for Cassino in May 1944 allowed the forces at Anzio beachhead to attempt a breakout on 23 May. It met with some success, but, rather than swinging east to cut off the Germans defending the Gustav line, Clark ordered his forces north to Rome, in direct contravention of Alexander's orders, allowing Kesselring's forces to escape northwards and foiling any chance of a decisive victory in Italy.

The war rumbled on through 1944. The 8th Army successfully breached the major German defensive barrier, the Gothic Line, in September 1944, but failed to exploit its advantage once more. It seemed that, after a year spent in the Italian mountains, the Allied army had forgotten how to fight a mobile battle. Alexander did at least tie down 20 or more German divisions throughout the campaign which could have been used in Normandy and, in the last month of the war, destroyed Army Group C before it could retire across the Alps.

LEFT: A flock of South African Shermans of the 6th South African Armoured Division in Fornace, Italy, awaits the order to advance on Bologna on 20 April 1945. The Sherman, in its many forms, was the mainstay of the tank armies of the Western Allies from 1942 onwards.

NORTH-WEST EUROPE

Normandy was not ideal tank country, but, once clear of the hedgerows, Allied armour raced towards the Rhine and victory.

Captain Basil Liddell Hart reckoned that the battle of El Alamein was a turning point in tank warfare after which 'armoured fighting changed its form ... and the form which ... took shape persisted not only in Africa but in the campaigns that followed in Europe. It was a more cautious form of action, at slower tempo. Concentrated punches were superseded by what has been aptly described as a process of "incessant sparring with anti-tank screens".' This was an accurate assessment, although at times operations proceeded with the speed of the early years of the war, Patton's breakout from the Normandy beachhead being a case in point. Generals still hoped for the decisive armoured breakthrough, but the days of sweeping *Blitzkrieg*-style tank advances had largely gone. There

LEFT: A PzKpfw VI Tiger I – the scourge of Allied tank crews in Normandy – of the 101st *Schwere Panzerabteilung*, advances along a road. Its frontal armour was practically impenetrable to Allied tank guns, while the Tiger's fearsome 88mm (3.45in) gun – likened by Allied troops to a 'telegraph pole' – could deal comfortably with any Allied tank deployed in the Normandy Campaign. It took a minimum of five M4 Shermans to stand a chance of knocking out a Tiger, four of them 'distracting' the German, while the other tried to sneak around to its rear.

ABOVE: An early British experiment with the DD (Duplex Drive) system designed by Nicholas Straussler fitted to a Valentine tank. This system kept an amphibian tank – universally the Sherman during the Normandy landings – afloat by means of a collapsible canvas screen. The tank was driven by two screws powered by the main engine while in the water.

were a number of reasons for this, such as the difficult terrain in Normandy and Italy and, perhaps more importantly, the increasing power of anti-tank weaponry and tactics, which meant that tanks had to become more cautious. The British officer Captain Ralph Ingersoll provides an excellent description of the approach that Allied armoured forces were forced to adopt in Europe:

'Tanks do not rush forward in the mechanised version of the flying wedge … They advance hesitatingly, like diffident fat boys coming across the floor at a party to ask for the next dance, stopping at the slightest excuse, going back, then coming on again, and always apparently seeking the longest way round. When they do have to cross a plain they postpone the evil moment as long as possible by clinging to the lower slopes of the nearest ridge until some invisible force pushes them unhappily into the open. When

they follow a road, they zigzag in a series of tangents to it, crossing it occasionally and staying on it only when there is no [other way] through difficult country. They are timid creatures.'

Armoured warfare had indeed changed.

PREPARATIONS FOR THE INVASION

Ever since the Dunkirk evacuation in 1940, the British had known that to defeat Germany they would have to land an army in northwest Europe. Yet, haunted by the memories of the slaughter of World War I, British military leaders showed considerable and understandable reluctance to undertake this monumental task. They had dabbled with the idea of invading the periphery of Nazi-occupied Europe, such as the Aegean or Norway, and strongly advocated that the main Anglo-American effort continue in the Mediterranean. Some proponents of strategic air power even argued that the continuation and intensification of the Allied bombing campaign could alone win the war. Nonetheless, their American allies were quite determined that the invasion of Europe and the march into Germany should be launched as soon as possible. The British were forced to accept the military logic of the American position and agreed to a major landing in France, later codenamed Overlord, at the Casablanca Conference in January 1943.

The Allied planners decided to land in Normandy largely because it was within Allied air cover, had firm and sheltered beaches, and was close to a major port: Cherbourg. American General Dwight Eisenhower had been appointed Supreme Commander of the Allied assault, and General Montgomery, former commander of the 8th Army, would lead the invasion's land forces. Immediately the original plan was altered, widening the beachhead and strengthening the invasion force to five divisions landed on the beaches, with support from various commando and Ranger units, and three airborne divisions dropped inshore to secure the flanks. They would be rapidly followed by the rest of the US 1st Army commanded by General Omar Bradley and the British 2nd Army led by General Sir Miles Dempsey. It would be a week, however, before the number of divisions ashore could be doubled.

HOBART'S 'FUNNIES'

One of the lessons learnt from the failed Dieppe Raid of 1942 was the importance of adequate armoured support for the assaulting infantry. Major-General Percy Hobart's 79th Armoured Division was responsible for developing the techniques and equipment that would spearhead the Allied invasion. The division's regiments were eventually equipped with a plethora of well-tested and largely very useful armoured vehicles designed to undertake a number of specialised tasks. Experience at El Alamein had proved that the flail – heavy chains suspended on a rotating drum in front of the tank – was the most effective tank-borne method of clearing a path through a minefield. The best design, the Sherman Crab, could clear a lane almost 3.3m (10ft) wide at the speed of 2km/h (1.25mph).

The division's most versatile vehicle was the AVRE (Assault Vehicle Royal

Engineers) based around the hull of a Churchill infantry tank. The AVRE carried a 290mm (11.4in) petard mortar designed for destroying bunkers and fortifications. It could be used with a wide variety of external fittings. It could carry a fascine which could be dropped into anti-ditches or trenches to allow other tanks to cross, or be fitted with a bobbin, a device which laid a carpet of hessian and metal tubing ahead of the vehicle to allow tanks and other vehicles to cross soft ground, such as a beach. Furthermore, it could lay a small box girder bridge with a 40-tonne capacity over gaps up to 9.1m (30ft) or could push mobile bailey or skid bridges into position. The AVRE was also able to place 'Goat' demolition charges (up to

817kg (1800lb) of HE) against an obstacle or fortification before reversing away and detonating the explosive. These tanks equipped the 1st Assault Brigade RE, consisting of three regiments of 60 AVRE each, and were to play a key role during the landings. Amongst the most fearsome weapons deployed by Hobart's division were flamethrower-armed Churchill tanks known as Crocodiles, which proved horribly effective against the dug-in defenders and their bunkers.

The most important problem was how to provide the first assault wave with

ABOVE: A Sherman Crab flail tank easily works its way through a barbed wire emplacement. The flail – a rotating drum with heavy chains attached which was fixed to the front of the tank – proved the quickest and most efficient method of clearing a path through a minefield. The chains would need replacing after several detonations, as they were literally blown apart.

armoured support. The specialist armour would also need the protection of direct gunfire from more conventional tanks. Perhaps the most important of Hobart's so-called 'Funnies' was the DD (Duplex Drive) 'swimming' tank. The DD tank was the product of engineer Nicholas Straussler, who developed an amphibian tank kept afloat by a collapsible canvas screen and driven by two small screws powered by the main engine. When the tank reached the shore, the buoyancy screen could be lowered and normal drive engaged; it could then operate as a conventional gun armed tank. Tests were carried out on the Tetrarch light tank and heavier Valentine, but the Sherman was the tank of choice for the Normandy landings. Used by a number of units of 79th Armoured Division, the DD Sherman was also the only 'Funny' tank used by the Americans, equipping the US 70th and 741st Tank Battalions.

GERMAN PREPARATIONS

By late 1943, it was obvious to the Germans that an invasion had to come; it was just a question of when and where. The German commanders, Hitler included, were inclined to believe the Allies would cross the Channel at its shortest point and land on the Pas de Calais. Soon after the fall of France, Hitler had ordered the construction of a line of coastal defences, known as the Atlantic Wall, to protect his Western empire. It was formidable in places, particularly around the major ports, but sparser elsewhere. Perhaps more serious was the low quality of troops defending it. It was only after November 1943 that the quality and quantity of the formations in France began to increase. Field Marshal von Rundstedt, the German Commander in Chief in the West, had 58 divisions under his command but half of these were static, tied to stretches of coastal defences. More important were his nine panzer and one panzergrenadier divisions, which would probably prove critical in any attempt to repel an Allied invasion. Von Rundstedt also disagreed with his subordinate, Rommel, who led Army Group B (made up of 15th Army) in the Pas de Calais, and the 7th Army protecting Normandy and Brittany. Rommel felt that once the Allies gained a foothold ashore they would be impossible to dislodge, and therefore he wanted to defeat the invasion on the beaches. To this end, he added new impetus to the strengthening of the Atlantic Wall. He also wanted his panzer divisions held as close to the coast as possible. Here he clashed with von

BELOW: An interesting selection of German armour during the fighting in northwest Europe, the Sturmpanzer IV *Brummbär* (Grizzly Bear) self-propelled gun in the foreground, a PzKpfw V Panther in the middle and what appears to be a turretless early panzer to the rear.

Rundstedt, who wanted to hold them back as a mobile reserve, which would deliver a crushing counterattack after the Allies had landed. Hitler's solution was compromise, which left both commanders dissatisfied; Rommel felt his forward defences were inadequately manned and von Rundstedt believed his panzer reserve was too small.

6 JUNE 1944: D-DAY

D-Day began just after midnight on 6 June 1944, when 23,400 Allied paratroopers were dropped on to the flanks of the invasion beaches. At 0630 hours, following a naval bombardment, the landing craft of the five assault divisions began their final run in to the invasion beaches which were codenamed, from west to east, Utah, Omaha, Gold, Juno and Sword. At Utah, a relatively lightly defended beach, the Germans were stunned by the preliminary bombardment. Their shock was compounded by the sight of Sherman tanks rising from the waves and opening fire on them. Of the 32 DD Shermans of US 70th Tank Battalion which were launched towards Utah, 28 made it ashore. The beach was very

rapidly secured with only light casualties suffered by the American 4th Division and its troops and vehicles were soon moving through the marshes behind the dunes.

The situation for US 1st Infantry Division on the neighbouring Omaha beach was very different. The Americans had eschewed the use of specialised armour, with the exception of the DD Sherman. Very few of those deployed made it to the beach. The seas off Omaha were heavy and the waves easily swamped the canvas screens of the DD tanks. By a serious and costly error of judgement, the tanks were launched 5487m (6000yds) out and each one sunk like a stone when it left the landing crafts' ramp. Yet, despite these appalling examples, the crews of the subsequent tanks showed extraordinary and fatalistic courage by following without hesitation. Only five of the 32 DD Shermans launched in the first wave made it to the beach. Those that did so arrived after the infantry, so the spearhead troops had to storm Omaha's defences without armoured support. The commanders of the LCTs (Landing Craft Tank) that followed had the sense to bring their craft into within 229m

ABOVE: The crew of a heavily camouflaged PzKpfw IV relax in the Normandy sunshine. The almost total Allied control of the air made the movement of German armour during daylight at best extremely hazardous, and fighter-bombers such as the Typhoon and Thunderbolt were a constant menace.

ABOVE: British infantry and an accompanying Sherman move out from the beaches. The availability of tanks in close support made the task of troops assaulting the German defences on the landing beaches considerably simpler. Where they were unavailable or in short supply – such as on Omaha – serious problems occurred.

RIGHT: A Tiger tank of the SS *Schwere Panzerabteilung* 101 moves through a Normandy town on 10 June 1944, four days after the initial landings. By mid-1944, Tigers were deployed in heavy tank battalions attached at corps and army level. Although capable of massive tactical success, there were never enough of these potent beasts available.

(250yds) of the beach before launching the DD tanks. Nonetheless, many of these tanks were destroyed once they had landed. The appalling confusion and wreckage strewn across the beach hampered the landing of more vehicles, many of which were also immediately destroyed. The Germans were well dug in and nearly prevented the Americans gaining a foothold there. By the end of the day, the Americans on Omaha suffered 2000 casualties, in contrast to the 197 lost on Utah.

The British and Canadians deployed a wide range of specialised armour from Hobart's 79th Armoured Division and this gave them a considerable advantage when it came to clearing the German defences. On Sword, 34 of the 40 DD Shermans reached the beach and did much to clear German resistance before the infantry landed. This first wave of amphibious tanks was soon followed by the specialised armour: the AVRE Churchills with their petard mortars, the Crocodile flamethrower tanks and the Sherman Crab flail tanks. These vehicles quickly broke through the beach defences and into the dunes beyond. At Juno, a few miles west, the Canadians also broke through the German defences, but at greater cost. Most of the DD tanks made it ashore after the infantry, although they proved useful in the fighting behind the towns beyond the beach. On Gold, again the tanks arrived late and were unable to provide support against the fierce German fire from their bunkers, most of which had survived the naval bombardment unscathed. As the AVREs and flail tanks began to arrive, the German resistance was subdued and the tanks and infantry moved into the countryside beyond. While it is easy to over-emphasise the importance of Hobart's Funnies in the clearing of British and Canadian beaches, it is worth contrasting their relatively rapid success to what happened to the Americans on Omaha, who did not enjoy such specialist armoured support. The real success was the DD tank, which seems to have had a considerable psychological effect on the defenders, in addition to its providing the infantry with direct fire support.

The only German panzer division close to the beaches was the 21st. Initially ordered to move against the British paratroopers east of the Orne River. General Marcks, commander of 84th Corps, halted this move, rightly believing the 127 PzKpfw IVs and 40 assault guns at the panzer division's disposal were better used against the British and Canadian beachheads. By late afternoon, the division was in place. Marcks, who had driven forward, told the commander of the 22nd Panzer Regiment, Colonel von Oppeln Bronikowski: 'Oppeln, if you don't succeed in driving the English into the sea, we've lost the war.' The panzers and panzergrenadiers then began to advance northwards. The division drove straight into the gap between Juno and Sword beaches. However, the attack faltered in open country against well-sited tanks and anti-tank guns. The Sherman Fireflies (a British variant of the Sherman, armed with the superb 17-pounder anti-tank gun) of the Staffordshire Yeomanry caused the Germans serious problems. Only a handful of panzergrenadiers reached the sea and the division was forced to pull back because of an airborne landing behind it which threatened to cut them off. The attack had cost 21st Panzer 70 of its 120 or so tanks.

THE STRUGGLE FOR CAEN

Montgomery had included the capture of Caen in his objectives for the first day. Only the tanks of the Staffordshires and the troops of the King's Own Shropshire Light Infantry had any chance of reaching the ancient town. However, the counterattack by the 21st Panzer Division ensured the British lost their momentum and shifted temporarily to the defensive. The 21st Panzer Division fell back to Caen and dug in, while overnight the 12th SS Panzer Division *Hitler Jugend* arrived to bolster the Germans' positions. On 7 June, Montgomery renewed his efforts to take Caen. The light Stuart tanks of 9th Canadian Brigade heading the advance of the 3rd Canadian Division collided with the leading elements of *Hitler Jugend*, which were preparing for an attack of their own. The SS tank men and panzergrenadiers mauled the Canadian tanks, then launched a furious counter-offensive. The fighting did not go all their own way, as the Canadians could call on vast amounts of fire support. The battle

ABOVE: A column of British Cromwell tanks moves up to its start line in Normandy on 25 July 1944. The Cromwell was far less used than the almost ubiquitous Sherman by British and Canadian tank units. Nonetheless, it was at least a vast improvement on most previous British designs and went some way towards restoring the qualitative balance with the Germans.

raged to and fro throughout 7 June and the following day. Although the *Hitler Jugend* had knocked the Canadian advance off balance, the SS had failed to push them back into the sea.

Normandy was rapidly becoming a battle of attrition in the dense hedgerows of the area. This terrain ideally suited the defender and engagements often took place at extremely close range. Both sides suffered constant losses in both men and materiel as the Allies built up their forces and the Germans rushed reinforcements to the front. Meanwhile, the British sought to break out from the bridgehead and the key to this remained the capture of Caen. Following the failure of the Canadians' frontal push, Montgomery

decided that he would try to envelop the city. On 12 June, after discovering a hole in the German defences, the veteran 7th Armoured Division moved through the gap to the southwest of Caen. The division initially made excellent progress, as the commander of the lead formation the 8th Hussars, Colonel Goulburn recorded: 'We are beginning to think we have obtained a complete breakthrough.' However, stiffening German resistance meant that the lead units probed eastwards in an attempt to maintain the pace of the advance. On the morning of the 13th, the advance was renewed and the 4th County of London Yeomanry (4th CLY) reached the town of Villers Bocage. Here the British advance was blunted single-

RIGHT: American troops in a M4A3 with 105mm (4.1in) gun followed by a Jeep liberate a French town. The somewhat too-high-for-comfort silhouette is evident, but the Sherman's reliability and excellent performance came to the fore once the Allies broke out of Normandy.

handedly by Captain Michael Wittmann of the 501st SS Heavy Tank Battalion. The British had halted outside the village when Wittmann swung around behind them. The first shot from his Tiger's 88mm (3.45in) gun destroyed the rearmost of 4th CLY's Cromwells, and the second dealt with the Sherman Firefly in front of it. He then proceeded to machine-gun the Rifle Brigade Company accompanying the tanks. Having dispatched the infantry, he went on to destroy the rest of 4th CLY's Cromwells further up in the village. Turning off the road, Wittmann attacked the rear of the British column, destroying the rearmost half-track, and then proceeded to move methodically along the column, shooting up all 25 vehicles. Although his Tiger was later disabled, Wittman was able to escape and muster enough armour from the nearby *Panzer Lehr* Division to counterattack and recapture the village. In the aftermath of this disaster, the whole 7th Armoured Division advance began to break down under pressure from *Panzer Lehr* and the recently arrived 2nd Panzer Division. The British had been fought to a standstill.

EXCELLENT TRAINING

The Germans adapted better to fighting in Normandy than their Allied opponents. Part of this was due to the excellence of German military doctrine and the superb integration of their tanks and supporting infantry, the panzer-grenadiers. The British were inclined to allow their infantry and tanks to become separated or operate almost independently of one another, and thus the tanks suffered when they came across a German anti-tank screen and had no infantry accompanying them available to clear out the defenders. There was also the problem of the qualitative difference between Allied and German tanks. The Sherman was roughly equal to the PzKpfw IV and far more reliable and manoeuvrable than any of its German opponents. However, it was utterly outclassed by the Panthers and Tigers deployed by many of the German panzer divisions. The Sherman's 75mm (2.95in) gun could not penetrate either the Panther or the Tiger's frontal armour, while a Panther could deal with a Sherman at 2743m (3000yds) and a Tiger

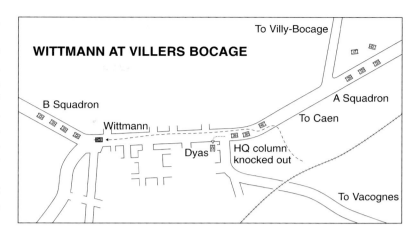

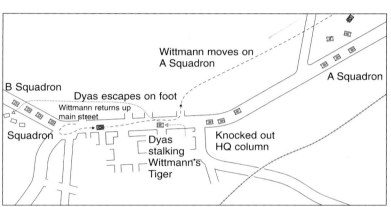

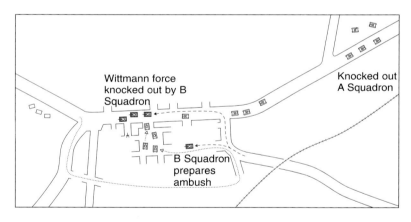

could at 1645m (1800yds). Even the up-gunned 76mm (3in) Sherman could only penetrate the front turret of a Panther at 549m (600yds), while, of course, the Panther could do the same at five times the distance and the Tiger at three. The British Cromwells and Churchills were not any better. Only when the Sherman was equipped with the British 17-pounder did it stand a chance. A British Churchill tank commander, Lieutenant Andrew Wilson, vividly described the imbalance faced by Allied tank men in recounting a pre-D-Day conversation:

'What do the Germans have most of?'

ABOVE: Wittmann's finest hour. His tank knocked out two British squadrons single-handedly at Villers Bocage, and caused serious delay to the British advance in the area. His greed for further success was his downfall, however, as he was knocked out in an ambush after returning to the fray.

'Panthers. The Panther can slice through a Churchill from a mile away.'

'And how does a Churchill get a Panther?'

'It creeps up on it. When it reaches close quarters, the gunner tries to bounce a shot off the underside of the Panther's gun mantlet. If he's lucky, it goes through a piece of thin armour above the driver's head.'

'Has anyone ever done it?'

'Yes, Davis in C Squadron. He's back with headquarters now trying to recover his nerve.'

'What's next on the list?'

'Tigers. The Tiger can get you from a mile and half.'

'And how does a Churchill get a Tiger?'

'It's supposed to get within 200 yards and put a shot through the periscope.'

'Has anyone one ever done it?'

'No.'

Add to this the excellent German man-portable anti-tank weapon, the *panzerfaust* which, while fairly short-ranged, would destroy almost any Allied tank, and it is not surprising that the Allied armoured forces struggled in Normandy, despite their vastly superior numbers.

EPSOM

The defeat at Villers Bocage meant that there would be no rapid British breakout. Meanwhile, another powerful German division had reached the front. The 2nd SS Panzer Division *Das Reich* had been based in southern France. Constant attacks by the French Resistance meant it did not arrive until the end of June. This additional armour, coupled with the imminent arrival of the 2nd SS Panzer Corps, allowed Rommel to begin planning a counterstroke to drive the Allies out of France. However, ULTRA intelligence warned Montgomery and he launched his own offensive, Operation Epsom, to draw the SS armour into battle, rather than allowing Rommel to use it as he hoped. Epsom was undertaken by General Richard O'Connor's 8th Corps including 11th Armoured Division, which attacked the German lines west of Caen. O'Connor's men made reasonable progress and reached the Odon, forcing Rommel to commit the SS Panzer Corps against the British. Both 9th and 10th SS Panzer Divisions were hurled against 11th Armoured and bloodily fought off, aided

by concentrated Allied naval and artillery fire. Then 11th Armoured was pulled back across the river, but Rommel's intended offensive was never properly started. When Epsom did not succeed, Montgomery turned to strategic air power. On the evening of 7 July, Allied bombers demolished Caen, which finally allowed British and Canadian troops to enter the city a month later than planned.

The Germans had moved to a new defensive line south of Caen, which was considerably deeper than any yet encountered in France. On 18 July, Montgomery launched Operation Goodwood, designed to outflank Caen and drive on the town of Falaise. It was again spearheaded by O'Connor's 8th Corps using all three British armoured divisions: 7th, 11th and Guards. Once again, the attack was preceded by massive artillery and air bombardment. However, the Germans were prepared, as German intelligence had for once accurately predicted the British intention. General Eberbach of Panzer Group West deployed five lines of tanks and anti-tank guns across the path of 8th Corp's intended advance. The British, spearheaded by 11th Armoured, initially made good progress, but, as had happened at Villers Bocage and during Epsom, German resistance soon began to take a terrible toll. On that day, 11th Armoured lost 126 tanks and Guards Armoured lost 60. The Canadians on their flank suffered equally badly. The Panthers of 1st SS Panzer Division *Leibstandarte* and the battered yet resilient 12th SS Panzer Division *Hitler Jugend* caused terrible losses. When Goodwood finally petered out, the British had lost 400 tanks, in all 36 per cent of their armoured strength in France. Such was Allied superiority in materiel that each armoured division was fully replenished within 36 hours. The Germans were not in the same position. In the more open country in which Goodwood was fought, the British had paid a price for their lack of a tank that measured up to the Panther and Tiger, as well as for their poor coordination between infantry and armour.

COBRA

As Goodwood sucked in the bulk of the German armour in Normandy, the Americans to the west began to prepare an offensive to capitalise on the weakened

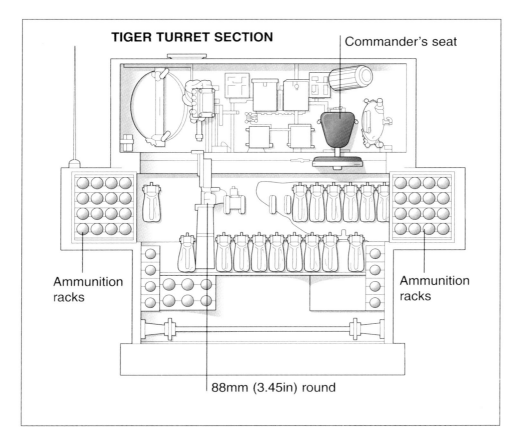

TIGER TURRET SECTION

Commander's seat

Ammunition racks

Ammunition racks

88mm (3.45in) round

LEFT: A cutaway view of the Tiger I showing the storage of ammunition in the hull spaces. Ammunition stowage areas were generally well armoured, as a hit that managed to penetrate the armour would tend to be fatal. The large size of the Tiger's gun meant that it carried a smaller ammunition load than most of its contemporaries.

German line in front of them. This would be the crowning Allied achievement of the campaign. General Omar Bradley's Army had pushed a mere 11km (6.8 miles) forward in two weeks of heavy fighting, but with Operation Cobra the speed of advance was due to change. As ever, it was preceded by a massive bombardment; the main weight of this fell on General Fritz Bayerlein's superb *Panzer Lehr* Division. *Panzer Lehr* was formed from demonstration units and, when it arrived in Normandy, it was lavishly equipped with tanks. By July, however, after 49 days of continuous fighting, it was down to 2200 men and 45 serviceable tanks. It held a 4.8km (3-mile) front south of the town of St Lô directly in Cobra's axis of advance. On the morning of 25 July, waves of US P-47 Thunderbolt fighter-bombers attacked the division with high explosives and napalm. They were followed by 400 medium bombers carrying 227kg (500lb) bombs. Then came 1500 B-17 Flying Fortress and B-24 Liberator heavy bombers, carrying a total of 3300 tonnes of bombs. They obliterated the positions beneath them; Panther tanks were picked up and hurled high into the air. Finally, 300 P-38

Lightning fighter-bombers attacked with fragmentation and napalm bombs. Nearly half *Panzer Lehr* died in the attack. Many hundreds more were killed by the 10,000 American guns that opened up the moment the air bombardment ceased. Bayerlein, a veteran from the desert, was ordered by Field Marshal von Kluge, who had replaced the wounded Rommel, to hold the position. He replied: 'Everyone

BELOW: General Leclerc of the Free French forces, and commander of the Second French Armoured Division. Here he watches tanks under his command rumble through the streets of Paris during the liberation of the capital on 25 August 1944.

is holding the front ... everyone. My grenadiers and pioneers, my anti-tank gunners, they're holding. None of them have left their positions, none. They're lying in their foxholes, still and mute, because they are dead. Dead, do you understand? Tell the field marshal that the *Panzer Lehr* is destroyed. Only the dead can still hold.' Extraordinarily, the division fought on until the American armour pushed it aside the following day.

If firepower was instrumental to Allied success in Normandy, another contribution came from an ingenious invention deployed in Cobra which restored the tanks' ability to manoeuvre in the bocage. The Rhino – a set of steel tusks welded onto the front of a Sherman – equipped hundreds of US 1st Army tanks, which enabled them to rip through the hedgerows. The US Army had pondered the problem of fighting in bocage since they had come ashore and Sergeant Curtis Culin of 102nd Cavalry Reconnaissance, 2nd Armoured Division, came up with the solution. Bradley's tanks could now move through the countryside while their opponents were forced to keep to the roads.

Thus, when the Americans finally shook themselves clear of *Panzer Lehr*, they were able to make remarkably rapid progress across open country. By 29 June, American tanks had advanced 48km (30 miles) to Avranches at the foot of the Normandy peninsula. Its capture opened up the entire German left flank in Normandy as four armoured divisions poured south of Coutances. Nonetheless, the Germans still put up remarkably stiff resistance. One particular battle near St Denis-le-Gast between the US 2nd Armoured Division and 2nd SS Panzer and 17th SS Panzergrenadier Divisions was described by one American officer as 'the most Godless sight I have ever witnessed on any battle field'. The dream of a return to mobile armoured warfare seemed to be becoming a reality. The Americans had just the man to exploit the situation: General George S. Patton.

Patton's 3rd Army became operational on 1 August and his armoured divisions drove into Brittany against almost no German resistance. The entire army was supposed to seize the major Brittany ports, but no more than a corps was needed, even though the actual ports

BELOW: Weary German troops of 6th SS Panzer Army file past a Panther in the Ardennes in December 1944. The sheer size of the mid to late German tanks is evident here. The 45-tonne Panther was originally intended to fill the role of medium tank, replacing the stalwart PzKpfw IIIs and IVs.

were heavily defended. Patton had quickly concluded that operations in Brittany should be kept to a minimum while the rest of his army turned eastwards to drive on the Seine. Bradley agreed on 3 August and Montgomery concurred, resisting the pressure of the logisticians to shift more resources to Brittany and speed the capture of its ports. As he told Brooke: 'The main business lies to the east.'

THE MORTAIN COUNTERATTACK

The collapse of the German position appeared imminent. A retreat to behind the Seine might have stabilised the situation, but Hitler's direct intervention ensured a German disaster. On 2 August, he ordered von Kluge to launch a strong armoured counteroffensive using 'all available panzer units, regardless of their present commitment' to recapture the neck of the Cotentin Peninsula and cut off all US forces in Brittany and south of Avranches. Von Kluge was full of doubt and cabled the German High Command, claiming that 'tanks are the backbone of our defence. Where these are withdrawn, our front will give way … If, as I foresee,

this plan does not succeed, catastrophe is inevitable.' Nonetheless, he managed to scrape together a panzer force consisting of the battered remains of 2nd Panzer, 1st SS Panzer and 2nd SS Panzer, along with the only fresh formation, 116th Panzer. The combined strength of these divisions was only 250 tanks. The attack launched on 7 August made some progress against the US 1st Army despite tough American resistance. Mortain was retaken and the four panzer divisions managed to penetrate about 17.7km (11 miles) into American lines. The following day, the Germans were subjected to the full force of Allied air power. The Americans also began to reinforce their positions. Although the Germans insisted upon counterattacking for a further four days, they made no more progress. This offensive only made the dire German situation worse, as it pushed much of their remaining armour westwards into a pocket that was rapidly closing around the Germans.

On 7 August, Montgomery launched the 1st Canadian Army southwards in a major offensive to capture Falaise. General Crerar, commanding the Canadians, mounted a carefully planned armoured

LEFT: A PzKpfw V Panther Ausf G on the offensive – albeit temporarily – in the Ardennes in December 1944. Allied command of the air forced the Germans to launch their counter-offensive during the worst possible weather in an effort to keep Allied aircraft on the ground and give their attack the best chance of success.

assault preceded by a heavy bombardment. The Canadians enjoyed considerable initial success, but the two exploitation divisions, Canadian 4th Armoured and Polish 1st Armoured, were inexperienced and could make little headway as resistance stiffened. The Germans had once again, by skilful use of their meagre armoured resources, blunted an Allied offensive. However, the rapid advance of elements of Patton's 3rd Army westwards, coupled with the Canadian offensive, gave Bradley the idea of trapping the bulk of the German forces in a pocket around Mortain. If the Canadians could capture Falaise, and Patton, whose lead divisions were at Le Mans, could drive north to Argentan, there would be only 23km (14.3 miles) separating the Canadian and American forces. If closed, an estimated 21 divisions of the German Army west of Falaise would be trapped. Montgomery immediately approved the plan.

THE FALAISE POCKET

Patton turned north and met virtually no opposition, reaching Argentan by the evening of 12 August. Patton pleaded with Bradley to let his forces advance all the way to Falaise, but was refused. The Canadians attacked again on 14 August, but did not capture Falaise for four days. In the meantime, the Germans pulled as much of their forces as possible eastwards in an attempt to escape the closing Allied pincers. The pocket was finally closed when Canadian and American troops met on 19 August. An attempt by what remained of 2nd SS Panzer Corps to smash a path into the pocket from outside was stoutly defeated. Figures vary as to the numbers of Germans trapped and the number that escaped. About 10,000 troops died there and an estimated 50,000 Germans were taken prisoner. Perhaps between 20,000 and 35,000 escaped. Precious little heavy equipment had been retrieved. The Allied advance maintained its momentum; however, to avoid being encircled again, the Germans managed to pull 240,000 men back over the Seine. Patton's troops reached the river on 19 August and his men were first across. By 25 August, all four Allied armies – Dempsey's 2nd British, Crerar's 1st Canadian, Hodges' 1st American and Patton's 3rd American – were across. The Normandy campaign was over.

The Allies drove eastwards at speed. On 25 August, Leclerc's French Armoured Division liberated Paris. Patton crossed the Meuse on 31 August and reached Metz on the Moselle the following day, pushing the German forces in front him of back in disarray. The Guards Armoured Division reached Brussels on 3 September after advancing 120km (75 miles) in one day. The 11th Armoured Division reached Antwerp on 4 September and found the port intact. The German position in the west seemed to have collapsed. The Germans could field maybe 100 tanks on the Western Front, as opposed to the Allies with at least 2000 in their armoured spearheads. Only logistical overstretch caused the Allied armies to pause as they raced to the very borders of the Reich. There were many senior Allied commanders who speculated that the war could be won in 1944.

Yet, as the Allied armies were slowed to a halt by the need to refuel and refit, the Germans' defences began to thicken. The British became entangled around Antwerp. The US 1st Army came up against the West Wall defences around Aachen and stopped. Even Patton to the south around Metz could make little progress, as he now faced the bulk of German forces in the west. Patton demanded additional resources so that 3rd Army could strike towards Frankfurt. However, Eisenhower was also faced with Montgomery's determination to break onto the north German plain by driving Dempsey's British 2nd Army rapidly through Holland and crossing the Rhine at Arnhem. Eisenhower could not provide the resources for the two plans, so he backed Montgomery.

Operation Market Garden, as Montgomery's plan was codenamed, was launched on 17 September 1944. It was the largest airborne operation ever mounted and the 16,500 paratroopers and 3500 glider-borne troops were given the task of securing the bridges in the path of 2nd Army's advance. The US 101st Airborne was dropped at Eindhoven, the US 82nd at Grave and Groesbeek, and the British 1st Airborne near Arnhem. However, after a promising start, the operation began to go terribly wrong. A number of mistakes had been made during Market Garden's preparation. Air reconnaissance had revealed the

presence of German armour in the area of Arnhem. The commander of Market Garden, Lieutenant General 'Boy' Browning, reckoned, however, 'I shouldn't trouble myself if I were you ... they are probably not serviceable at any rate.' He failed to inform 1st Airborne Division of the tanks' presence. In fact, those tanks happened to belong to the veteran 9th and 10th Panzer Divisions, which were refitting in the area, and they would play a decisive part in the battle. The RAF also refused to drop the paratroopers close to Arnhem as heavy flak concentrations were believed to be in the area, and thus the paratroopers were landed 9–12km (5.6–7.5 miles) west of the bridge. Only a single battalion of the Parachute Regiment made it to Arnhem bridge, where they met the battle-hardened SS panzergrenadiers. The other paratroopers tried to reach and relieve the battalion at the bridge, but found

themselves facing the Panther and Tiger tanks and self-propelled artillery of the SS panzer divisions with little more than rifles, Sten guns and grenades. Meanwhile, Guards Armoured Division leading Horrocks's 30th Corps was making terribly slow time in its effort to relieve the paratroopers. Although the American airborne divisions had seized and held their objectives, the tardy advance of the British armour was even further hampered by fierce German counterattacks. By the time Horrocks's 30th Corps reached Arnhem, the brave paratroopers had been driven from the bridge and the Germans had managed to bring artillery and armour across it. Out of the 10,005 men of the 1st Airborne Division, only 2163 managed to escape to British lines. If anything, Arnhem proved that lightly armed troops stood no chance against tanks. The slow advance of the British armoured forces and their failure

ABOVE: An American M10 Tank Destroyer. The US Army somewhat unnecessarily separated its tank destroyer battalions from the rest of its armoured forces, and the tank destroyers were very often committed to unsuitable tasks such acting in an assault gun role.

ABOVE: Free French Shermans advance in the Saar region at the end of 1944. All Free French units were equipped with Shermans, which were readily available, although at the end of the war at least one regular French Army unit used captured German Panthers.

to reach the paratroopers at Arnhem meant that the Rhine was not crossed and the war would continue into 1945.

What the fighting in France demonstrated again and again was the quality of the German Army and their very skilful use of their limited tank resources in the defensive. Heavily outnumbered, particularly with regard to materiel, and subjected to the largely unrestrained weight of Allied air power, the Germans consistently fought the Allied armies to a standstill. The doctrinal combination of tanks and infantry was a potent and reliable combination. In contrast, the failure of the Allies, and particularly the British, to coordinate their tanks and troops properly proved a serious constraint to success. Yet it was the Allies who prevailed, and at a reasonably low cost in men. The overwhelming and steady application of firepower eventually won out, despite the manifold skills of the German Army. It also should be noted that, once the Allies broke out of the Normandy bridgehead, the Sherman showed its merits. Only a tank as reliable as the Sherman could have maintained the remarkable pace and length of the Allied advance during late 1944.

As the front stabilised along the German border and there were some local successes in the Ardennes, Hitler, encouraged by the news, declared to the OKW on 16 September 1944: 'I have just made a momentous decision, I shall go over to the counterattack. That is to say, here, out of the Ardennes, with the objective Antwerp.' Hitler had decided his only hope lay in a gamble to knock one of his opponents out the war, and the best chance lay in an offensive in the west. His generals were horrified, considering his plan of a single thrust on Antwerp, cutting off the bulk of Montgomery's 21st Army Group, far beyond the scope of the German Army in late 1944. Model, commanding Army Group B, was damning, claiming that 'this plan doesn't have damned leg to stand on!... If it succeeds it will be a miracle.'

NEW PANZER ARMY

Hitler was able to strip a number of divisions from the Eastern Front – one of the few advantages of Soviet success shortening the front. He created the 6th SS Panzer Army made up of four SS panzer and five infantry divisions. This formation would spearhead the main thrust from the northern Ardennes. Simultaneously, another new panzer army, General Hasso von Manteuffel's 5th, of three panzer and four infantry divisions, would attack towards Bastogne. To the south the weakest force, Erich Brandenberger's 7th Army, of four infantry divisions, would protect the flank. Model was commander of the whole operation. The key to the offensive were the seven panzer divisions: Sepp Dietrich's 1st SS *Leibstandarte*, 12th SS *Hitler Jugend*, 2nd SS *Das Reich* and 9th SS *Hohenstaufen,* and Manteuffel's 116th, 2nd and *Panzer Lehr*. All were under strength. In theory, they should have fielded a total of 490 Panthers, but no more than 340 were available. The *Luftwaffe* could muster 1000 aircraft, but the German commanders preferred to rely on bad weather to keep the Allied air forces out of the skies.

Facing this German assault was the weakest sector in the Allied line. Lieutenant General Hodges' 1st US Army was responsible for the Ardennes, but most of his strength was committed to the Aachen area. Considering the Ardennes unsuitable for offensive operations (despite the events of 1940), he had only five recuperating or green divisions covering over 130km (81 miles) of front, 99th and 106th from his 5th Corps and 28th and 4th from his 8th Corps, with 9th Armoured in reserve. ULTRA revealed the German build-up, but was wrongly interpreted, and the Germans imposed strict radio silence. Furthermore Allied air reconnaissance flights were kept on the ground by bad weather. Both Bradley and Montgomery reckoned a German offensive extremely unlikely.

Surprise was therefore complete when, aided by searchlights reflected from the low clouds, the Germans attacked at 0530 hours on 16 December 1944. They were aided, although not significantly, by Otto Skorzeny's 150th SS Brigade, dressed in American uniforms and equipped with captured American vehicles and Panthers disguised as M-10 Tank Destroyers. Dietrich's advance was spearheaded by *Kampfgruppe* Peiper, a reinforced armoured regiment from *Leibstandarte* commanded by Jochen Peiper. This force was to advance as rapidly as possible towards Antwerp. Behind Peiper came an SS battalion of 30

King Tigers. These massive tanks were unsuitable for a quick advance. From 17–19 December, Peiper managed to press forwards some 40 km (25 miles). The mounting American resistance in Peiper's path exposed the rawness of the SS troops. They tended to engage the opposition rather than bypass it, which had been a central precept of *Blitzkrieg*. Meanwhile, traffic blocked up behind, clogging the roads and slowing Dietrich. As Peiper's advance halted, Dietrich sought to develop new axes of advance and thus maintain the momentum of the advance in the north. Although *Hitler Jugend* managed to capture Dom Bütgeneach, its advance also soon stalled, despite the use of a number of potent *Jagdpanzer* IV/70s and *Jagdpanther* tank destroyers.

To the south, Manteuffel met with more success. He punched through 28th and 106th US Divisions, and his panzers raced for the two important centres of the local road network, St Vith and Bastogne. At St Vith, the Americans put up a stout defence, aided by the 7th US Armoured Division. However, by 22

ABOVE: 'Old Blood and Guts', General George S. Patton, commander of the US 3rd Army and most successful US armoured commander in World War II. His drive and élan were crucial in the rapid Allied drive to the borders of Germany and the crossing of the Rhine. He died in an air crash shortly after the war's end in 1945.

ABOVE: A massive 76-tonne *Jagdtiger* is examined by American troops. Although packing an enormous 128mm (5in) gun, the *Jadgtiger*, the heaviest armoured fighting vehicle to see regular service in World War II, was underpowered and unreliable, making it little more than a (barely) moveable pillbox.

December, the defenders pulled back behind the river Salm. At Bastogne, 101st Airborne Division and elements of 10th Armoured were rushed into the area and dug in around the town. Manteuffel's 2nd Panzer Division skirted the town and pushed on, while *Panzer Lehr* encircled the Americans on 21 December. By 23 December, 2nd Panzer was within sight of the Meuse bridges. This was the high point of the German advance; the division ran out of petrol and the thrust ground to a halt.

The remarkably stiff American opposition was partially due to the skilful shifting of American military strength by the Allied commanders. Bradley had initially thought that the offensive was merely a spoiling attack, but Eisenhower was more troubled and he ordered the transfer of the 7th and 10th Armoured Divisions to 1st US Army. When the Allied commanders met on 19 December, Eisenhower told his subordinates, 'the present situation is to be regarded as one of opportunity for us and not of disaster. There will only be cheerful faces at this table.' Patton made a typically extravagant statement: 'Hell, let's have the guts to let the sons of bitches go all the way to Paris. Then we'll really cut them off and chew 'em up!' Of course, Patton's suggestion was ignored, but the shoulders of the salient were reinforced, forcing the Germans into an ever-shrinking frontage. Patton, whose army was to the south, was told to counterattack in the Bastogne area. As he said, 'this time the Kraut has stuck his head in a meat grinder and this

time I've got hold of the handle.' On 22 December, Patton counterattacked with one armoured and two infantry divisions. Brandenberger's 7th Army put up tough resistance, but Patton made steady progress. The following day the weather cleared, allowing the Allies to resupply the Bastogne pocket and reassert air superiority. The Americans reached Bastogne on 26 December.

By now, the German commanders were convinced that to continue was pointless, yet Hitler persevered. On New Year's Day, at his insistence, Manteuffel's army, now reinforced by 1st SS Panzer Corps, attacked again at Bastogne in a desperate effort to snatch victory from the jaws of defeat. Five German divisions attacked the corridor Patton had driven to Bastogne road and briefly cut the Bastogne-Arlon before it was recaptured by American tanks. The raw 11th US Armoured Division took heavy casualties, but managed to repulse the assault. The fighting rumbled on for some days and Eisenhower persuaded Montgomery, who had taken charge of 1st US Army, to attack from the north to link up with Patton. Meanwhile, there was one final failed German attack on Bastogne by *Hitler Jugend* and 15th Panzergrenadier Division on 4 January. Until 11 January, the Allies slowly pushed forward, but then the massive Soviet winter offensive forced Hitler to strip the Ardennes for the Eastern Front. The Allied advance picked up pace in the face of lessened resistance, and 1st and 3rd US Armies linked up on 16 January. Patton failed to surround large numbers of German forces in a pocket, but the Americans had certainly made the Germans pay.

The last attempt at *Blitzkrieg* had failed. The vital air superiority was missing. The Americans proved tougher and better led than Germany's opponents earlier in the war. The Allies had reacted with remarkable swiftness and the US Army's extraordinary mobility and flexibility had been the key to success. In four days, the number of infantry divisions had doubled and the armour tripled in the Ardennes. The men responsible for executing the plan, Model and von Rundstedt, had predicted the operation would fail and they were right. The Germans lost about 100,000 men and almost all the tanks and aircraft committed, about 25 per cent of total stocks. The Ardennes offensive destroyed vital reserves of manpower, tanks, aircraft and fuel. The Allies had taken similar casualties, but these could quickly and easily be replaced, although the final offensive on Germany had to be delayed.

THE CROSSING OF THE RHINE

The Western Allies had built up overwhelming strength for their assault on the Rhine. The main thrust would come from Montgomery, who was assigned the 9th US Army in addition to the 1st Canadian and 2nd British Armies. Most American generals resented this somewhat, and put vigorous efforts into their own sectors. On 7 March, tanks of Patton's 3rd US Army broke out of the Ardennes and reached the Rhine near Coblenz in three days. However, the bridges across the Rhine were blown. To the north, the US 1st Army was luckier, capturing the bridge at Remagen, near Bonn. Reserves were rushed up and a vital bridgehead secured. Bradley, the army group commander, reckoned this would 'burst [the enemy] right open' if the bridgehead were exploited. However, it did not fit in with Montgomery's plan and Eisenhower told Bradley not to push

substantial forces into the bridgehead. Bradley turned Patton loose to the south and, by 21 March, he had cleared a large stretch of the west bank of the river and was able to cross the river almost unopposed at Oppenheim. Hitler, shocked by the news, called for an immediate counterattack, but was told that only five tanks from a nearby tank depot were available. Thus, the American advance proceeded almost unhindered.

By now, Montgomery was ready to cross the river near Wesel with 25 divisions. He was faced by only five weak German divisions. On 23 March, the attack was preceded by a 3000-gun bombardment and heavy air attack. The infantry, supported by DD swimming tanks, established bridgeheads with little resistance. The US 9th Army lost only about 40 men. Montgomery did not sanction a general advance until he had built up his forces. The main hindrance to his armour's advance was the rubble created by Allied bombers, which slowed their forward progress far more effectively than the Germans ever could. Indeed, most German troops were far keener to surrender to the Western Allies than fight them. This contrasted somewhat with what was going on in the east.

BELOW: The Churchill Crocodile belches flame. The Crocodile, one of Hobart's 'Funnies' – a flamethrower-equipped Churchill Mark VII – proved terribly effective against entrenched and fortified positions, and was understandably much feared by the Germans. This Crocodile of the 79th Armoured Division is being used at the end of the war to clear up the concentration camp at Belsen.

CHAPTER EIGHT

STALIN'S REVENGE

After the mass armoured battle at Kursk, the Red Army's tanks took less than two years to reach the capital of the Third Reich.

The stunning German success at Kharkov in March 1943 was a rare return to the rapid armoured advances that had characterised the heady days of *Blitzkrieg*. Paul Hausser's three elite SS panzergrenadier divisions – *Leibstandarte*, *Das Reich* and *Totenkopf* – in conjunction with Hermann Hoth's 4th Panzer Army, shattered Soviet General Vatutin's South-West Front and led to the recapture of Kharkov. The spring thaw brought the German advance to an end, yet the brilliant counterstroke had stabilised the front, leaving a huge Russian salient in the line, 161km (100 miles) wide and 113km (70 miles) deep, centred on the city of Kursk. Here would be fought the largest tank battle in history, one which changed the course of the war. After Kursk, the Soviets permanently held the initiative.

LEFT: A T-34 burns in the Soviet Union in 1943 after being knocked out by a column of Tigers. By the middle of 1943, the Germans had largely redressed the qualitative imbalance that had been caused by the appearance of the T-34 in 1941, although large numbers of PzKpfw IVs and even IIIs remained in service. The new generation of German tanks – most importantly, the Tiger and the Panther – was beginning to become available in reasonable numbers in time for the renewal of the German offensive in the summer of 1943.

119

ABOVE: PzKpfw IVs at Kursk equipped with their distinctive *schurzen* (skirt) side armour. This extra 5mm armour provided some protection against Soviet anti-tank rifles and the hollow-charged anti-tank round introduced in 1943. The tanks are accompanied by SdKfz 251 half-track armoured personnel carriers, carrying the division's panzergrenadiers into battle.

After two years of bitter struggle, the *Wehrmacht* was in no position to launch a full-scale offensive in the East. Yet the strategic question remained as to what policy the Germans should undertake in 1943. Heinz Guderian had been recalled to service as the Inspector General of Armoured Troops in February and was painstakingly rebuilding the *Wehrmacht*'s battered panzer arm. Powerful new tanks, particularly the Tiger and the untried Panther, were beginning to enter service. Guderian was determined that his careful work should not be frittered away, and he argued in March 1943 that Germany should forego launching a strategic offensive that year. Instead, he took a long-term view, believing that Germany needed a strong and effective armoured reserve, which might be able to resume the offensive in 1944. Manstein similarly rejected the idea of an attack. He felt that Germany should employ an 'elastic' defence using superior German staff work and mobile tactics to deliver devastating counter blows whenever the Soviets overstretched themselves.

Hitler, however, had other ideas. He needed a victory in 1943 to reassure his wavering allies. His chief of staff, Colonel General Kurt Zeitzler, provided him with such a possibility. However, Zeitzler's plan, Operation Citadel (or *Zitadelle*) – the destruction of the Kursk salient – had

one major flaw: the plan itself was obvious to anyone with even a basic conception of strategy. Manstein and Guderian firmly set themselves against Citadel, as did Colonel General Walter Model, whose 9th Army would have do much of the fighting. Nonetheless the plan gained enough support to be approved, despite the fact that Hitler admitted to Guderian: 'Whenever I think of this attack my stomach turns over.'

To the north of the salient, Model's 9th Army was to break through on a line between Kursk-Orel highway and railway and then drive southwards to Kursk. To achieve this, Model had 15 infantry divisions and seven panzer and panzergrenadier divisions. To the south, the bulk of Army Group South's best units had been assembled in Hermann Hoth's 4th Panzer Army and Army Detachment *Kempf*, a total of nine panzer and panzergrenadier divisions and eight infantry divisions.

Hoth's command was the most powerful armed force ever assembled for an offensive under a single commander in German military history. It consisted of the elite *Grossdeutschland* Division, 2nd SS Panzer Corps containing SS panzergrenadier divisions *Leibstandarte*, *Das Reich* and *Totenkopf*, five panzer divisions, 10th Panzer (Panther) Brigade and two infantry divisions. Hoth's Army was concentrated on a 48km (30-mile) front between Belograd and Gertsovka. Army Detachment *Kempf* would provide vigorous flank protection. In total, the Germans massed 900,000 troops and 2700 armoured vehicles for Kursk.

The possibility of a German attack on the Kursk salient was equally obvious to Soviet High Command. Furthermore, the penetration of German High Command by the 'Lucy' spy ring ensured that Stalin also knew the prospective date for the offensive and much of the detail. The Soviets thus set about turning the bulge into an impregnable fortress. Mobilising vast numbers of civilian workers – 105,000 in April, rising to 300,000 in June – 4827km (3000 miles) of defensive trenches were dug, connecting a vast network of bunkers, anti-tank positions and strongpoints, positioned to provide mutual support. The German armour would be channelled into the Soviet fields of fire by carefully placed minefields. Some 400,000 mines were laid in the Kursk salient in places to a density of 2500 anti-personnel and 2200 anti-tank mines per mile of the front. The Russians crammed seven armies into the bulge,

supported by 20,000 guns, a third of which were anti-tank weapons. Reserve forces of a tank army and two infantry armies were concentrated 150km (94 miles) behind. These reserves built additional defensive belts. When all the preparations were complete, 1,336,000 men, 2900 aircraft and 3444 tanks sat in or behind eight defensive belts stretching back 177km (110 miles). As much as 75 per cent of the entire Soviet tank force was assembled at Kursk. Stalin and Supreme Commander Marshal Zhukov's strategy for Kursk was simple: wear down the Germans' resources and then counterattack.

THE BATTLE OF KURSK

The German offensive was delayed until 5 July because of Hitler's determination to have more Tigers and Panthers available. Guderian had argued that the Panther was not yet ready for battle. Despite the delay, Hitler was adamant that the offensive should go ahead. The Soviet defenders did not know exactly when it would be launched. On the evening of 4 July, General Konstantin Rokossovsky, commander of the Central Front facing Model's 9th Army, gained what he

BELOW: A StuG III Ausf G assault gun complete with *schurzen* moves past entrenched infantry at Kursk. Early StuG IIIs had been designed as infantry support guns, but latter models such as the Ausf G were armed with an L/48 75mm (2.95in) gun, which was capable of taking on tanks. Although not an ideal tank-killer, the turretless StuG III was at least relatively simple to produce and thus increasingly equipped panzer formations as the war progressed and demands on the German economy increased.

needed. A Soviet patrol captured a prisoner who revealed that the Germans would attack at 0330 hours the following morning. Rokossovsky thus ordered his artillery to open fire on the German positions at 0220 hours, severely disrupting and delaying their attack. It was only by 0500 hours that Model's forces on the north of the salient began to advance. He initially relied very heavily on his infantry divisions, committing only the 20th Panzer Division in the first wave. To the south, the movement forward of the 4th Panzer Army made the Soviet commander Vatutin order an artillery barrage at 0230 hours. An hour later the Germans replied with a tremendous barrage which, according to official reports, fired more shells than the entire Polish and French campaign put together. Then at 0400 hours the 4th Army went on to the

offensive. Two panzer corps with 700 tanks rolled into the Soviet 6th Guards Army in front of them.

The basic German tank tactic used at Kursk was a series of advances based around the armoured formation known as the *Panzerkeile* (panzer wedge). Heavy Tiger tanks spearheaded the tip of the wedge, and the Panthers (where available), PzKpfw IVs, PzKpfw IIIs and assault guns echeloned off the flanks. Behind the tanks came the infantry and heavy forces with mortars and artillery. As Alan Clark notes in his history of the war on the Eastern Front, *Barbarossa*:

'This tactic amounted to a rejection of the traditional principle of the Panzer army, as a sword, to be used in a deep, narrow thrust to the enemy's rear, and substituted an axe which was to break down the opposing front along a

BELOW: Massed German armour moves past German infantry prior to the opening of the battle of Kursk in July 1943. Kursk was the largest tank battle of World War II and the last major German offensive in the East. After the *Wehrmacht*'s panzer armies had been blunted at Kursk, the initiative lay henceforth with the Soviets.

considerable length. It had been forced on the Germans by the tenacity of the Red Army in holding close to the sides of the breach, and the multiplication of their fire power in the last year, which made independent action by the Panzers too dangerous – at least in the early stages of the battle.'

Basil Liddell Hart wrote that, after El Alamein, tanks were no longer used in deep and rapid thrusts; rather tank warfare was characterised by the constant sparring of tanks and infantry with lines of anti-tank defences. This was certainly the case at Kursk on a vast scale. Model to the north and Manstein to the south were essentially using the same tactics that Montgomery used in North Africa: infantry supported by armour to penetrate the enemy's defensive line, hoping that enough armour would be left to exploit the breakthrough. This may have worked at Alamein with considerable material superiority for the Allies, but at Kursk the strengths were roughly even and Soviet defence was organised in such a way that much of their armour could be held back until later in the battle.

The Germans immediately met with remarkably stiff resistance. A Tiger crewman recalled:

'As we advanced the Russian artillery ploughed the earth around us. Ivan, with his usual cunning, had held his fire in the weeks before, and even that morning when our own guns were pounding him. But now the whole front was a girdle of flashes. It seemed as if we were driving into a ring of flame. Four times our valiant "Rosinante" shuddered under a direct hit, and we thanked the fates for the strength of our good Krupp steel.'

Yet that steel did not always keep out the Soviet artillery, nor were the mine-fields completely cleared. When this was combined with the density of the Red Army's anti-tank guns – concentrated in a group of up to 10 guns under a single commander, who targeted one tank at a time – German armoured losses soon mounted. These were worsened by Manstein's instruction that, in order to maintain the momentum of the advance, 'in no circumstances' were the tanks to stop and help those which had been disabled. The crews in these tanks were to maintain fire from static positions. This had fatal consequences for those unfortunate men,

given the density of Soviet anti-tank guns and the large numbers of determined tank-killing squads.

The official history of the elite *Grossdeutschland* (*GD*) Panzergrenadier Division vividly described the struggle to break through well-prepared Soviet defences:

'The Panzer Regiment *GD* and the Panther brigade were supposed to attack … however they had the misfortune to drive into a minefield that had escaped notice until then – and this even before reaching the Bolshevik trenches! It was enough to make one sick. Soldiers and officers alike feared that the entire affair was going to pot. The tanks were stuck fast, bogged down on the tops of their tracks, and to make matters worse the enemy was firing at them with anti-tank rifles, anti-tank guns and artillery. The fusiliers advance

BELOW: Ammunition resupply of a T-34 Model 1943 (nicknamed 'Mickey Mouse' by the Germans due to the distinctive shape formed by the commander's and loader's hatches when opened together). The whole four-man crew is shown here as the main armament's 76.2mm (3in) round is passed through the driver's hatch and into the ammunition bins in the floor of the hull.

without tanks – what can they do? The tanks do not follow. Scarcely does the enemy notice the precarious situation of the fusiliers when he launches a counter-attack supported by numerous close support aircraft. The infantry companies of III Panzer-Fusilier Regiment *GD* … walked straight into ruin. Even the heavy company suffered 50 killed and wounded

RIGHT: The attack on Ponyri during the Kursk offensive. The Soviets were well aware that the offensive was coming and took the opportunity to prepare in-depth defences. Minefields were sown, barbed wire laid down, tanks dug in to defensive strongpoints and artillery zeroed in on likely chokepoints. When the Germans eventually attacked, it was to the credit of the men on the ground that they managed to advance at all.

BELOW: A Panther and supporting infantry preparing to advance on the Eastern Front. The all-arms battle and tank-infantry cooperation were vital elements in the successful prosecution of tank warfare in World War II.

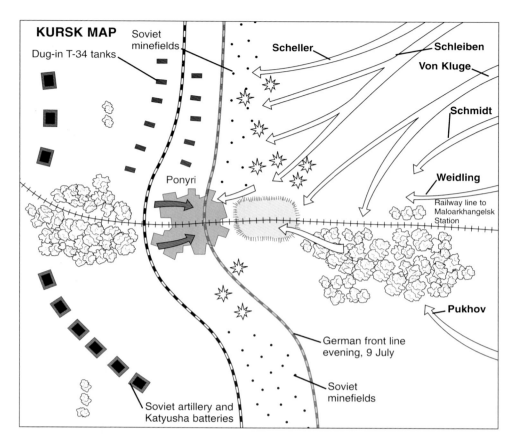

KURSK MAP
Dug-in T-34 tanks
Soviet minefields
Scheller
Schleiben
Von Kluge
Schmidt
Weidling
Ponyri
Railway line to Maloarkhangelsk Station
German front line evening, 9 July
Soviet minefields
Pukhov
Soviet artillery and Katyusha batteries

in a few hours. The pioneers were moved up immediately and they began to clear a path through the mine-infested terrain. Ten more hours had to pass before the first tanks and self-propelled guns got through and reached the infantry.'

As ever, once the infantry were separated from the tanks, problems occurred. When the opposite happened and the tanks – which had been told to push on regardless – forged ahead, the infantry were met by Soviet machine-gun nests and mortar positions that had strict orders to ignore the tanks.

LACK OF GERMAN SUCCESS

As the depth and the strength of the Russian defences became increasingly apparent, the Germans failed to make the inroads that had been expected. On the northern edge of the salient, infantry divisions with armoured support such as independent Tiger and Ferdinand sections plus 20th Panzer Division made the best progress, but, even so, their advances were at some considerable cost. To the south, 2nd SS Panzer Corps also showed great determination, as it slogged through the belts of German defences. The 41 Tigers available to it and the renowned élan of the SS units meant that it managed to penetrate some 20km (12 miles) into the Soviet lines.

Fierce Soviet counterattacks forced the 9th Army to commit more and more armour, including the 9th and 18th Panzer Divisions, and fighting intensified around the town of Ponyri, which eventually involved some 1000 German tanks in action along a 9.6km (6-mile) front. In response to the superiority of the Tiger's 88mm (3.45in) gun, Rokossovsky had all his tanks dug in where possible. The fighting around this village went on for six days and earned it the title of the 'Stalingrad of Kursk'. By 9 July, Model told Kluge that a break-through to Kursk was extremely unlikely, although he continued to attack until the operation was halted four days later. Tank after tank attack by the Germans was broken up by the dug-in T-34s, anti-tank guns and Soviet tank-hunting infantry. Eventually, all of the 9th Army's Panzer Divisions were committed, yet the crucial breakthrough was never achieved.

To the south, the Soviet commander Vatutin realised that the Germans had done better than expected, particularly 2nd SS Panzer Corps. Stalin diverted key forces to Vatutin's front, including the 1st Tank Army with its 640 tanks. Vatutin initially wanted to counterattack, but was persuaded to dig in the tanks as had been done to the north of the salient. Yet the SS still continued to advance remorse-lessly. Forty-eighth Panzer Corps had made reasonable, if costly, progress, too. Hoth's forces had managed to advance another 15km (9.1 miles) by 11 July. The following day, the 2nd SS Panzer Corps broke through the final Soviet trench line near the village of Prokhorovka. Vatutin was aware that, with nearly 900 German tanks (600 of Hoth's Panzer Army and Kempf's 300) bearing down on his positions from the south and west, he was in considerable danger. The Germans might well be able to roll up the entire Soviet position in the south of the Kursk salient. Therefore, he launched the bulk of Paval Rotmistov's 5th Guards Tank Army in a counterattack against the SS panzer-grenadier divisions.

That morning, 600 tanks of Hausser's corps and just fewer than 900 tanks of Rotmistrov's army clashed around Prok-horovka. This was mitigated somewhat by the technical superiority of the German Tigers and Panthers. Indeed, not all the Soviet tanks of the 5th Guards Army were T-34s. As well as 501 T-34s, there were 264 light T-70s and 35 British-built Churchills. There was also a number of SU-76 regiments, but none of the potent SU-152s, which had caused the Germans considerable problems. The SS divisions advanced in their familiar *Panzerkeile* wedge formations – the Tigers flanked by the PzKpfw IIIs and IVs – into a massive Soviet barrage. Meanwhile, the first of wave after wave of T-34s drove headlong obliquely at the German line. Conscious of the superiority of the Tigers and the Panthers over the T-34s at long range, Rotmistrov had ordered his tank crews to close with the enemy as quickly as possible, in direct contradiction to normal tactical procedure. As the Soviet official history described, the proximity of the ensuing mêlée helped the Russians:

'It destroyed the enemy's ability to control his leading units and subunits. The close combat deprived the Tigers of the advantages, which their powerful gun and thick armour conferred, and they were successfully shot up at close range by the T-34s. Immense numbers of tanks were mixed up all over the battlefield; there was neither time nor space to disengage and reform ranks. Fired at short range, shells penetrated front and side armour. There were frequent explosions as ammunition blew up, throwing tank turrets dozens of yards from their stricken vehicles … On the scorched black earth, smashed tanks were blazing like torches. It was difficult to tell who was attacking and who was defending.'

As smoke from burning tanks and thrown-up dust obscured the battlefield, it soon became impossible to call up artillery and air support. As Soviet General Kirill Moskalenko recalled, 'There was no place for manoeuvre. The tank men were forced to fire at point blank.' There were cases of Soviet tanks ramming their opponents after they had run out of ammunition. The fierce fighting continued throughout the day but the Germans were stopped. As Rotmistrov observed:

'More than 700 tanks were put out of action on both sides in the battle. Dead bodies, destroyed tanks, crushed guns and numerous shell craters dotted the battlefield. There was not a single blade of grass to be seen; only burnt, black and smouldering earth throughout the entire depth of our attack – up to eight miles.'

It had cost him 50 per cent of the 5th Guards Tank Army. Overall, Kursk cost the Soviet Union almost 50 per cent of its tank strength, although many of these damaged tanks were able to be recovered from the battlefield. For the Germans, however, the losses were proportionately far greater; some 300 Panzers including 70 Tigers were lost at Prokhorovka. These could not be so easily replaced. Manstein, Hausser and Hoth were convinced that the Germans could advance no further. Therefore, coupling the events at Kursk with the Allied landings in Sicily, Hitler cancelled Citadel on 13 July, a strategic victory for the Soviets. It was a major turning point in the war. Guderian summed up the implications of Kursk thus:

'By the failure of Citadel we had suffered a decisive defeat. The armoured formations, reformed and re-equipped with so much effort, had lost heavily both in men and equipment and would now be unemployable for a long time to come. It was problematical whether they could be rehabilitated in time to defend the Eastern Front; as to being able to use them in defence of the Western Front against the Allied landings that threatened for next spring, this was even more questionable. Needless to say the Russians exploited their victory to the full. There were to be no more periods of quiet on the Eastern Front. From now on the enemy were in undisputed possession of the initiative.'

CLEARING THE SOVIET UNION

The German failure at Kursk meant that Kharkov now constituted a German salient and Stalin immediately ordered its recapture by the rebuilt 5th Guards Army of Pavel Rotmistrov. Hitler refused to allow the city to be abandoned, despite repeated requests by its defenders. Nonetheless, SS Panzer Division *Das Reich* badly mauled Rotmistrov's elite unit, destroying 420 tanks. Even in the aftermath of the disaster at Kursk, German tactical and technical superiority could inflict heavy local defeats on the best units that the Soviet Union had to offer. However, *Das Reich* with its Panthers and Tigers, plus the infantry divisions of the *Wehrmacht's* 11th Corps, could not hold against the four Soviet armies eventually committed against them. The Germans finally evacuated Kharkov on 22 August 1943.

The Soviets continued to make headway, if somewhat slowly, and towards the end of August the offensive widened. The rhythm of the Soviet offensives that summer – an 'alternating series of strokes at different points, each temporarily suspended when its impetus waned in the face of stiffening resistance, each so aimed as to pave the way for the next, and all timed to react on one another' – was likened by Liddell Hart to Foch's general offensive of 1918. Certainly there were considerable parallels, given the combination of manoeuvre and attrition that characterised the tank war on the Eastern Front from 1943 onwards.

The Germans – as in 1918 – had to hurry their reserves from one place to another, while those reserves were progressively worn down. The immense skill of the Germans in defence – German armour might well strike decisively against the Soviets' flank or rear – meant that Soviet losses were

invariably heavier than those of the Germans. Yet these were losses that the Soviets could afford. The attrition of the *Wehrmacht*'s resources was speeded by Hitler's refusal to sanction retreat.

German exhaustion and increasing Soviet operational skill led to a gradual quickening of the Soviet advance as the summer campaign of 1943 progressed. Talented Soviet commanders such as Vatutin and Rokossovsky were able to exploit German weak points, aided by the increased mobility provided by American lend-lease trucks. Furthermore, new Soviet tanks were entering service, particularly the T-34/85 with its excellent 85mm (3.35in) gun, which went some way to restoring the qualitative balance. The quantitative margin remained massively in the Soviets' favour.

ABOVE: Tigers formed the spearhead of the *Panzerkeile* (panzer wedge) at Kursk, while lighter panzers protected the sides.

BELOW: The tenacity of Soviet tank-killing infantry squads caused panzer crews inordinate problems.

The panzer divisions acted as 'fire brigades', constantly shuttled from one crisis spot to another. This practice became standard throughout 1943 and 1944. Encirclement became ever more common as Hitler refused to allow his units to retreat. Early 1944 was characterised by a series of cauldron battles (*Kesselschlachten*) to break these encirclements. Invariably the armoured formations spearheaded the counterblow westwards. The Germans could still inflict stunning blows on the Soviets. In January 1944, one regiment of 34 Tigers and 47 Panthers under the command of Lieutenant Colonel Dr Franz Bäke tried to stop the advance of five Soviet tank corps on Vinnitsa, in the process destroying 267 tanks and 156 guns in five days of fighting at the cost of one Tiger and four Panthers. However, it was never enough. In 1944, German tank production peaked at 19,000 tanks and assault guns; the Soviet Union alone produced 29,000 tanks and self-propelled guns. This does not include the vast output of the Western Allies now on mainland Europe.

THE DRIVE INTO POLAND

Stalin had promised his allies an offensive in the summer of 1944 in support of the Normandy landings. He was as good as his word and Operation Bagration, as the massive assault was codenamed, demonstrated how much the Soviets had learnt over three years of warfare. Indeed, elements of the campaign bore a remarkable resemblance to the 'deep operations' outlined by Tukhachevsky in the early 1930s. On the anniversary of Barbarossa, on 22 June 1944, in the wake of partisan attacks and heavy air-raids, Soviet reconnaissance units began to probe the German positions, followed by the main weight of the Soviet advance the following day. Three Soviet fronts were launched against German Army Group Centre. A massive opening barrage was eschewed in favour of surprise. Soviet tanks and infantry with artillery close behind rolled forwards, breaking through the German lines. Soviet commanders were ordered to leave pockets of resistance – as the Germans had done in 1941 – and push on regardless. Large numbers of *Kesselschlachten* ensued.

In a just over a week, Bagration turned into a massive success. Field Marshal Model was given command of the Army Group Centre in an effort to stop the collapse, but the only option he could see was withdrawal. Hitler, of course, expressly forbade this, thereby adding to the disaster. A 402km (250-mile) wide and 160km (100-mile) deep hole was torn out of the German front. Minsk fell on 3 July, giving the Soviets 300,000 prisoners. Stalin asked Zhukov if he could continue the advance into eastern Poland and reach the Vistula. Zhukov replied this could be done with little difficulty. One million men and 2000 tanks were moved to the drive onto the Polish capital and the gateway to Berlin. On 25 July 1944, the first Soviet tanks units reached the river and were soon establishing tenaciously held bridgeheads on the other side of Vistula, where the offensive halted. Bagration showed how far the Soviet armies had come in terms of equipment, leadership and combat ability. It was one of the most sophisticated and sustained operations of the war.

Stalin decided that he should get the credit for the final operations against Germany. Zhukov was posted to 1st Belorussian Front and Rokossovsky shifted to 2nd Belorussian Front. These two formations would lead the drive into the heart of Germany. When Stalin assumed command in November 1944, about 800km (500 miles) separated the Soviet armies stretched out along the Vistula from their prize.

On 12 January 1945, after months of careful planning, the Soviets launched their second great offensive. The Vistula-Oder Operation launched over six million Soviet troops against some two million Germans and 190,000 of their allies. Many German units were scratch regiments of under-aged conscripts and older men, desperately short of tanks, fuel and ammunition. The 2nd and 3rd Belorussian Fronts with 1.6 million men drove into East Prussia and began to clear the Baltic coast. Zhukov swept the Germans from central Poland in a little over two weeks. On 29 January, he had reached the banks of the Oder and had Berlin within his sight. At times, the Soviet armies were covering 50 miles per day, troops clinging onto T-34s as they drove an increasingly demoralised German army and streams of frightened refugees in front of them. Yet these battles were

hard fought – once the war reached German soil, losses began to rise again.

Zhukov's advance halted on the Oder for a number of reasons. The Soviets were overstretched and at the end of their supply lines. The Germans had also decided that the defence of the Oder was vital, and the bulk of German reinforcements went east. Thus the line on the river was held, albeit temporarily.

SPRING AWAKENING

Hitler still looked for offensive opportunities and decided to attempt to relieve Budapest. On 18 January, the 4th SS Panzer Corps of 3rd SS Panzer Division *Totenkopf* and 5th SS Panzer Division *Wiking* opened an offensive towards the Hungarian capital. It covered 64km (40 miles) in the first day and reached within 24km (15 miles) of its target. Even as the offensive ground to a halt in the face of massive resistance, Hitler was sufficiently encouraged to believe that victory was at hand. He ordered Dietrich's 6th SS Panzer Army from the Ardennes to Hungary. Guderian yet again protested, believing Dietrich's

formidable formation would be of far more use employed against the main Russian advance in Poland.

Nonetheless, when the 6th SS Panzer Army arrived and subsequently attacked, it met with some success. Spearheaded by 1st SS Panzer Corps, the Germans made considerable progress when they attacked on 17 February. The 150 tanks and assault guns smashed the Soviet 7th Guards Army, yet this was the last German operational victory. Its final major offensive, Operation Spring Awakening, was intended to destroy the 3rd Ukrainian Front and recapture Budapest. Some 877 tanks and assault guns from 11 panzer divisions were scraped together. Although the Soviet commander Tolbikin had only 407 tanks, he had approximately the same number of men as the Germans and ample warning of their intentions. He set about preparing a Kursk-style defence in depth of three defensive belts several miles deep. The attack began on 5 March 1945: 2nd Panzer, 6th SS Panzer and 6th Army attacked across low-lying and waterlogged ground, crisscrossed by canals and drainage ditches. The fighting

ABOVE: A column of T-34/85s advances through the wartorn countryside. As the new German Panthers and Tigers appeared on the battlefield in 1943, the 76.2mm (3in) gun equipping the T-34 was found to be increasingly inadequate. The Soviet response was to up-gun the superlative T-34 with an 85mm (3.34in) gun and new three-man turret. The transition required no lengthy design process nor major disruption of the production lines.

ABOVE: Rows of the huge 70-tonne PzKpfw VI Tiger II tank preparing for Operation Spring Awakening. This massive vehicle was almost invulnerable to any available Allied tank gun and was armed with the potent KwK L/71 88mm (3.45in) gun and was therefore a formidable defensive weapon. It was, however, unreliable and there were too few available to stem the Soviet advance.

degenerated into an attritional killing match and the Germans were less able to endure the losses. Spring Awakening petered out between 9 and 14 February, with the Germans advancing little more than 20km (12.5 miles) from their start line. It cost Germany over 500 tanks. Some of the *Wehrmacht*'s best panzer formations had been frittered away

CAPTURE OF BERLIN

The Soviet plan to capture Berlin was straightforward. Zhukov's 1st Belorussian front would attack from the Oder bridgeheads in a frontal assault on the city across the Seelöw Heights, while elements of his forces encircled the city to the north. Marshal Konev's 1st Ukrainian Front was to encircle it from the south. Rokossovsky's 2nd Belorussian Front would support to the north. Between them, they could muster 2.5 million men, 6250 tanks and armoured vehicles and 7500 aircraft.

On 16 April, Zhukov opened his offensive in a predawn attack on the Seelöw Heights. Despite a preliminary bombardment and air strike, the Soviet tanks met with determined German resistance. Suicidal bravery on the part of some German defenders against the vastly superior numbers of Soviet armour and infantry halted the attack. Determined groups armed often only with light weapons, *panzerfausts* and mines fought on despite the hopelessness of their position. By the 18th, Zhukov's tanks had made two sizeable dents in the German line, but they had not broken through. Stalin ordered him to encircle Berlin from the north, while Rokossovsky brought his forces in for support. Konev, meanwhile, was making good progress to the south.

Zhukov had not committed his tank armies to the first assault, and, determined not to be beaten, he threw them at the German positions. At last the Germans began to crack. The 56th Panzer Corps – with very few panzers indeed – had held the full brunt of Zhukov's assault across the Seelöw Heights for two days, but the

breaking point had finally come. Three of Zhukov's armies finally reached Berlin's outer defensive ring on 21 April, and the city was encircled by 25 April.

Berlin was now a massive fortress defended by a few regular German troops, conscripted old men and the Hitler Youth. The Germans fought for every street, house and room. As has been shown elsewhere, the urban environment is extremely dangerous for a tank. Close ranges, hiding places and limited room to manoeuvre make armoured vehicles extremely vulnerable to defenders with mines, *panzerfausts* and Molotov cocktails. The Soviet tank men solved the threat from the German *panzerfausts* by attaching mattresses to the front of their tanks to break up the impact of the rocket's warhead. The T-34 drivers also took to driving through buildings. Close armour and infantry cooperation was essential to protect the tanks from German tank-hunter squads. The Soviets applied massive firepower to ease their advance, but the Germans fought on stubbornly.

By 27 April 1945, the Red Army had reached Potsdamer Platz, just a few hundred yards from Hitler's bunker. On the afternoon of 30 April, the Soviets stormed the Reichstag, where the German defenders fought to almost the last man and last bullet. Hitler shot himself that same day. General Weidling, Berlin's military commander, surrendered the city on 2 May. All German forces finally surrendered on 7 May 1945.

By 1945, the role of the tank had shifted considerably; while still very much 'Queen of the Battlefield' and the benchmark by which opposing forces were judged, it was not the dominant force it had been in the first years of war. The tank's seeming invincibility had been negated by other forces. Air power could be just as decisive, but the real change was in the power of defences. Anti-tank guns had become progressively more powerful and infantry now had access to effective man-portable anti-tank weapons such as the bazooka and the *panzerfaust*. The tank struggled in difficult terrain such as Italy, Normandy and urban environments such as Stalingrad and Berlin. The power of defences had turned the advance of armoured units into a slow, attritional slogging match. Rarely were the tanks able to make the rapid sweeping advances that had characterised the *Blitzkrieg* and war in the desert. Far more typical was the 'incessant sparring with anti-tank screens' identified by Liddell Hart, as typified by Kursk, Epsom, the Ardennes Offensive and even the Seelöw Heights. Tanks were reliant on infantry to break through the enemy lines, and the key development in tank warfare in the second half of the war was the Allies finally learning this lesson and applying it in the offensive. The Germans had known it all along.

ABOVE: To the victor the spoils. The T-34 was a real war-winner. Here a pair of T-34 Model 1943s advances through Leipzig in Germany after the war's end in June 1945. The T-34 was such a successful and prolific design that it would remain in front-line service with some Warsaw Pact armies until the 1970s.

CHAPTER NINE

THE COLD WAR IN EUROPE

After Germany's collapse, the Cold War broke out in Europe, spurring on the development of new tank models and tactics.

The German surrender on 8 May 1945 did not solve all of Europe's problems. The Soviet and Western Allied tank armies came to halt and, for a while, there was much celebration. Yet the erstwhile allies eyed each other warily across the ruins of Germany. The Soviet dominance of Eastern and Central Europe was a military fact. The Red Army had advanced 160km (100 miles) west of Berlin and occupied the eastern halves of Austria and Czechoslovakia, including Vienna and Prague. The Soviets also dominated the Balkans. Stalin insisted on keeping the Red Army's territorial gains as a matter of security. Given the destruction wrought and sacrifices made by the Soviet Union, it was hardly surprising that Stalin was determined to create a Soviet-dominated Eastern Europe as a buffer zone against future aggression. As Lenin put it: 'As long as capitalism and socialism

LEFT: One of the last Cold War designs, the Soviet T-80 main battle tank. A development of the highly successful T-72, the T-80 is armed with a 125mm (4.9in) gun capable of firing the AT-8 Songster anti-tank missile. For much of the second half of the twentieth century, Germany was divided into two huge armed camps ready to conduct mass armoured warfare at a moment's notice. Tank design was dominated by the design requirements dictated by the North German plain's geography and the need for an increased ability to survive in a threat-rich environment.

ABOVE: The Cold War fought by proxy – Cuban T-34/85s on the streets of the Angolan provincial city of Huambo in 1975. The Cubans fought on the side of the Communist MPLA in the Angolan civil war, which broke out following the withdrawal of the Portuguese colonial authorities. Despite their age, the T-34/85s gave good and effective service.

exist, we cannot live in peace; in the end, one or other will triumph. A funeral dirge will be sung either over the Soviet Republic or over Capitalism.'

Even before the end of the war, there were those on the side of the Western Allies who were expressing similar views. This distrust heightened in the first months of peace. George Kennan of the US State Department famously summarised in the Long Telegram the threat that he perceived from the Soviets: 'They have learned to seek security only in patient but deadly struggle for total

destruction of rival power, never in compacts and compromises with it.' Kennan's view was echoed by Winston Churchill, now out of power, when in March 1946 he made a speech at Fulton, Missouri, asserting that from 'from Stettin in the Baltic, to Trieste on the Adriatic, an iron curtain has descended across the continent'. Later in the same speech, he added: 'From what I have seen of our Russian friends and allies during the war, I am convinced that there is nothing they admire more than military strength and nothing for which they have less respect

RIGHT: T-54s on the streets of Budapest in 1956. The brutal suppression of the Hungarian uprising in 1956 showed that the tank could be effectively used as an instrument of repression as well as on the battlefield in conventional war. Nonetheless, despite being armed with little more than Molotov cocktails, the Hungarian street-fighters killed and wounded 2200 Soviet troops in the two-week battle for Budapest.

than military weakness.' He urged the West to react with firmness to Soviet pressure. The US president, Harry Truman, responded by committing the United States to the containment of the Soviet threat, the cornerstone of US foreign policy for more than a generation.

It was all very well to talk of containment, but Western military strength had been rapidly run down in the aftermath of World War II. Truman committed US military power to the defence of Europe and, in conjunction with Britain, France, Belgium, the Netherlands, Luxembourg, Norway, Denmark, Italy, Portugal, Iceland and Canada, formed the North Atlantic Treaty Organisation (NATO) in April 1949. The purpose of this alliance was to defend against attack by the Soviet Union and, in the wake of the Berlin Crisis and the Korean War, most countries, particularly the United States and Britain, increased their defence spending. West Germany was rearmed and entered NATO in 1955. The Soviet Union responded by forming the Warsaw Pact Treaty Organisation in the same year. The Warsaw Pact included the Soviet Union's satellite states in Eastern and Central Europe: East Germany, Poland, Hungary, Romania, Bulgaria, Czechoslovakia and Albania (which left in 1961). The line-up for the Cold War in Europe had been solidified in the two treaty organisations, although France would later leave NATO, while Greece, Turkey and Spain would join.

The main area of possible armed confrontation was the border between West and East Germany. After West Germany's accession to NATO, the Western Alliance intended to fight the war as close to the West German border as possible, rather than to retreat to a natural barrier such as the Rhine in the event of a Soviet invasion, as had been the earliest defensive plans. The tank remained the mainstay of both NATO and the Warsaw Pact countries, but it did not remain the centrepiece of their defence strategies for long. The adoption of massive retaliation as the centrepiece of US strategy meant that NATO really relied on the nuclear deterrent for much of the Cold War. Nuclear weapons gave them defence on the cheap, as they are relatively inexpensive to maintain, unlike infantry and tanks. The presence of US

and NATO troops in Germany was really to act as a trip-wire, rather than a shield, for Western Europe. That trip-wire would trigger the use of US nuclear weapons in the event of Soviet aggression. Similar developments had taken place in Soviet military thinking in the early 1950s. As part of its 'Revolution and Strategy', the Soviet Union moved away from the manoeuvre style of warfare that had served it so well in the last years of World War II against Germany and towards the use of nuclear firepower in land warfare, seeing manoeuvre and firepower as essentially interchangeable.

The firepower made available to both armies by nuclear weapons did at least ensure that the tank remained central to

BELOW: A diagram showing the various measures that can be used to stop a tank. Combined with effective anti-tank weaponry, proper physical defences can break up an attack.

HOW TO STOP A TANK

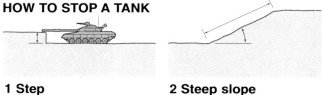

1 Step
On firm ground, the step must be at least 1.5m (5ft) high, and on softer ground at least 2m (6ft 7in) high.

2 Steep slope
A slope of over 30 degrees and greater than 12m (39ft) in length will be an obstacle for most tanks. It will also leave them very vulnerable to anti-armour weapons as they go over the crest.

3 Crater
The crater must be at least 1.8m (6ft) deep and 6m (20ft) wide to provide an effective obstacle.

4 Ditch
Purpose-built anti-tank ditches must have a minimum depth of 1.5m (5ft) on hard ground or 2m (6ft 7in) in soft earth. The ditch must be at least 3m (10ft) across and the spoil pile, placed on the opposite side to the approach, at least 1.2m (4ft) high.

5 Woodland
Any forest or plantation with regularly spaced trees less than 5m apart and with minimum trunk diameters of 60cm for pine and equivalents, and 50cm for oak and other hardwoods, will block movement by tanks.

6 Soft ground
Any ground with a bearing of less than 3.6kg (8lb) per 2.5cm² (square inch) will bog down a tank.

7 River
Rivers more than 150m (500ft) wide cannot be bridged by engineer-launched bridges, and if it is over 1.5m (5ft) deep it cannot be forded. Tanks would have to be ferried across or fitted with their snorkelling kit.

8 Dry gap
Any dry gap more than 20m (66ft) across cannot be bridged by most bridging equipment mounted on an armoured vehicle. Again, it must be at least 1.5m (5ft) deep in hard ground and 2m (6ft 7in) deep in soft earth.

BELOW: Polish Warsaw Pact troops in NBC protective suits hose down T-54 tanks on exercise. Despite the emphasis placed on nuclear weapons throughout the Cold War, the tank remained the centrepiece of both NATO and Warsaw Pact armies. For one thing it provided a method of providing some protection for troops on the chemical and nuclear battlefield.

their conventional arsenals. This was largely because it provided a way of protecting its crew from the dangers of the nuclear, biological and chemical environment that might well characterise a modern European war. Tank design therefore continued apace throughout the Cold War period and it remained, to quote British Defence Secretary Denis Healey, the 'virility symbol' of modern armies. As noted elsewhere, tanks are in essence a compromise between mobility, firepower and protection. The major armies came to differing conclusions about that balance, based largely on their experiences of World War II. Of course,

some changes did result from later conflicts such as the Korean and Arab–Israeli wars. Therefore, with a strategy based on the attack, the Soviet Army opted for fast, manoeuvrable tanks with good firepower. Protection came lower down the list, as casualties were a relatively low priority in an army with such vast resources of manpower. The British, chastened by the experience of producing tanks and guns inferior to their German opponents throughout World War II, were determined never to be outgunned again. Accordingly, they gave firepower the top priority, followed closely by protection, with mobility coming a very distant third.

TANK GUNNERY TECHNIQUES

Standard range adjustment

When you cannot clearly see the fall of shot, apply standard range adjustment until you bracket the target. The standard adjustment is + or − 200 metres (650ft) at up to 1500 metres (5000ft), and + or − 400 metres (1310ft) at longer ranges. If a tank platoon operates together like this it can get rounds on target faster than if the vehicles fought independently.

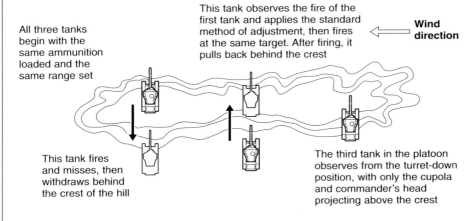

All three tanks begin with the same ammunition loaded and the same range set

This tank observes the fire of the first tank and applies the standard method of adjustment, then fires at the same target. After firing, it pulls back behind the crest

Wind direction

This tank fires and misses, then withdraws behind the crest of the hill

The third tank in the platoon observes from the turret-down position, with only the cupola and commander's head projecting above the crest

Burst on target method

This method is faster because the gunner operates without further reference to the tank commander. He notes where the shell lands using the reticle on his sight, adjusts his aim, and fires again.

Wind direction

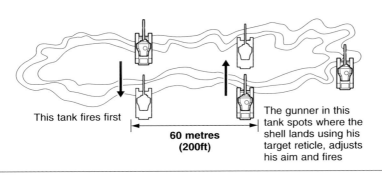

This tank fires first

60 metres (200ft)

The gunner in this tank spots where the shell lands using his target reticle, adjusts his aim and fires

LEFT: Using terrain to hide behind, modern main battle tanks can 'pop up' for their shot before retreating behind cover again, leaving their still-concealed colleagues to observe the fall of shot.

BELOW: An example of a pre-prepared defensive position or 'tank slot' for a tank. Dug by a unit's engineer detachment, each tank would have several slots dug for it to move between during an enemy attack. With only the turret visible, it would prove a hard target to hit.

As a result, British tanks were invariably the heaviest in service throughout the Cold War. The Americans fell somewhere in the middle with speed and manoeuvrability as their priority, firepower second, and protection third. Given the vast superiority of Soviet numbers facing them, all the NATO armies needed a considerable qualitative advantage in their tanks.

LAND WAR DOCTRINES

The Soviet Union progressively moved away from its adoption of nuclear weapons as the centrepiece for its land war doctrine. By the 1970s, the commanders of the Red Army had

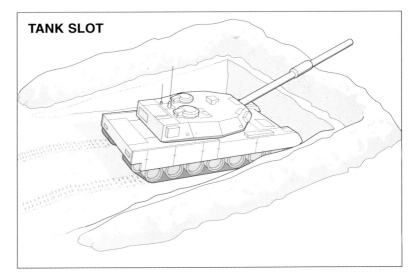

TANK SLOT

rediscovered the joys of 'Deep Battle' as the prospect of fighting a successful conventional war in Europe seemed more possible. The Soviets experimented with the World War II concept of the manoeuvre group, bringing it up to date. The first trials of the 'operational manoeuvre group' (OMG) occurred during the SAPAD 81 (West 81) manoeuvres in Poland and the western Soviet Union in 1981. These were the largest Warsaw Pact exercises for a decade, and involved some 100,000 personnel. The OMG was an important development in Soviet land doctrine, consisting of reinforced armoured divisions held back in reserve behind the main front. They would then exploit the gap created by other troops and drive deep into the enemy rear, converting a tactical success into a strategic one at the operational level.

BELOW: East German T-72s race across the countryside during an exercise. Warsaw Pact exercises in the 1970s and 1980s convinced Red Army commanders that a return to manoeuvre warfare was possible, and led to the reintroduction of World War II–style 'manoeuvre groups' intended to exploit breakthroughs in the enemy's defences.

The return to manoeuvre warfare by the Soviets had implications for NATO. In 1967, NATO introduced 'Flexible Response' as its basic strategy. This moved the emphasis away from massive nuclear retaliation and allowed NATO a more measured and graduated response to Soviet aggression, with a range of conventional and nuclear options. Shifting the reliance back to conventional means of defence meant that NATO first had to improve its land forces and, secondly, come up with a method of defeating a Soviet attack. This was initially a fighting withdrawal on a continuous front, giving up as little West German territory as possible and subjecting the Soviet attack to attrition. Critics of this plan considered it particularly vulnerable to the new Soviet doctrine. The solution was the adoption of manoeuvre warfare by the United States, which had traditionally relied upon attrition. Following the American defeat in Vietnam, the United States sought new means of using their superior technology and training to defeat the Soviet Union. The result was 'Air Land Battle'. This was adopted by the US Army in 1982 and took many of its ideas from the German, Soviet and Israeli experiences of warfare. The intention was to enable the US armed forces to outfight and outmanoeuvre the Warsaw Pact by taking the offensive. This was very much the application of air power, air mobility and tanks in a 'three-dimensional extended battlefield'. Although it was never tested in Europe, this soon became the basis of NATO doctrine, which moved away from attritional war fighting to manoeuvrist thinking.

TANK DESIGN

Throughout the Cold War, the Soviet tank force held the initiative and the West reacted. Soviet designers were innovative and considerably less conservative than their Western counterparts. The Soviets entered the Cold War with their battle-tested T–34/85 complemented by the JS3 heavy tank, carrying a 122mm (4.75in) gun, by far the most heavy and powerful weapon of any tank of that era. These were both formidable threats and the West produced a number of tanks specifically to counter the JS3. The JS3 was eventually succeeded by the T–10, which had even better armour, gun and engine, although it was phased out in the mid–1960s. The first post–war Soviet medium tank, the T–54, entered service in 1954. It served with all the armies of the Warsaw Pact and was in production for about 30 years. In total, 95,000 T–54s and T–55s (an improved version) were built and still made up 85 per cent of the non-Soviet Warsaw Pact's tank inventory at the end of the Cold War. It was well protected and armed for its time and had excellent cross-country performance. The T–62 was a stretched version of the T–54/55 with a 115mm (4.5in) smoothbore gun (the first to enter service anywhere in the world).

It was a fairly mediocre tank and only served with the Red Army. The first new generation tank was the T-64, with a new 125mm (4.75in) smoothbore gun and automatic loader that enabled the crew to be reduced to three men. It was the mainstay of the Warsaw Pact tank forces for much of the Cold War. The T-72 was produced in parallel to the T-64 and was cheaper and easier to maintain, while still retaining the firepower improvements of the T-64. The last in this family was the T-80, which was essentially an improved T-64 with a completely new gas turbine engine. This was issued to the front-line Soviet tank units towards the end of the Cold War. The Soviet tanks were built in vast numbers and were constantly upgraded and rebuilt. As new models appeared, older models were shifted to lower category units, then to reserve units and, finally, to storage depots. Built for an offensive role, the Soviet Army produced tanks at least 10 tonnes lighter than Western vehicles and also showed some considerable innovation, using such devices as automatic loaders that were perfected long before their opponent's designers had managed to do so. Soviet tanks were never used in anger against Western tanks in Europe and, when they did meet in the Middle East and Asia, they generally proved inferior. However, these tanks were not crewed by Warsaw Pact personnel, and the situation might have been very different had they been used against NATO.

Four of the NATO nations – France, West Germany, Britain and the United States – designed and built tanks. Although there was much talk about collaborative projects and NATO standards, there was nothing like this degree of standardisation amongst the Warsaw Pact countries. The British 105mm (4.1in) L7 gun was common throughout all NATO tanks, except those built by the French. The Korean War convinced the Americans of the need to replace their World War II veterans, the M4 and the M26. The M47 and M48 were rushed into service and suffered considerable problems. The M48 was redesigned and improved, and thus was given a new designation. As the M60, it served for many years as the army's standard medium tank. With the collapse of the American–German MBT70 project, the US Army turned to a Chrysler tank design, which entered production as the M1 Abrams and eventually entered service in 1982. This has since been upgraded as the M1A1, mounting a German Rheinmetall 120mm (4.7in) smoothbore gun. The British, having suffered from somewhat mediocre tank designs throughout World War II, finally hit upon a winner with the Centurion at the start of the Cold War. It was steadily up-gunned, eventually taking the L7 105mm (4.1in), and was heavier than all of its contemporaries. It gave excellent service to the Israelis. The Centurion was replaced in British service in 1967 by the Chieftain, another extremely heavy and well-armed tank

which initially suffered considerable problems with its engines and transmission. Its replacement was the Challenger, with a new hull and gas turbine engine, but the same 120mm (4.7in) gun. The West German tank industry produced just two tank designs during the Cold War, but they were both outstanding models: the Leopard I and Leopard II. The Leopard I became virtually the standard NATO tank, equipping the Danish, Canadian, Dutch, Norwegian, Belgian, Italian and West German armies. The French AMX-30 entered production in 1967. It was considerably lighter than other NATO tanks and had a unique 105mm (4.1in) rifled cannon. The French struggled to find a replacement for the AMX-30 in the late 1980s, although the Leclerc was about to enter production as the Cold War ended.

ABOVE: The low silhouette of the Swedish Stridsvagen 103 is evident in comparison to the Swedish Army Centurion by its side. The Strv 103 was an interesting design in which, in an effort to keep the tank as low as possible, the gun remained fixed in the azimuth and was aimed by traversing the vehicle and elevated by means of its suspension. Although an innovative design, the Strv 103 has had little influence on subsequent developments in tank technology.

By the tail end of the Cold War, the Soviet Union could bring to bear about two and a half times the amount of armour of NATO at the strategic level. Of course, that advantage would not have been evenly spread, as Soviet operational doctrine included the massing of forces to achieve local superiority. So that 1:2.6 advantage might well be converted to 1:6 or even 1:10 by careful Soviet planning and preparation, as the Red Army had regularly achieved between 1944 and 1945. Thus one should not assume that each NATO tank would have faced three Warsaw Pact tanks. Some would have faced 10 or more, and some none. So the question is whether or not the quality of NATO tanks could make up the quantitative difference. There are historical examples of smaller armies beating larger armies with more tanks; German panzers destroyed Soviet tanks at a ratio of about 5:1 throughout 1943. In Korea, US tanks achieved a similar ratio. The Israeli army has outfought larger tank forces time and time again with odds similar to those facing NATO. Quality can overcome quantity and this is

what NATO evidently intended, as its tanks were more sophisticated than the Soviet Union's, and its crews better trained. NATO tank tactics stressed long-range engagements to wear down the enemy's tanks at a longer distance. Thus, their tanks had to use more advanced range-finding equipment and better fire-control systems than those equipping their Soviet opponents.

DESIGN DEVELOPMENTS

The traditional focus of tank design has been firepower, mobility and protection. Thus, in comparing NATO and Warsaw Pact tanks, it is worth analysing the developments in these spheres throughout the Cold War. Until the 1970s, tank armour consisted, as it always had done, of homogenous steel, with the thickest armour to the front. Sloping armour had been becoming more common since the groundbreaking use of it on the T-34 in World War II. The increasing use of shaped-charge explosive warheads, particularly on anti-tank rockets and missiles, led to the introduction of non-metallic armours. This process was

BELOW: A British infantryman talks to the commander of a Chieftain tank in August 1978, via a telephone attached to the rear of the vehicle. The Chieftain was an extremely heavy and well-armed tank, specifically designed to fight a defensive campaign in Europe.

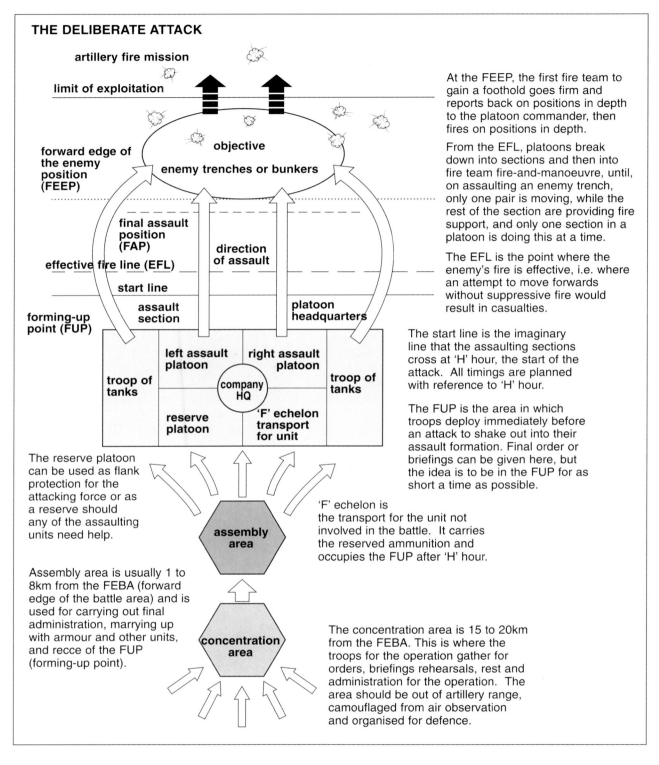

THE DELIBERATE ATTACK

artillery fire mission

limit of exploitation

forward edge of the enemy position (FEEP)

objective
enemy trenches or bunkers

final assault position (FAP)

effective fire line (EFL)

direction of assault

start line

forming-up point (FUP)

assault section

platoon headquarters

left assault platoon

right assault platoon

troop of tanks

company HQ

troop of tanks

reserve platoon

'F' echelon transport for unit

assembly area

concentration area

At the FEEP, the first fire team to gain a foothold goes firm and reports back on positions in depth to the platoon commander, then fires on positions in depth.

From the EFL, platoons break down into sections and then into fire team fire-and-manoeuvre, until, on assaulting an enemy trench, only one pair is moving, while the rest of the section are providing fire support, and only one section in a platoon is doing this at a time.

The EFL is the point where the enemy's fire is effective, i.e. where an attempt to move forwards without suppressive fire would result in casualties.

The start line is the imaginary line that the assaulting sections cross at 'H' hour, the start of the attack. All timings are planned with reference to 'H' hour.

The FUP is the area in which troops deploy immediately before an attack to shake out into their assault formation. Final order or briefings can be given here, but the idea is to be in the FUP for as short a time as possible.

The reserve platoon can be used as flank protection for the attacking force or as a reserve should any of the assaulting units need help.

'F' echelon is the transport for the unit not involved in the battle. It carries the reserved ammunition and occupies the FUP after 'H' hour.

Assembly area is usually 1 to 8km from the FEBA (forward edge of the battle area) and is used for carrying out final administration, marrying up with armour and other units, and recce of the FUP (forming-up point).

The concentration area is 15 to 20km from the FEBA. This is where the troops for the operation gather for orders, briefings rehearsals, rest and administration for the operation. The area should be out of artillery range, camouflaged from air observation and organised for defence.

pioneered by the British in the late 1960s and early 1970s with their Chobham armour, which was created by mixing conventional armour plate with layers of ceramic material, and effectively defeated the menace of the HEAT round. It is currently incorporated in the latest generation of NATO tanks such as the M1A1 Abrams, Challenger and Leopard II.

However, it does not affect tank–versus–tank fighting using kinetic energy rounds to any great extent. The Soviets began introducing a similar system in the early 1980s. A cheaper solution was reactive armour, which first appeared on Israeli tanks in 1982. Reactive armour consists of small, explosive blocks, which are detonated when hit by a shaped charge.

ABOVE: Cold War offensive thinking for a limited attack on a fixed enemy position by an infantry company supported by two troops of tanks.

ABOVE: West German Leopard I tanks demonstrate their fording ability by crossing a river in Western Europe. The Leopard I was the first German tank design built after World War II; it equipped a number of NATO members' tank forces.

The Soviets acquired samples of the Israeli system from the Syrians and reactive armour was fitted to T-64, T-67 and T-80 tanks in the mid- to late 1980s. The most advanced form of tank armour is American depleted uranium armour, which is an evolutionary development from Chobham and incorporates a depleted uranium mesh inside the layer of steel in the armour. It will probably enter service with the upgraded Abrams tank. On the whole, the final generation of Cold War NATO tanks was better protected than its Soviet counterparts.

In the question of tank firepower, it has largely been an issue of increasing the high-velocity kinetic energy weapons or the chemical energy weapons such as the shaped charge. With the kinetic energy attack, it has been a case of fabricating rounds of ever-denser material – first steel, then tungsten carbide, and finally depleted uranium – and increasing the velocity with which the projectile is delivered. By the end of the period, NATO and Warsaw Pact guns, usually in the 120 to 125mm (4.7–4.9in) class, had fairly similar penetration capabilities. The way NATO took the lead was with aiming devices and stabilisation of the main armament. Tanks such as the Leopard II,

the M1 Abrams and the Challenger can accurately engage targets at 2000m (2188yds) while moving at speed. As for aiming devices, most tanks use an optical range finder, although the British produced a simple system in which a machine gun mounted coaxially with the main gun was used to find the range. The modern use of laser designation has greatly increased tank gun accuracy.

PETROL VERSUS DIESEL

At the start of the Cold War, all Soviet tanks were diesel powered and all Western tanks used petrol. Although petrol provided a better power-to-weight ratio than diesel, fuel consumption was high and thus shortened the tanks' range. Petrol is also more flammable. In the intervening years, NATO converted to diesel or turbo-charged diesel, which improved range and also safety. In the 1980s, the US Army introduced a gas turbine engine for the M1 Abrams, which offered considerable power for its size. The generation of tanks introduced in the 1980s all followed suit. This new generation of engines has helped offset the growing weight of modern tanks.

In the Cold War, NATO tanks enjoyed certain qualitative advantages,

which would probably have allowed them a superior kill ratio to that of the Warsaw Pact tanks. How far this would have countered the Warsaw Pact's quantitative superiority is open to question. Of course tanks would not have fought alone and would not solely have decided the outcome of any war in Europe. In discussions over what might have happened had the Cold War become hot, they cannot in actuality be considered in isolation from other weapon systems.

ABOVE: The pinnacle of Cold War tank design, the M1 Abrams. The M1 began to enter service in Europe in the 1980s and represented a considerable leap in capability over its predecessor, the M60. Its composite armour and, on the later M1A1 version, its 120mm smoothbore gun coupled with superior American electronic and sighting devices, also put the M1 considerably ahead of its main Soviet rivals.

LEFT: Modern main battle tanks are equipped with various devices to improve the crew's ability to survive, and the M1 Abrams is no exception.

M1 ABRAMS CREW PROTECTION SYSTEM

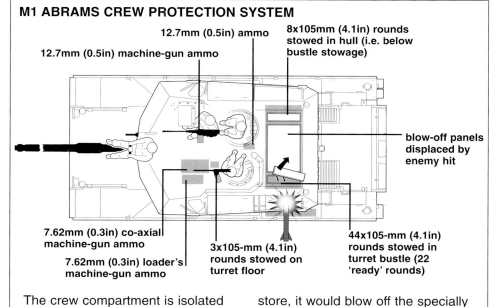

12.7mm (0.5in) ammo

12.7mm (0.5in) machine-gun ammo

8x105mm (4.1in) rounds stowed in hull (i.e. below bustle stowage)

blow-off panels displaced by enemy hit

7.62mm (0.3in) co-axial machine-gun ammo

7.62mm (0.3in) loader's machine-gun ammo

3x105-mm (4.1in) rounds stowed on turret floor

44x105-mm (4.1in) rounds stowed in turret bustle (22 'ready' rounds)

The crew compartment is isolated from the main ammunition storage area by sliding armoured doors. If a shell penetrated the ammunition store, it would blow off the specially fitted top panels and the crew would be safe – providing the armoured doors were shut.

CHAPTER TEN

HOT WAR POST-1945

The ideas of *Blitzkrieg* survived the end of World War II and were adopted by the Israelis in the numerous Middle Eastern wars.

The Middle East has probably witnessed more conflict and turbulence than any other region in the post-war world. The tension here has largely centred on the state of Israel and its Arab neighbours. In the series of wars that have occurred since the foundation of Israel, the tank has played a central role. The region has proved something of testbed for Western and Soviet technology, as the West, particularly the United States, was the main backer of Israel and the Arab nations were largely supplied by the Soviet Union. Many new weapons systems made their debuts during these conflicts, particularly the anti-armour missile, which made a spectacular and effective entrance during the 1973 Yom Kippur War. Indeed, the experience of armoured warfare led Israel to make innovative advances in tank design, culminating in one of the most important and influential post-war tank designs, the Merkava. The fluctuating fortunes of the post-war tank and changes in armoured tactics were

LEFT: An Israeli M48 Patton crosses the Suez Canal during the 1973 Yom Kippur War. The crossing of the canal allowed the Israelis to drive deep into the Egyptian rear, threatening both its missile defences and its rear areas, and thus forcing the Egyptians to sue for peace. Despite lacking the latest equipment, the Israelis were experts in armoured warfare and were able to defeat their numerically superior Arab enemies on several occasions in the twentieth century. Their success against the Arab's Soviet-supplied equipment was closely studied by NATO.

145

ABOVE: A column of Israeli French-built AMX-13s rolls through the desert in 1956. Ever aware of the limited manpower resources available to the Israeli state, the Israeli Army bought the light tanks and up-gunned them, as they had done with other tanks which they had managed to obtain from various sources.

RIGHT: An Egyptian Soviet built Su-100 self-propelled gun destroyed by British paratroopers during the Anglo-French 1956 attempt to seize the Suez Canal. The attack was launched in conjunction with an Israeli drive into the Sinai Desert. While militarily successful, the operation was politically disastrous for the British and the French, who operated without American support.

well illustrated by the stunning Israeli *Blitzkrieg* in 1967 and the prematurely heralded 'death of the tank' in 1973.

THE OPENING ROUND

The British had ruled Palestine from World War I until 1948 under a League of Nations mandate. Unable to resolve the differences between the Jews and Arabs, the British decided on partition, but, when they left in June 1948, there

was no agreement in place. Despite the efforts of the newly formed United Nations, the intransigence of all sides meant that Israel's neighbours decided to crush the new nation at birth. However, the Israeli tank arm was not the highly trained and well-equipped force that it was in later wars. The Israelis had stolen, salvaged and bought an eclectic variety of tanks: Cromwells stolen or salvaged from British stocks, illegally imported pre–World

War II French Hotchkiss light tanks and old Shermans acquired from Italy and the Philippines. These were formed into the 8th Armoured Brigade under Yitzhak Sabeh. This rag-tag formation faced the considerably better equipped tank forces of Lebanon, Syria, Jordan, Egypt and Iraq.

The 8th Armoured Brigade carried out a number of operations during the War of Independence. They forced back the Jordanian advance along the Jerusalem Road. The Jordanians had proved to have one of the more capable Arab armies and were the only ones to make any gains during the war. Israeli armoured forces captured the British-built fort of Suweidan in the Negev Desert. Two battalions pushed into Sinai, defeating an Egyptian counterattack as part of the operations that encircled an Egyptian Army in the coastal Gaza area. A second armoured brigade, the 7th, was also formed during the War of Independence and, hastily equipped with armoured cars and half-tracks, saw service in the operations that secured Galilee. The invasion of Egyptian territory was enough to bring the Arab states to the table to discuss peace. These peace negotiations were to result in an enlarged Israel, but, despite the sizeable Jordanian gains west of the Jordan River and the Gaza Strip going to Egypt, much resentment remained.

THE SUEZ CRISIS
The Israelis wasted no time in improving their tank forces and developing a distinct armoured doctrine based on the principles of mobility, assault and surprise. Surrounded by hostile nations, the Israeli Defence Force (IDF) intended to fight a short, intensely destructive war against a much larger enemy. Given Israel's size, there was no question of sustained defence in depth. Ironically, the Israelis, particularly the deputy commander of 7th Armoured Brigade, Lieutenant Colonel Uri Ben Ari, drew heavily on the memoirs of wartime German panzer commanders. There was also something of an arms race going on in the early to mid-1950s.

In 1955, Czechoslovakia supplied the Egyptians with large quantities of Eastern bloc equipment. As the Egyptians were supporting anti-French forces in Algeria, the French retaliated by sending the Israelis 250 Shermans and light tanks. In addition, tank protection had developed somewhat in the 10 years since the end of World War II, so the Israelis up-gunned some of their Shermans with French CN 75-50 guns.

Tension between Israel and the Egyptian leader Gamal Abdul Nasser increased during 1956 and, in October 1956, flared into open war with an Israeli invasion of the Sinai Peninsula. The Israeli action was encouraged by the British and French, who resented Nasser's earlier nationalisation of the Suez Canal. Thanks to the French, the IDF was equipped

with conventional Shermans (a variety of models including the M4A1 and M4A2), up-gunned 'Super' Shermans, Shermans with French FL10 turrets (similar to those used on the French AMX-13) and French AMX-13 light tanks. Meanwhile, the Egyptians fielded a range of armour including Shermans and Centurions (and older British types such as the Valentine), but 230 T-34/85s formed the majority of the Egyptian armour. In addition to the T-34s, Czechoslovakia also sent some JS3s, 200 BTR-152 armoured troop carriers and 100 SU-100 self-propelled guns.

In the tank battles in the Sinai in 1956, Egypt's armour was totally outclassed by

ABOVE: An Israeli Sherman in the desert. The Israelis were always short of tanks, both new and old, and were forced to use an eclectic mix of types, most of which they up-gunned (including all the Shermans in their stocks), in order to keep the veteran tanks capable of fighting the latest Soviet equipment.

Israel's. It was not so much a question of superior Israeli equipment as it was better training, motivation and tactics. In the initial assault on the Sinai, tanks were left out of the attack. However, Ben Ari, now commanding the 7th Armoured Brigade, argued for a more active role. His force helped the infantry capture the well-defended village of Kusseima and then drove quickly into the Egyptian rear, destroying the equivalent of three infantry brigades in an hour. The Israeli commander, Moshe Dayan, was somewhat alarmed as his armour disappeared westwards in pursuit of the enemy, but, as he recognised, it was 'better to be engaged in restraining the noble stallion than in prodding a reluctant mule'. So Dayan, recognising the opportunity, accelerated the whole Sinai operation to keep up with Ben Ari's armour. They reached the Suez Canal, 250km (153 miles) away, in 100 hours, fighting a number of battles through Egyptian defensive positions and routing an Egyptian armoured brigade in the process. Although much aided by the destruction of Egyptian air force on the ground by the British and French, it was a remarkable *Blitzkrieg*-style victory. In their attack to take the Sinai, the Israelis knocked out 26 T-34/85s, one T-34 command tank, six SU-100s, 40 Sherman Mk 3s and 12 MS/FL10s, 15 Valentines, 40 Archers and 60 BTR-152s. Egyptian tanks, fighting a desperate rearguard action as they retreated to the Suez Canal, were not only knocked out by Israeli tanks but also suffered from Israeli air strikes that badly mauled the T-34s and

SU-100s exposed in the open ground of the Sinai Desert.

British and French forces invaded Egypt in conjunction with the Israeli attack. An Anglo-French amphibious and air assault on Port Said, at the northern end of the Suez Canal, was followed by a push by British and French forces down the canal. The Anglo-French force soon came into contact with Egyptian forces defending the area and the fear was the effect that heavy tanks such as the JS3 could have on the British and French forces. In the end, the only armoured engagement came with SU-100 tanks when British paratroopers knocked out four SU-100s of the Egyptian 53rd Artillery battery on 5 November.

THE 1967 'SIX-DAY' WAR

The experience of 1956 converted Dayan and the IDF was reorganised as a wholly mechanised force, with the tank at the centre of Israeli doctrine and tactics. New armoured brigades were formed and a fresh re-equipment programme initiated. The Shermans were up-gunned with a French 105mm (4.1in) cannon. Major General Israel Tal, worried by losses to vital tank crew, insisted on the purchase of heavily armoured 50-tonne British Centurions.

Therefore, the Israeli tank force for the war of 1967 was much improved on the 1956 war: Centurions, M48 Pattons, Shermans and AMX-13s. Crews were also better trained and disciplined as a result of Tal's reforms, and had the experience of the 1956 war under their belts. This experience would show itself in the

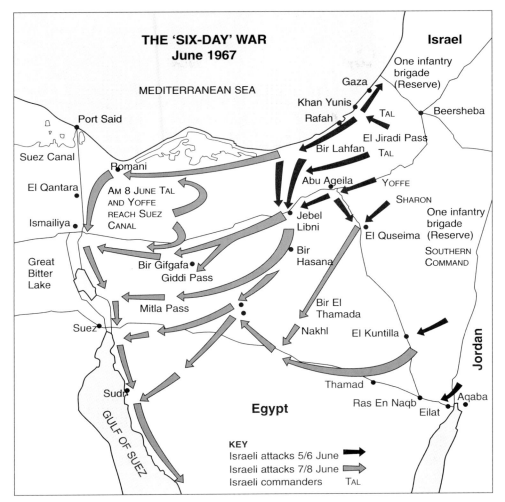

THE 'SIX-DAY' WAR
June 1967

MEDITERRANEAN SEA

Israel

One infantry brigade (Reserve)

Gaza

Khan Yunis

Rafah

TAL

Beersheba

El Jiradi Pass

Bir Lahfan

TAL

Port Said

Suez Canal

Romani

El Qantara

Am 8 June Tal and Yoffe reach Suez Canal

Ismailiya

Great Bitter Lake

Bir Gifgafa

Giddi Pass

Mitla Pass

Suez

Abu Ageila

YOFFE

Jebel Libni

SHARON

One infantry brigade (Reserve)

Bir Hasana

El Quseima

SOUTHERN COMMAND

Bir El Thamada

Nakhl

El Kuntilla

Jordan

Sudr

Thamad

Ras En Naqb

Aqaba

Eilat

Egypt

GULF OF SUEZ

KEY
Israeli attacks 5/6 June
Israeli attacks 7/8 June
Israeli commanders TAL

LEFT: The 'Six-Day' War was a remarkable Israeli victory in 1967, pre-empting an Arab attack on Israel. The Israeli armoured forces, working in harmony with the air force, smashed through the Egyptian Army and reached the Suez Canal in days.

BELOW: Assembled Israeli armour – AMX-13s and American-built M3 half-tracks in Gaza. Ironically, Israeli generals drew much inspiration from the German theories of *Blitzkrieg* and, by 1967, had a fully mechanised force with a well-integrated mobile infantry component.

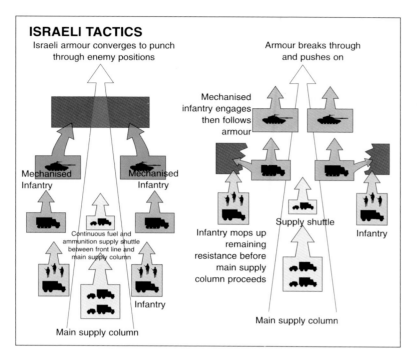

ISRAELI TACTICS

Israeli armour converges to punch through enemy positions

Armour breaks through and pushes on

Mechanised infantry engages then follows armour

Mechanised Infantry

Mechanised Infantry

Continuous fuel and ammunition supply shuttle between front line and main supply column

Infantry mops up remaining resistance before main supply column proceeds

Supply shuttle

Infantry

Infantry

Main supply column

Main supply column

ABOVE: This diagram demonstrates how the Israelis emphasised the importance of getting supplies through to the front line. By doing so, the pace of advance would not be slowed by tanks waiting to rearm or refuel, and the pressure on their opponents would be maintained.

RIGHT: An Egyptian T-34/85 heading into battle against the Israelis in the Sinai in October 1973. The T-34/85 had been the mainstay of Egyptian armoured forces in 1956 and, although as good as any tank in the Israeli arsenal at that stage, by 1973 it was not suitable for use in the front-line units.

'Six-Day' War, when Israeli forces, in the space of only five and a half days, routed three Arab armies.

THREE ARAB ARMIES

When the next Arab-Israeli War erupted in June 1967 (the famous 'Six-Day' War), Israel faced Egypt, Syria and Jordan. While newer T-54s were being absorbed into the Egyptian and Syrian armies, the veteran T-34/85 was still a mainstay of the armoured forces of Israel's Arab foes. In the Sinai peninsula along the Egyptian–Israeli border, the Egyptian 7th Infantry division defending Rafah had 100 T-34/85s and JS3s; the important junction at Abu Agheila was held by the 2nd Infantry division with 100 T-34/85s and T-54s; the 3rd Infantry division stationed near Djebel Libni had a further 100 T-34/85s and T-54s; and the 6th Mechanised division to the south was also equipped with a mixture of T-34/85s and T-54s.

When the war started on 5 June 1967, an Israeli offensive tore through the Egyptian defensive positions in the Sinai. A pre-emptive strike by Israeli warplanes had destroyed the Arab air force on the ground and this left the Arab ground forces bereft of top cover. The Israeli tanks made short shrift of the JS3s and the more modern T-54s in an enveloping manoeuvre, which allowed them to attack the heavy Soviet tanks from behind. In the mobile warfare of the Sinai, the Israelis advanced rapidly to the Suez Canal, brushing aside the tanks of the Egyptian Army. At one point, Israeli and Egyptian tanks became so entangled that the Israeli general Avraham Yoffe ordered his tanks to move sharply to the right of the road and then shoot any machines that stayed where they were. It was all over in less than four days. Basil

Liddell Hart reckoned the 'Six-Day' War was the 'perfect *Blitzkrieg*', and the 'superb' and 'subtle' operation a vindication of his own theories. Egyptian losses were heavy: of the 935 Egyptian tanks that had started the war, 820 had been lost by the end of hostilities (291 T-54s, 82 T-55s, 251 T-34/85s, 72 JS 3s, 51 SU-100s, 29 PT-76s and some 50 Shermans and M4/FL10s). Israeli losses were some 122 tanks, many of which were able to be repaired as the Israelis controlled the battlefield.

On the Golan front between the Israelis and Syrians, the Syrian tanks proved to be no match for the modern Israeli armour. The Syrian armoured force defending the Golan Heights consisted of the 14th and 44th Armour Brigades and was made up of wartime PzKpfw IVs, T-34s, T-54s and SU-100s. On 9 June, the Israelis assaulted the Syrian positions and, while there was none of the large-scale tank engagements of the Sinai front, the Israelis lost many tanks in taking the hilly and difficult Golan Heights from the Syrians.

THE 1973 YOM KIPPUR WAR

In order to protect the eastern bank of the Suez Canal, Israel established the Bar-Lev Line of fortifications. Some argued strongly against this. Israel's Tal and paratroop general Ariel Sharon reckoned that such rigid defence contradicted the Israeli doctrine of mobile warfare; rather, the armour should be held back to counterattack any crossing of the canal.

BELOW: The next generation of Soviet armour – an Egyptian T-62 in Sinai in 1973. The Arabs were largely supplied with equipment by the Soviet Union, while the Israelis relied on the West, particularly France and the United States.

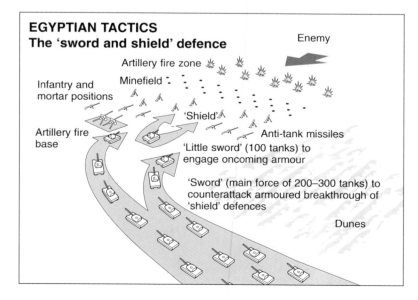

ABOVE: A column of Israeli M48 medium tanks moving south to the Suez Canal during the Yom Kippur War. The fighting in 1973 initially proved chastening for the Israelis, as they underrated their Egyptian opponents before hastily counter-attacking. They suffered very heavily at the hands of Egyptian infantry equipped with Soviet anti-tank missiles.

BELOW: The 'sword and shield' tactics used by the Egyptians in 1967 followed tactical doctrine devised by their Soviet advisers.

Tal and the Israeli advocates of the tank were convinced that Israel could not afford to be drawn into a defensive war of attrition, which it would inevitably lose. 'So that is why we gave the priority to the offensive,' said Tal. He continued:

'The tool on land, the tool to wage an offensive war on land, especially in the Middle East, is the armoured mobile formation. So by nature we had to act in the manner, along the lines of *Blitzkrieg*, you see. So even if there were no theories of the *Blitzkrieg*, we would do it, because the situation forced us to do it.'

Yet during the build-up to the war of 1973, the Israeli troops on the Bar-Lev Line were forced to endure frequent bombardment in their defensive bunkers. When the Syrians and Egyptians attacked simultaneously in October, the Israelis

found themselves fighting desperate defensive battles and forced to launch what Tal described as 'piecemeal counterattacks against large well organised forces – in direct contradiction to the principles of armoured warfare'. The success of 1967 had bred a sense of complacency in the Israelis, yet the Syrians and Egyptians had prepared carefully for the attack in 1973. They were not the second-rate enemy the Israelis believed them to be.

THE DAY OF ATONEMENT

The Syrians and Egyptians attacked simultaneously on 6 October 1973: Yom Kippur, the Jewish Day of Atonement. The Syrians attacked across the Golan Heights and the Egyptians crossed the Suez Canal, assaulting the Bar-Lev Line and breaking into the Sinai. Both Arab armies showed considerable skill and innovation in their initial operations. The Syrians had assembled their large tank force in front of the Israelis on Mount Hermon, but employing their tanks in hull-down defensive positions convinced the Israelis that the build-up was not for offensive purposes.

On 6 October, three Syrian mechanised divisions, the 5th, 7th and 9th, well equipped with about 600 Soviet T-54s, T-55s and the latest T-64s, rolled forwards in the wake of an artillery barrage and air strikes. They were followed by 1st and 3rd Armoured Divisions and their three mechanised or armoured brigades, adding another 1000 main battle tanks to the Syrian strength. As one Israeli tank commander recalled,

'I never knew there were so many tanks in all the world.'

The Syrians' three spearhead brigades were tasked with cracking the Israelis' defences, to allow the armoured divisions to break through into the Galilean hills beyond. They faced some substantial Israeli defences, in particular a 4.5m (15ft) deep anti-tank ditch and extensive minefields. The Syrians employed a whole range of specialised armour – armoured bulldozers, bridge-layer tanks and flail tanks – in an effort to breach the Israeli line. Their armour was protected from air attack by anti-aircraft missiles. Yet, despite surprise and a wealth of new weaponry, it was not enough. As Lieutenant Colonel Avigdor Kahalani, commander of the 77th Battalion of the famous 7th Armoured Brigade said of the new T-62, 'This newest ghost in the Soviet–Syrian arsenal was as destroyable as the T-54 and T-55 which preceded it.'

Although the 50 or so Centurions of 7th Armoured Brigade were hopelessly outnumbered, the Israelis put up extraordinary resistance. Moshe Dayan, now Israeli defence minister, had ordered the brigade to stand and fight, and this they did. Its commander, Colonel Ben Gal, profited from his excellent combination of tank infantry and artillery firepower. The Centurion tanks, using the British system of tank ranging with the secondary armament as a preliminary to main armament fire, ensured a large number of long-range and first-shot kills. However, the Syrians kept coming in almost endless numbers until the Israelis were firing at almost point-blank range. After four days of desperate fighting, Kahalani was able to report to Ben Gal: 'We've stopped them. It's quite a sight. The valley is full of burning and abandoned hardware.' Indeed, the Israelis were able, once they had brought reinforcements, to shift onto the offensive, retaking the areas lost in the Syrians' initial advance and finally moving into Syria itself. A mere 177 Israeli tanks had defeated a massive force of 1400 Syrian machines.

BELOW: The Super Sherman seen on the Syrian Front in October 1973. This World War II veteran served the Israeli Defence Force well throughout most of the second half of the twentieth century. Armed with a French 105mm (4.1in) gun, this tank held its own in the Yom Kippur War.

The Egyptian force that attacked across the Suez Canal was even larger, with 1700 tanks and 2500 armed vehicles. They, too, managed to prepare for their attack without the Israelis noticing and, on the night of 5 October, launched an amphibious assault across the Suez Canal that captured the Israeli Bar-Lev Line. Using high-powered water hoses and bulldozers, the Egyptians shifted the sand embankment built by the Israelis as a defensive measure on the east bank of the canal and, using Soviet-supplied pontoon bridges and ferries, armour and infantry were across the canal in sizeable numbers by 7 October.

LIMITED ADVANCE

By 8 October, Egypt had pushed the 2nd and 3rd Armies, some 100,000 men and over 1000 tanks, across the canal and had established a defensive perimeter along the east bank. Meanwhile, the integrated ZSU (a Russian mobile anti-aircraft gun system) SAM (surface-to-air) air-defence systems gave top cover and countered the feared Israeli air strikes. The Arabs'

widespread use of wire-guided anti-tank missiles (such as the 'Snapper' and the 'Sagger') also blunted the Israelis' traditional superiority in tanks. As the Egyptian chief of staff, Saad el Shazly noted, the Israeli armoured response was 'the first combat between the essentially World War II concept of armour and infantry weapons of the next generation'.

The Israelis unwisely and hastily counterattacked with two armoured divisions in the Sinai on 8 October, only to see their armour brigades ambushed with heavy losses by the Egyptians and the surviving tank crews paraded on Egyptian television. As the war unfolded, the Israelis instituted countermeasures against the Arab missiles and SAM batteries, but at first these cheap and portable weapons gave the Arabs the military edge. The Israelis lost 260 tanks in two days. An Israeli tank commander provides a account of his first encounter with the new weapons. He noticed what he initially thought were old tree trunks dotted amongst the dunes. These turned out to be men and he wondered why

BELOW: A column of Israeli M48 tanks and jeeps rolls forwards past watching infantry as they return to the east bank of the Suez Canal after the Yom Kippur War. The Israeli Defence Force has been the most impressive exponent of tank warfare in the post-war world.

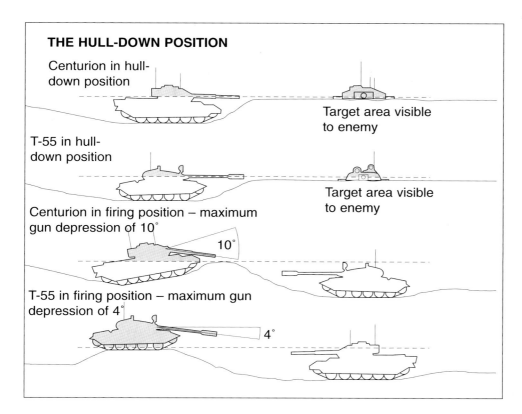

THE HULL-DOWN POSITION

Centurion in hull-down position

Target area visible to enemy

T-55 in hull-down position

Target area visible to enemy

Centurion in firing position – maximum gun depression of 10°

10°

T-55 in firing position – maximum gun depression of 4°

4°

LEFT: This diagram shows how the Israeli Centurion's ability to depress its main gun by 10 degrees gave it a significant advantage over the Egyptian and Syrian T-55s, as the Centurion could effectively engage the Arab tanks from a hull-down position without exposing its more vulnerable parts.

they were standing there still and solitary as his tanks raced towards them. Then, 'suddenly all hell broke loose. A barrage of missiles was being fired at us. Many of our tanks were hit. We had never come up against anything like this before.'

The Arabs' military success on 6 October surprised the Egyptian leader Anwar Sadat and unduly emboldened him to further military action, as he wanted to push on and make even bigger gains. Shazly argued that further advances into Sinai would take the Egyptian ground forces out of the range of their SAMs and expose them to air attack by the Israelis or, as he put it: 'Tanks without air cover are sitting ducks.'

The second phase of the October war began on 14 October with Sadat's ill-judged offensive. On 14 October, the Egyptians launched a huge tank offensive in the Sinai, involving some 2000 tanks on both sides, surpassed only in numbers of tanks by the battle of Kursk in World War II. The Israelis had been able to shift strong armoured reinforcements from the Golan and therefore the tank ratio was only two to one in the Egyptians' favour. This was mitigated even more by the better quality of the Israeli tanks. The Israelis also knew the ground and their air force was now managing to play a role.

The Israeli defenders stopped both flanks of the Egyptian advance, forcing the Egyptian commanders to commit most of their reserves. They put almost 1000 tanks in the field that day and lost at least half of them. The Israelis needed to end the war quickly, however, and decided to attack across the canal in an effort to take the Egyptian armies from behind and clear the SAM sites in the area. Thus, on 15 October, Major General

BELOW: A Syrian P-55 mine clearance tank seen after the ceasefire agreement in 1974. The P-55 was an adapted T-55 fitted with strengthened metal rollers to detonate any mines in its path.

ABOVE: An Israeli Defence Force Centurion stationed in an overwatch position in South Lebanon in 1982, after the Israeli invasion of that country. The Centurion, a British design dating from the very end of World War II, was upgunned to carry a 105mm (4.1in) gun. Like the Sherman, the Centurion served the Israeli Defence Force for many decades.

Arik Sharon drove his forces towards the canal. One of his brigades hit the southern flank of the Egyptian 21st Armoured Division and a large tank battle developed in an area known to the Israelis as the Chinese Farm. Sharon did, however, manage to get some tanks across the canal, plus a brigade of paratroops. Once a bridge was thrown across, large amounts of Israeli armour crossed the canal and drove into the Egyptian rear. As the Egyptian general Shazly noted: 'swift armoured thrusts with close air support against unprepared men was the sort of war that the Israelis excelled'. The Egyptian 3rd Army was surrounded and cut off at Suez City and, by the time Sadat managed to secure a ceasefire, the Israelis were also advancing north to cut off the Egyptian 2nd Army.

The Yom Kippur War therefore was an Israeli victory, but one bought at some cost, not least some 830 battle tanks. Many Western commentators gleefully pronounced the war proof of the 'death of the tank' and that the new generation of anti-tank missiles such as the 'Sagger' and also the handheld RPG 7 had proved immensely effective, perhaps causing about a third of Israeli tank casualties around the canal. This, however, was wishful thinking, as there can be no doubt that the tank retained its dominance in land warfare. It was the weapon with which the Israelis retook

the initiative and was instrumental in their defeat of both the Egyptians and the Syrians. There was no thought within the Israeli Army of reducing the role of the tank in future and they pressed on with a new design, the Merkava, implementing the lessons learnt during the 1973 war.

THE MERKAVA

The Israelis could ill afford the losses to their tank crews, and thus decided to produce a tank that enhanced a crew's ability to survive. To quote Patrick Wright in his recent work *Tank*, tank design represents a 'triangular reconciliation of three partly contradictory parameters: firepower, mobility and protection. A tank is inevitably a compromise because gains according to one parameter often entail losses in another and every tank producing nation has evolved its own tank triangle as its designers and engineers have struggled to come to terms with this intractable fact.'

Thus, in their new tank design, the Merkava, the Israelis gave priority to protection. However, Major General Israel Tal rejected the whole concept of the tank triangle. He claimed that the Merkava is unique because it is founded upon the belief that protection should not be considered as a separate parameter alongside mobility and firepower: 'what we say is that the tank is a synthesis or a compromise between firepower and

mobility and not the synthesis of the three parameters'. He stressed that 'you strive to produce a machine that would provide firepower and mobility. Protection is only a by-product like the gun, the engine and everything else.' This synthesis, according to Tal, 'is our original approach and the most important difference between our design and the rest of the world'.

Traditional tank design largely considers protection a matter of armoured plate, shielding the crew and the working systems of the tank. The Israelis, however, reconceived the concept of protection. Protection contributes to mobility, enabling the tank to close with the enemy, and also to firepower, as most weapon systems are more effective at closer range. To quote Tal again: 'so in that respect, the capability of the tank to launch a very high volume of fire is an outcome not only of the gun but also its protection, whether it can absorb many direct hits and face the enemy close. Its firepower is stronger and naturally in the same way its mobility is increased too. So this is the most basic thing that makes the Merkava a different tank from any other tank.'

The Israelis also divided the concept of protection. The tank's armour protected itself and its systems, and also the crew. According to Tal: 'these two parameters are completely different from one another. We can provide protection to people inside a tank, many many more times than to the entire system we call a tank.' The Merkava was designed with this in mind and the survival of the crew was the most important factor. The crew are placed at the centre of the vehicle, with the engine in front of them to provide additional protection. It is estimated that 75 per cent of the weight of the Merkava is involved in the protection of the crew, whereas, in a conventional tank, the proportion may only be 50–55 per cent. Indeed, the result is a very tough tank, which does not have much propensity to burn, traditionally a terrible killer of tank crews. The IDF estimated 26 per cent of soldiers wounded in battle would suffer from burns, but the Merkava is designed to prevent this. The fighting compartment is entirely dry and electrically operated, and the crew have no contact with fuel or even hydraulic oil.

THE LEBANON

Not one of the 50 or so soldiers wounded in the Merkava in the Lebanon suffered burns as the result of fire. Tanks in the Lebanon have taken numerous hits without being penetrated. It is a tank created by soldiers out of their experience and it has served well in the Lebanon. The Merkava spearheaded the 1982 invasion and was instrumental in the mauling inflicted on Syria's 1st Armoured Division.

ABOVE: The best tank in the world? The superlative Merkava. Designed in the wake of the experiences of the Yom Kippur War, where the IDF suffered serious losses to its highly trained and extremely valuable tank crews, the Merkava is an extremely tough armoured fighting vehicle with protection of the crew at the absolute centre of its concept. To this end, uniquely in modern tanks, the engine is mounted at the front of the tank to give added protection.

CHAPTER ELEVEN

LIMITED WAR: 1945 ONWARDS

Total, open warfare has been rare since 1945, but tank crews have had to learn to fight limited wars, each bound by their own rules.

T his study has generally concentrated on the use of the tank in high-intensity war – usually total war – such as World War I and World War II and, arguably, the Arab–Israeli conflict. However, the tank has been used in many minor conflicts and limited wars. The theory of limited war grew out of the US retreat from a strategy of massive retaliation, a somewhat inflexible doctrine which tended to exacerbate a crisis and risked triggering a nuclear exchange. Thus, in an effort to introduce more flexibility into US foreign and military policy, and to contain Communist expansion in peripheral areas, they came up with 'Limited War Theory', and exercised restraint in political aims, mobilisation of resources, geography and weaponry. The wars examined below all conform to this pattern, at least in terms of US involvement. This does not imply that the wars were anything but

LEFT: Master of the Battlefield – the M1A1 Abrams in the Gulf War of 1991. American armoured technology and design, and the 'AirLand Battle' were emphatically vindicated during the war against Saddam Hussein's Iraqi forces. Sophisticated computer technology allowed tanks, aircraft and missiles to combine in the effort to knock out the Iraqi forces. To quote one Iraqi battalion commander, 'When I went to Kuwait I had 39 tanks. After six weeks of air bombardment, I had 32 left. After twenty minutes in actions against the M1s, I had none.'

TANK WARFARE

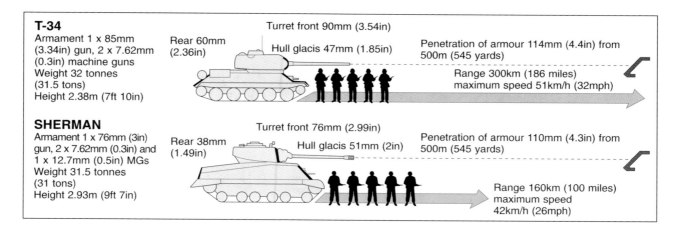

T-34
Armament 1 x 85mm
(3.34in) gun, 2 x 7.62mm
(0.3in) machine guns
Weight 32 tonnes
(31.5 tons)
Height 2.38m (7ft 10in)

Rear 60mm
(2.36in)

Turret front 90mm (3.54in)

Hull glacis 47mm (1.85in)

Penetration of armour 114mm (4.4in) from
500m (545 yards)

Range 300km (186 miles)
maximum speed 51km/h (32mph)

SHERMAN
Armament 1 x 76mm (3in)
gun, 2 x 7.62mm (0.3in) and
1 x 12.7mm (0.5in) MGs
Weight 31.5 tonnes
(31 tons)
Height 2.93m (9ft 7in)

Rear 38mm
(1.49in)

Turret front 76mm (2.99in)

Hull glacis 51mm (2in)

Penetration of armour 110mm (4.3in) from
500m (545 yards)

Range 160km (100 miles)
maximum speed
42km/h (26mph)

ABOVE: A comparison between the main protagonists of the Korean War. The North Koreans were equipped with the excellent T-34/85, but their tactics were lacking.

BELOW: A US Army Sherman tank in the harsh, mountainous terrain of Korea. The geography of Korea did not suit extensive armoured operations.

total for the unfortunate populations of Korea and Vietnam, nor do they provide anything but case studies. The use of the tank in the post-war world has been extensive and it would be impossible to examine its role in all conflicts. Thus the various wars in Africa, the Indo–Pakistan conflict of 1971 – which involved the extensive use of tanks, with 45 Pakistani M47 Pattons and 15 Indian Centurions destroyed in two days of bitter fighting – China's numerous wars with its neighbours, and the Iran–Iraq War are all arbitrarily ignored.

THE KOREAN WAR

The Korean War was very much a limited war for the United States, which restricted its commitment both in terms of manpower and weaponry. However, it did see the first encounter between US and Soviet tanks. The war was fought largely using armour which had entered service during World War II, and the terrain of the predominantly mountainous country did not suit armoured operations. In June 1950, 100,000 Communist North Korean troops attacked South Korea, capturing the capital, Seoul, on 28 June. The North

160

Korean Army pushed south to expel the remaining enemy troops from the peninsula, spearheaded by their 150 Soviet-supplied T-34/85s. Tanks of the North Korean 105th Brigade formed the van of the attack. With three regiments of 40 T-34 tanks apiece, the 105th Brigade, named in May 1949, had been formed in Sa-dong in 1947 as the 115th Tank regiment. It was the North Korean Army's elite unit, and given the nickname of 'The Tiger's Cave Sadong Unit'. Using this armoured formation, the North Koreans had managed to break the South Korean Army. However, the South Korean Army enjoyed rapid US support, led by General Douglas MacArthur. North Korean tanks were brought up against American armour, as the Americans attempted to first halt and then roll back their advance.

To combat the T-34s, the US Army had the M26 Pershing, armed with a 90mm (3.5in) gun, and World War II

Shermans. At first, the T-34s met little real opposition. The South Korean Army was poorly equipped and the North Koreans swept all before them. The first encounter between the Americans and North Korean T-34s involved lighter M24s ('Chaffees') of the American 24th Infantry Division. In July 1950, three M24s fought a delaying action against a powerful force of T-34/85s. In an unequal contest, two M24s were lost, but not before knocking out one T-34. These early encounters were salutary for the Americans, and left them with the uneasy feeling that the T-34 was impervious to their weapons.

The M26 Pershing was underpowered for the hilly terrain of the Korean peninsula and at first the Americans had to rely on their Shermans to counter the North Korean armour. But improvements to the M26 and the Shermans (M4A3) gradually gave them the edge. In a series of engagements at

BELOW: A Sherman of the 2nd US Infantry Division operating in the fire-support role in Korea in July 1952. The establishment of air superiority by UN forces and the obvious ascendancy of American armoured training and tactics meant that, for the most part, UN tanks in combat provided direct-fire support for the infantry.

Obang-ni ridge and in a valley near Taegu known as the 'Bowling Alley', large numbers of T-34s were destroyed by ground-attack aircraft, the fire of M-26 tanks and 88mm (3.45in) rockets. This engagement re-established American confidence and shattered the legend of T-34 invincibility. By the end of the war, superior American tanks and training proved themselves against the North Koreans, and achieved kill ratios of roughly five to one. Yet US dominance of the air ensured that the North Koreans and their Chinese allies had no opportunity to mass their precious armour for concerted operations. For the most part, American tanks and also those of their United Nations allies, such as the British with their new Centurions, provided a means of direct fire support for the infantry.

VIETNAM

Vietnam also corresponded to US limited war theory. The political aim was to preserve the South Vietnamese regime; attempting to overthrow the Communist North might well have widened the war to include the Soviet Union and China. US military involvement was geographically

purely limited to operations in the south, with the odd incursion across the border into Cambodia and Laos. Furthermore, the United States did not employ its full range of weaponry. But, although nuclear bombs were not used, they did employ a limited number of tanks.

As in Korea, the terrain in Vietnam did not lend itself to tank operations. The French had used armour to limited effect during their 10-year struggle with the Communist insurgents between 1946 and 1956. A number of Chaffee light tanks had provided fire support during the disastrous French defeat at Dien Bien Phu in 1954, and French mobile operations had been similarly unsuccessful. Therefore, as US commitment to South Vietnam increased in the early 1960s as the pressure from the North grew, the US military had serious doubts as to the utility of tanks. The South Vietnamese Army used M24 Chaffee tanks and M113 armoured personnel carriers to some effect, but the United States may not have deployed tanks at all had not the two Marine Corps battalions sent to Vietnam in 1965 brought their organic armour with them. The jungle over which much of the Vietnam War was fought precluded

BELOW: An American infantryman inspects a wrecked North Korean T-34/85. Although an extremely potent tank in its day, when crewed by North Koreans, the T-34/85 failed to achieve the success that it had had in the hands of the Red Army five or six years earlier against the Germans.

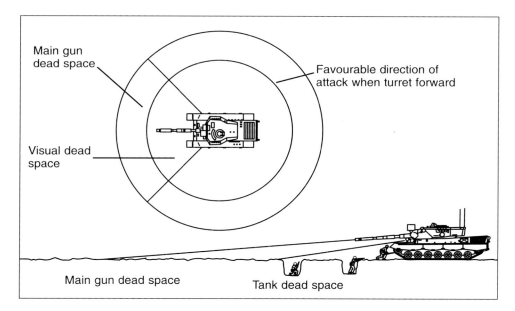

Main gun
dead space

Favourable direction of
attack when turret forward

Visual dead
space

Main gun dead space

Tank dead space

LEFT: A modern main battle
tank can be vulnerable to
infantry armed with anti-
tank weaponry. The visibility
from a tank is poor and
concealed soldiers can wait
for a tank to approach them,
unobserved. A favoured tactic
in World War II was for
infantry to allow tanks to
roll past them before
engaging them in their
poorly armoured rear.

their widespread employment, but the M48A3 Patton medium tank proved a useful addition to the US arsenal in certain tactical situations. Tanks were used to protect convoys and as a rapid reaction force if convoys or patrols ran into trouble. They also were involved in numerous search-and-destroy missions and were a useful addition to perimeter defence of US bases. In urban operations,

such as the battle for Hue, the Patton provided vital direct-fire support. Its 90mm (3.5in) gun proved useful against bunkers, although, given the type of combat that they were involved in, the tank crews stowed very few armoured piercing rounds. The main mix of shell types was HE, white phosphorous and a horribly effective flechette anti-personnel round called a beehive. The main

BELOW: Infantry of the 3rd US Division accompany a M26/46 Pershing on patrol in South Korea in August 1954. The Pershing replaced the Sherman in US service.

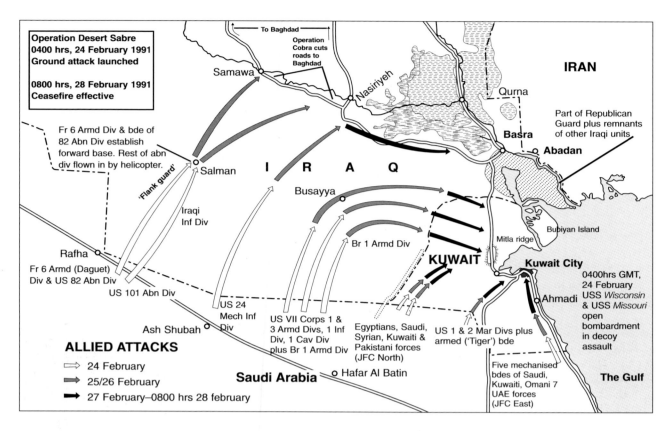

Operation Desert Sabre
0400 hrs, 24 February 1991
Ground attack launched

0800 hrs, 28 February 1991
Ceasefire effective

To Baghdad

Operation
Cobra cuts
roads to
Baghdad

Samawa

Nasiriyeh

IRAN

Qurna

Basra

Abadan

Part of Republican
Guard plus remnants
of other Iraqi units

Fr 6 Armd Div & bde of
82 Abn Div establish
forward base. Rest of abn
div flown in by helicopter.

Salman

'Flank guard'

I R A Q

Busayya

Iraqi
Inf Div

Br 1 Armd Div

Bubiyan Island

Mitla ridge

KUWAIT

Kuwait City

Rafha

Fr 6 Armd (Daguet)
Div & US 82 Abn Div

US 101 Abn Div

US 24
Mech Inf
Div

US VII Corps 1 &
3 Armd Divs, 1 Inf
Div, 1 Cav Div
plus Br 1 Armd Div

Egyptians, Saudi,
Syrian, Kuwaiti &
Pakistani forces
(JFC North)

US 1 & 2 Mar Divs plus
armed ('Tiger') bde

Ahmadi

0400hrs GMT,
24 February
USS *Wisconsin*
& USS *Missouri*
open
bombardment
in decoy
assault

Ash Shubah

ALLIED ATTACKS

⇨ 24 February

➡ 25/26 February

➡ 27 February–0800 hrs 28 february

Saudi Arabia

Hafar Al Batin

Five mechanised
bdes of Saudi,
Kuwaiti, Omani 7
UAE forces
(JFC East)

The Gulf

ABOVE: The 1991 Gulf War took place in perfect tank country. The long-range visibility, excellent weather and flat terrain gave the more sophisticated tanks of the Allies a significant advantage over the Soviet-supplied Iraqi vehicles. In a classic hook manoeuvre, Operation Desert Sabre outflanked the Iraqi defenders and hit what remained of their defences from the rear.

Communist anti-tank weaponry was based around light man-portable systems such as the RPG-7 – which the Patton was reasonably secure against, although the M113 was much less so – the recoilless rifle, and mines. Tank-to-tank combat was non-existent.

In 1969, the new and extremely unpopular American light tank, the M551 Sheridan, was committed to combat. It was unreliable, prone to burn if penetrated, and comparatively vulnerable to mines, although its 152mm (6in) gun/missile-launcher fired an extremely effective beehive round. The Australian 1st Armoured Regiment used the heavily armoured Centurion, which was immune to almost all North Vietnamese countermeasures. By 1969, the United States and its allies were deploying over 600 tanks in Vietnam. Although militarily speaking, such firepower enabled them to inflict massive casualties on their enemy, politically it could not win the war for the United States.

THE GULF WAR: 1990–1991

The experience of the United States in Vietnam led them to rethink the strategy of limited war. Moving away from the attritional policies they had employed in

that war, they adopted the doctrine of 'Manoeuvre War', as characterised by 'AirLand Battle', which was intended to allow US forces to fight to win within the limited parameters set out by the politicians. Saddam Hussein's Iraqi army invaded Kuwait on 2 August 1990. Backed by the relevant United Nations resolutions, the United States, in conjunction with a vast coalition of her Western allies, sympathetic Arab states and nations from all over the world, set about putting AirLand Battle into practice to gain the limited aim of liberating Kuwait. They were not concerned with the invasion of Iraq, nor with the overthrow of the Iraqi leader.

The Iraqis possessed a large and, at least on paper, formidable army, of 955,000 men and 5500 main battle tanks. These were a mixture of T-55s, T-64s and 1000 modern T-72s. A large proportion of these sat threateningly on the Saudi Arabian border. The first American troops reached Saudi Arabia on 9 August and, within a month, the UN coalition had amassed 665,000 troops and 3600 tanks in theatre. From a military point of view, it might have been better for Saddam Hussein to attack further and inflict an unacceptable number of casualties before the coalition was properly in place. From a political perspective, he could have pulled out of Kuwait, retaining perhaps Bubiyan Island and some of the northern oilfields. Instead, however, he simply continued to pour troops into Kuwait, packing some 43 divisions into the country and digging them in along the frontier. Many of the Iraqis' older tanks were also dug in into this defensive line. Saddam Hussein held back his best formation, the Republican Guard, ready to counterattack the Coalition forces that had been worn down by breaking through his dug-in divisions.

Although the possibility of a frontal assault coupled with a amphibious landing was seriously considered, the coalition commander, US General Norman Schwarzkopf, decided against

this, preferring instead to institute a large, sweeping encirclement of the bulk of the Iraqi forces by driving his best armoured forces through the weaker-held Iraqi border to the west before turning behind the enemy. Before he would commit his troops, however, he decided that the Iraqis needed softening up. Thus he launched a prolonged preparatory air bombardment on the night of 16 January 1991. The Allies rapidly gained air supremacy and then set about degrading the Iraqi ability to fight. Command and control targets were destroyed with precision guided missiles, while Iraqi Army positions were carpet-bombed by B-52s night after night. Despite the adoption of manoeuvre warfare, this was attrition in its classic form.

BELOW: An M48 medium tank provides direct-fire support for American ground troops in Vietnam. With tank-to-tank combat almost non-existent, this was the main role of US armour during this war and thus tanks carried a load of HE, phosphorous and flechette, rather than conventional armour-piercing shells.

RIGHT: The process of aiming and firing the main armament of a tank. Once the gunner has successfully 'lased' the target, on-board computers calculate the necessary deflection and automatically point the gun to the correct angle for a hit, leaving the gunner only to fire the gun on the commander's instructions.

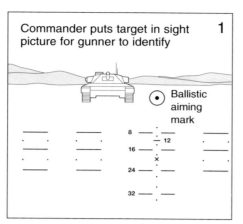

Commander puts target in sight picture for gunner to identify 1

Ballistic aiming mark

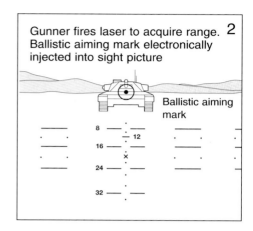

Gunner fires laser to acquire range. 2 Ballistic aiming mark electronically injected into sight picture

Ballistic aiming mark

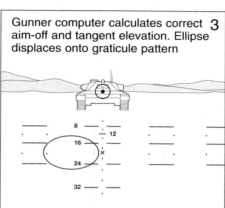

Gunner computer calculates correct 3 aim-off and tangent elevation. Ellipse displaces onto graticule pattern

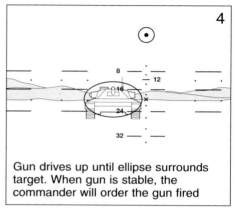

Gun drives up until ellipse surrounds target. When gun is stable, the commander will order the gun fired

To keep Saddam's forces in place, Schwarzkopf based the mechanised and armoured forces of Kuwait, Saudi Arabia, Oman, Qatar and United Arab Emirates, plus two US Marine Divisions and a brigade from US 2nd Armoured Division, in front of the bulk of the Iraqi Army in Kuwait. The main armoured punch would come from the US VII Corps made up of 1st and 3rd US Armoured Divisions, 1st Armoured Cavalry Division, 1st Infantry Division (Mechanised) and British 1st Armoured Division. Further west still, the US XVIII Airborne Corps, comprising French 6th Light Armoured Division, US 82nd Airborne, 101st Airborne (Air Assault), 24th Infantry (Mechanised) Divisions, and 3rd Armoured Cavalry Regiment, would use its airborne and land mobility to move as quickly as possible through Iraqi territory to establish a blocking position on the Euphrates.

ASSAULT ON KUWAIT

The land assault began on 24 February 1991. US Marines and Arab members of the coalition began an assault on Iraqi positions in southern Kuwait. Far to the west, the XVIII Airborne Corps sprinted deep into Iraq. By the end of the day, 101st Airborne, using helicopters, had established a position 80km (50 miles) across the border. The main armoured thrust from General Fred Franks's VII Corps was launched that afternoon ahead of schedule, as Schwarzkopf had received intelligence that the Iraqis were beginning to withdraw from Kuwait City, destroying everything of value. The US 1st Infantry Division punched the hole through the Iraqi line, and British 1st Armoured Division, operating exactly as a Soviet-style pperational manoeuvre group, passed through the American formation to exploit the breach in the Iraqi defences. In conjunction with the American divisions, they drove north before turning eastwards to engage the bulk of the Iraqi Army.

Iraqi resistance was almost non-existent; the demoralised troops had been pounded into virtual submission by Coalition air power. Command and communications structure and, perhaps more seriously, unit cohesion had broken down. The Iraqis surrendered in droves. Only the Republican Guard put up

anything resembling organised resistance, but the divisions that attempted to take on the American and British armour of VII Corps were promptly destroyed. The forces driving into southern Kuwait had

little problem in overcoming the broken Iraqi forces. Major Richard Shirreff, of Challenger-equipped B Squadron of 14th/20th King's Hussars of British 1st Armoured Division, provides an excellent

ABOVE: British 1st Armoured Division in the Gulf – a mixture of Challenger tanks, Warrior personnel carriers and various support vehicles.

DISCARDING SABOT ROUNDS

Armour-piercing fin-stabilised discarding sabot (APFSDS) rounds owe their strange shape to the need for maximum velocity. The radius of the projectile is much smaller than that of the gun, so the projectile is fired from a disproportionately large cartridge case

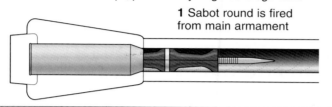

1 Sabot round is fired from main armament

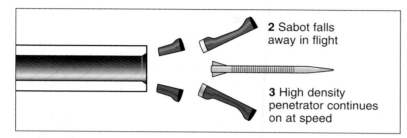

2 Sabot falls away in flight

3 High density penetrator continues on at speed

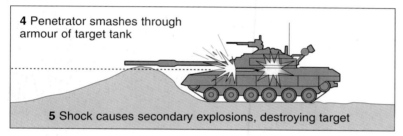

4 Penetrator smashes through armour of target tank

5 Shock causes secondary explosions, destroying target

ABOVE: Modern anti-tank ammunition is usually of the penetrator type, relying on sheer velocity to destroy a target. The impact of a solid tungsten penetrator literally smashes up the tank with the subsequent shock waves. The fins on the penetrator give it much greater stability.

RIGHT: Tanks from the Egyptian 3rd Armoured Brigade use phosphorous to create a smokescreen to cover their advance across the Iraqi desert.

description of the nature of war in the Gulf in 1991:

'At first light (26 February) we had a clearer view of our night's work. Burning tank hulks and the debris of battle littered the desert; disconsolate groups of Iraqis wandered about in a daze looking for someone to accept their surrender! All the T-55s destroyed by B Squadron with APFSDS or HESH had been dug in facing south and most had died with their guns traversed right as they faced the sudden, deadly threat from the flank. A few been destroyed as they attempted to reverse out of their tank scraps. Seldom can the dangers of digging tanks in as mobile pill boxes have been more graphically illustrated.'

The US 24th Mechanised Infantry Division reached the southern bank of the Euphrates, isolating Iraqi forces in Kuwait, save for the Basra road, up which the Iraqis fled, pounded by Coalition airpower. When Coalition forces reached the road, they were appalled by the destruction wrought. Although important elements managed to escape before the ceasefire was reached on 26 February, the Iraqi Army had been decisively defeated. Altogether 42 Iraqi divisions had been destroyed. Estimates of the numbers of

Iraqi dead vary from 25,000 to 100,000: most commentators accept a rough figure in the area of 60,000. As many as 80,000 prisoners were taken and 3700 tanks were captured or destroyed. Coalition casualties were extraordinarily light, with only 150 killed of the 500 taken. Western tanks – the M1 Abrams and the Challenger in particular – emphatically proved their superiority over the Soviet tanks used by the Iraqis. Their ability to fight effectively at night was particularly important. Western armoured tactics were also vindicated, although the AirLand Battle employed in the Gulf had included large elements of attrition. Here was all-arms *Blitzkrieg* applied with overwhelming effectiveness and at minimal cost to the attacker.

THE FUTURE

The demise of the tank has been forecast many times. From its mediocre debut on the Somme, through the drastic reduction of the tank's strategic role at the end of World War II, to the use of anti-tank missiles during the Yom Kippur War, the power of anti-tank defences has more

than once apparently signalled the end of the tank's mastery of the battlefield. The struggle between armour and anti-armour continues, and neither side has gained a clear advantage. Compound armour such as that pioneered by Chobham has seriously degraded the efficiency of many chemical-energy based HEAT (High Explosive Anti-Tank) and HESH (High Explosive Squash Head) shaped charge anti-tank weapons, which is the basis of all anti-tank missiles, as well as some tank gun rounds. HEAT rounds use an explosive-backed cone to melt through the tank's armour plate, utilising the focused energy of hot gas, molten copper or plasma. HESH relies on its plastic explosive to distort on impact, increasing the area of contact between explosive and armoured plate. A shock wave is sent through the armour, which releases a scab of metal from the inside surface. Explosive Reactive Armour (ERA) is a useful and cheap additional protection and has used been by most major tank armies, either to up-armour their older tanks or to give additional protection to more modern tanks using

ABOVE: An M60 equipped with bulldozer and appliqué reactive armour blocks in the Gulf. In a throwback to Hobart's 'Funnies' of World War II, Coalition forces used a whole range of specialised armour to break through the considerable defences behind which the bulk of Iraqi forces sat.

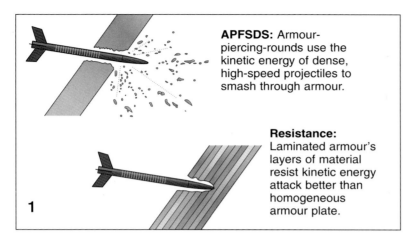

APFSDS: Armour-piercing-rounds use the kinetic energy of dense, high-speed projectiles to smash through armour.

Resistance: Laminated armour's layers of material resist kinetic energy attack better than homogeneous armour plate.

1

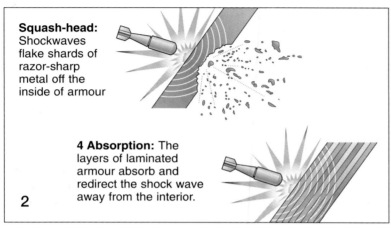

Squash-head: Shockwaves flake shards of razor-sharp metal off the inside of armour

4 Absorption: The layers of laminated armour absorb and redirect the shock wave away from the interior.

2

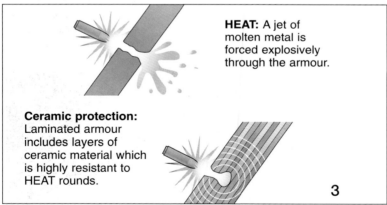

HEAT: A jet of molten metal is forced explosively through the armour.

Ceramic protection: Laminated armour includes layers of ceramic material which is highly resistant to HEAT rounds.

3

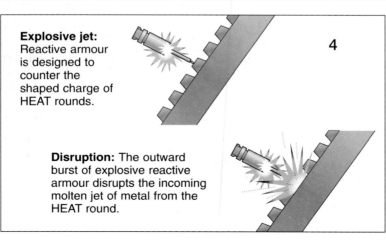

Explosive jet: Reactive armour is designed to counter the shaped charge of HEAT rounds.

4

Disruption: The outward burst of explosive reactive armour disrupts the incoming molten jet of metal from the HEAT round.

compound armour. In conjunction, these armours drastically reduce the usefulness of the current generation of infantry and helicopter mounted anti-tank weapon systems. However, helicopter and infantry weapons capable of overcoming reactive armour are beginning to enter service. These are tandem-shaped charge missiles which, carrying two shaped charges as they do, one going off after the other, might well penetrate compound or reactive armour, but probably not both. The effectiveness of these weapons is unproven and they are considerably heavier than traditional shaped charge weapons and much more difficult for a man to carry.

Most tank guns use solid shot projectiles that rely on kinetic energy (KE) for tank-to-tank combat. KE attacks have consistently been the most successful. Currently the only defence remains thick armour plate, which can be sloped for greater protection. The Rheinmetall smoothbore 120mm (4.7in) gun uses Armour Piercing Fin Stabilised Discarding Sabot (APFSDS) where the round's velocity is increased by fitting sabot fins that are stripped away by air resistance to reveal a long, thin arrow of hard metal – usually tungsten or depleted uranium – concentrating the energy from the gun and increasing penetration. These Rheinmetall guns, mounted on the US Army M1A1 and M1A2 Abrams, can produce muzzle velocities of 1650–1700m/s (1805–1860yds/s), which could comfortably destroy Iraqi T-72s at extreme ranges.

NEW ARMOURS

To produce such velocities requires a large and heavy gun, not the sort of thing infantry and helicopters can carry around. In response, depleted uranium armour will probably enter service in the next generation of tanks, unless health concerns over its use hold sway. More revolutionary still, the US Army Research Laboratory is working on armour systems based on Momentum Transfer Armour (MTA) technology to defeat KE attacks. MTA resembles the common ERA brick, but the laboratory's intention is to dispense with the high explosive normally associated with ERA and replace it with electromagnetic energy. The research remains far from practical application.

Other modern weapons attempt to target the areas of the tank where the armour is thinnest, such as its top. Top armour attack is typically undertaken by an air burst projectile which splits into submunitions (smaller projectiles or bomblets). These are usually individually guided to their target by its engine heat, infra-red or radar signature. However, such munitions are enormously expensive and can be defeated with comparatively simple countermeasures such as fitting a sheet of metal over the engine and thus shielding its infra-red signature. These submunitions rely on the shaped charge principle and can be defeated by reactive armour. The purpose of this argument is only to show that there is still no clear advantage between tanks' armour and anti-armour weapons. Since its introduction into warfare, there has never been a time when the tank has been totally invulnerable. This remains the case and thus its vulnerability, or invulnerability, should not be overstated.

Other systems have risen and vied for supremacy with the tank on the modern battlefield, most obviously the attack helicopter. The tank can be extremely at risk from the weapon systems carried by a helicopter. However, although the helicopter has high mobility and vast

firepower, it does not have the durability of the tank. It requires constant replenishment. It cannot loiter for extended periods, nor can it occupy ground. In the practice of manoeuvre warfare, a mobile, high-firepower and high-durability ground-based vehicle remains vital.

NEW GENERATION

The current generation and proposed next generation of tanks are not much different to their predecessors, at least in appearance. The Abrams M1A2 looks very much like the M1A1 upon which it is based. The differences are largely internal and electronic. In the aftermath of the Gulf War, the Americans discovered a number of cases of friendly fire, or blue-on-blue, casualties. These unfortunate incidents resulted from a lack of 'situational awareness', aggravated by the long combat ranges. As General Gordon Sullivan recalled: 'As we started down that road, we realised that with digital technology, we could have almost perfect situational awareness.' Full integration with all other arms was possible under airborne and satellite control. Troops could be familiarised with a theatre's terrain from the Defence Mapping Agency and the Topographic Engineering

OPPOSITE: Modern technology has had as great an impact on tank defensive systems as offensive systems. Ceramic or laminated armour can provide an effective defence against most forms of tank ammunition, and explosive reactive armour is a cheap way of improving a tank's safety. Reactive armour is often seen on older vehicles to compensate for their lack of laminated armour.

BELOW: A British Challenger II in the Kulen Vakuf area of Bosnia in 1996. Although armour has proved of limited utility in conflicts such as Vietnam and Afghanistan, the presence of heavy armour in the hands of peacekeeping forces in low-intensity operations such as those undertaken in the Balkans can have a useful calming effect on the warring factions.

RIGHT: French Leclerc tanks leaving the GIAT Industries Roanne factory for delivery to the French Army in January 1996. The Leclerc is an excellent design of main battle tank, but, after the end of the Cold War, the tank's role in a modern combat environment is being questioned and the huge fleets of armoured vehicles that once occupied central Europe have all been decommissioned or sold.

Centre before they were sent to fight in, say, Bosnia or Somalia.

The Americans are determined to dispense with Clausewitz's 'fog of war'. The M1A2 will have an expanded computer memory and be able to operate the wider battlefield management system. The Americans intend to put this in place across all platforms, as well as improved armour. It will be in service for a number of decades yet, as will the Challenger II, Leopard II, Leclerc and T-90 variants, all of which will be constantly upgraded over the next quarter of a century. It will also probably be replaced by the M1A3. What happens after that is another question. The

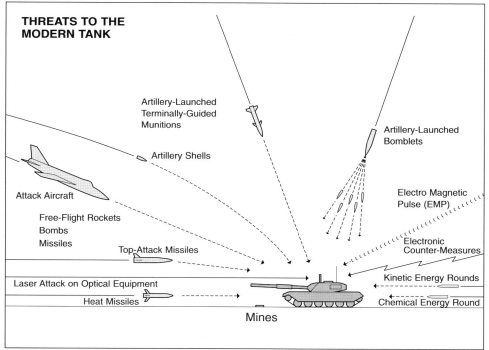

THREATS TO THE MODERN TANK

Artillery-Launched Terminally-Guided Munitions

Artillery Shells

Artillery-Launched Bomblets

Attack Aircraft

Free-Flight Rockets
Bombs
Missiles

Top-Attack Missiles

Electro Magnetic Pulse (EMP)

Electronic Counter-Measures

Laser Attack on Optical Equipment

Kinetic Energy Rounds

Heat Missiles

Chemical Energy Round

Mines

ABOVE: The M1A2 Abrams – the latest generation of American tank. Taking into account the lessons of the Gulf War, the M1A2 has a wide range of new electrical and electronic systems, the intention being to provide complete 'situational awareness' and avoid the friendly-fire incidents of the Gulf War.

LEFT: The battlefield is now such a threat-rich environment for the tank that many observers question its value to the modern army. However it seems likely that the tank will remain part of every professional army's arsenal for some time yet.

British firm Vickers has commissioned a light (40-tonne), plastic electric powered tank, which was revealed to the media in March 2000. The Americans talk in terms of their future main battle tank as 'riding on an electro-magnetic cushion'. Yet the concept remains what Sullivan describes as a 'mobile protected space with a direct fire weapon', or, in other words, a tank. While the future of military technology may well lie in nanotechnology and robotics, for the foreseeable future – that is, most of the twenty-first century – the twentieth-century concept of a weapon system that provides mobility, firepower and protection – the tank – will remain.

Bibliography

Barnet, Correlli *The Desert Generals*, Pan, London, 1960.

Bidwell, Shelford *World War III*, Hamlyn, London, 1978

Calovcoressi, Peter, Wint, Guy and Pritchard, John *Total War*, Penguin, London, 1989.

Carrel, Paul *Hitler Moves East, 1941-43*, Schiffer, Atglen, 1965.

Carrel, Paul *Scorched Earth: Hitler's War on Russia 1943-44*, Schiffer, Atglen, 1970.

Carrel, Paul *Invasion! They're Coming!* Schiffer, Atglen, 1995.

Chandler, David and Beckett, Ian (eds), *The Oxford Illustrated History of the British Army*, Oxford University Press, 1994.

Chamberlain, Peter and Ellis, Chris *Tanks of World War One*, London, 1969

Chaney, Otto P. *Zhukov*, David and Charles, Newton Abbot

Clancy, Tom *Armoured Warfare*, Harper Collins, London, 1996.

Clark, Alan *Barbarossa*, Cassell, London, 1965.

Condon, Richard W. *The Winter War: Russia against Finland*, London, 1973.

Cooper, Matthew and Lucas, James *Panzer*, Macdonald and Jane's, London, 1976.

Cooper, Matthew and Lucas, James *Panzer Grenadiers*, Macdonald and Jane's, London, 1977.

Dear, I.C.B. and Foot, M.R.D. *The Oxford Companion to the Second World War*, Oxford University Press, Oxford, 1995.

De La Billière, Peter *Storm Command*, Harper Collins, London, 1993.

De La Billière, Peter *Looking for Trouble*, Harper Collins, London, 1995.

Deighton, Len *Blitzkrieg. From the Rise of Hitler to the Fall of Dunkirk*. Grafton, London, 1985.

Edwards, Roger *Panzer: A Revolution in Warfare, 1939–1945*, Arms and Armour, London, 1989.

Eisenhower, Dwight D. *Crusade in Europe*, Heinemann, London, 1948.

Ellis, John *The Sharp End*, Pimlico, London, 1980.

Erikson, John *The Road to Berlin*, Weidenfeld and Nicolson, 1983.

D'Este, Carlo *Decision in Normandy*, Pan, London, 1983.

Ford, Roger *The Tiger Tank*, Spellmount, Staplehurst, 1998.

Forty, George *United States Tanks of World War II in Action*, Poole, 1983.

Fuller, John F. *Tanks in the Great War 1914–1918*. London, 1920.

Glantz, David and House, Jonathan *The Battle of Kursk*, Ian Allen, Shepperton, 1999.

Guderian, Heinz *Panzer Leader*, Futura, London, 1952.

Hackett, John *The Third World War*, Sphere, London, 1978.

Hamilton, Nigel *Monty: The Making of a General, 1887-1942*, Hamlyn, London, 1981.

Hamilton, Nigel *Monty: Master of the Battlefield, 1942-44*, Coronet, London, 1983.

Hamilton, Nigel *Monty: The Field Marshal, 1944-1976*, Sceptre, London, 1986.

Hart, Stephen *Montgomery and Colossal Cracks*, Praeger, Westport, 2000.

Hart, Stephen and Hart, Russell *Weapons and Fighting Tactics of the Waffen SS*, Spellmount, Staplehurst, 1999.

Hastings, Max *Overlord*, Pan, London, 1984.

Healy, Mark *Kursk 1943*, Osprey, London, 1993.

Hills, George *The Battle for Madrid*, London, 1977

Hughes, Matthew and Mann, Christopher *The T-34 Tank*, Spellmount, Staplehurst, 1999.

Hughes, Matthew and Mann, Christopher *The Panther Tank*, Spellmount, Staplehurst, 2000.

Hughes, Matthew and Mann, Christopher *Fighting Techniques of a Panzergrenadier*, Cassell, London, 2000.

Insight Team of the Sunday Times, *The Yom Kippur War*, Doubleday, New York, 1974.

Isaacs, Jeremy and Downing, Taylor *Cold War*, Bantam, London, 1998.

Jentz, Thomas *Germany's Panther Tank*, Schiffer, Atglen, 1995.

Keegan, John (ed), *Churchill's Generals*, Grove Weidenfeld, London, 1991.

Liddell Hart, Basil *The Other Side of the Hill*, Pan, London, 1948.

Liddell Hart, Basil *History of the Second World War*, Perigee, New York, 1971.

Lucas, James *Germany's Elite Panzer Force: Grossdeutschland*, MacDonald and Janes, London, 1978.

Macksey, Kenneth *Panzer Division: The Mailed Fist*, Purnell, London, 1968.

Macksey, Kenneth *Rommel: Battles and Campaigns*, Arms and Armour, London, 1979.

Messenger, Charles *A Century of Warfare*, Harper Colllins, London, 1995.

Miller, David *The Cold War: A Military History*, John Murray, London, 1998.

Milsom, John *Armoured Fighting Vehicles*, Hamlyn, London, 1972.

Montgomery, Bernard Law *The Memoirs of Field Marshal Montgomery*, Collins, London, 1958.

Neillands, Robin *The Desert Rats: 7th Armoured Division 1940-1945*, London, 1997.

Newton, Steven *German Battle Tactics on the Russian Front, 1941–45*, Schiffer, Atglen, 1994.

Overy, Richard *Russia's War*, Allen Lane, London, 1997.

Perret, Bryan *Knights of the Black Cross*, Robert Hale, London, 1986.

Perret, Bryan *Iron Fist*, Arms and Armour, London, 1995.

Schwarzkopf, Norman *It Doesn't Take a Hero*, Bantam, London, 1992.

Seaton, Albert *The Fall of Fortress Europe, 1943–45*, B.T. Batsford, London, 1981.

Shirer, William L. *The Collapse of the Third Republic: An Inquiry into the Fall of France in 1940*, London, 1970.

Shukman (ed), Harold *Stalin's Generals*, Weidenfeld and Nicolson, London, 1993.

Spaeter, Helmuth *The History of Panzerkorps Grossdeutschland*, Vol 2, Fedorowicz, Winnipeg, 1958.

Sydnor, Charles *Soldiers of Destruction*, Princeton University Press, Princeton, 1977.

Taylor, A.J.P. *The Second World War*, Hamish Hamilton, London, 1975.

Townshend, Charles (ed), *The Oxford Illustrated History of Modern War*, Oxford University Press, Oxford, 1997.

Walker, Martin *The Cold War*, Fourth Estate, London, 1993.

Whiting, Charles *The Last Assault*, Leo Cooper, London, 1994.

Wright, Patrick *Tank*, Faber and Faber, London, 2000.

Zaloga, Steven *Tank War – Central Front: NATO versus Warsaw Pact*, Osprey, London, 1989.

Zaloga, Steven and Madej, Victor *The Polish Campaign 1939*, New York, 1991.

Index